Shakespeare Confidential

C. V. Berney

Forever Press
2017

Published by

Forever Press
PO Box 263
Somerville MA 02143
www.foreverpress.org

Copyright©2017

©2017 C. V. Berney

2nd printing, January 2018

ISBN: 978-0-9989289-1-3

Cover image

Winking Bard by Katherine Berney
(after Martin Droeshout)

Cover design by William Boyle, Rory
McCarthy and Katherine Berney

All images courtesy of WikiMedia Commons
or derived from pre-1930 print sources.

Figure 7 (*Rosencrantz and Guildenstern are Dead* starring Daniel Radcliffe and Joshua McGuire) courtesy of the Old Vic, London. Photo by Manuel Harlan.

To Carole

Table of Contents

Confidential Video Bard

1	*A Midsummer Night's Dream*	1
2	*Love's Labor's Lost*	7
3	Who Is Jacquenetta?	11
4	*As You Like It*	16
5	*Midsummer Night's Dream* Revisited	21
6	*Titus Andronicus*	25
7	Three *Lears*	30
8	*Taming of the Shrew*	34
9	*Taming of the Shrew* Revisited	37
10	*Merchant of Venice*	41
11	Legend of the Round-Earthers	47
12	Mathematical Models of Stratfordian Persistence	50
13	Six Reasons Why Stratfordian 'Scholarship' Is So Bad	58

Sir Walter Scott as Paleo-Oxfordian

14	*Kenilworth*	60
15	*The Abbot*	63
16	*The Monastery*	69
17	In Search of Rosencrantz and Guildenstern	77

The Spanish Tragedy

18	Who Wrote *The Spanish Tragedy*?	93
19	Hidden Allusions (Spain)	102
20	More Hidden Allusions (England)	116
21	The Burbage Elegy	130

Robert Dudley, Earl of Leicester

22	*Leicester's Commonwealth*: Portrait of a Serial Killer?	133
23	The Earl of Leicester in the Plays of Shakespeare	145
24	Who Is Parolles?	156

25	Robert, Earl of Essex—Who's Your Daddy?	162
26	*Two Gentlemen of Verona*: Questions Answered	169
27	Plays on 'Oxford'	174
28	Gilbert and the Bard	176
29	*Billy Budd* and The Monument	182
30	Defending John le Carré	196
31	Listening to *The Winter's Tale*	197
32	*Cymbeline*: the Hidden History Play	219
33	Further Curiosities of *Cymbeline*	228

Illustrations

Fig. 1.   Johannes Vermeer's "The Milkmaid" (p. 12)
Fig. 2.   Models of Academic Behavior (p. 52)
Fig. 3   Time Evolution, Exponential (p. 54)
Fig. 4   Time Evolution, Gaussian (p. 55)
Fig. 5   Welbeck portrait of the 17th Earl of Oxford (p. 67)
Fig. 6.   Tycho Brahe and Arch (p. 78)
Fig. 7.   *Rosencrantz and Guildenstern Are Dead* (p. 84)
Fig. 8.   Robert Dudley, Earl of Leicester (p. 159)
Fig. 9.   Lettice Knollys (p. 160)
Fig. 10.   Drawings of Robert Devereux, Walter Devereux, and Robert Dudley (p. 164)
Fig. 11.   Coat of Arms of the Earls of Oxford (p. 185)
Fig. 12.   Mildred Cooke (p. 206)
Fig. 13.   Elizabeth of York (p. 222)
Fig. 14.   Henry Tudor (p. 235)

Introduction

The summer after my freshman year in college I worked as a pulp tester in the local paper mill. It was a full-time job, but since I had no social life, I had plenty of spare time. So I embarked on an ambitious program of reading. It included Homer's *Odyssey*, James Joyce's *Ulysses*, and a biography of Shakespeare. The only thing I remember from all this reading is that Homer liked the phrase "wine-dark sea." And that I was disappointed in the Shakespeare book, which gave me absolutely no insight into the plays.

Thirty-six years later I was in the Humanities Library at MIT. I idly picked up a book displayed on the Browsing Table. It was *The Mysterious William Shakespeare* by Charlton Ogburn Jr., and as I read it I became completely absorbed. Here was the story of a man—Edward de Vere, the 17th Earl of Oxford— who *could* have written the plays, and whose life illuminated every one of them.

Some time after that, my wife noticed a paragraph in the *Boston Globe* announcing a meeting of a group called 'the Shakespeare Oxford Society'. We attended, and I gradually got involved in their activities. I started by reviewing performances of the Shakespeare plays that had been preserved on a primitive medium we called 'videotape'. These writings were published in the SOS newsletter under the heading 'Confidential Video Bard', and they form the first section of this book. As I became steeped in Oxfordian lore, my outlook broadened, and the topics became more substantive (e.g., 'In Search of Rosencrantz and Guildenstern'). As the years rolled on, I continued to comment on topics that caught my eye, and finally I thought, 'Why not put all this wisdom together in one package?' Hence this book.

Acknowledgments. I thank my lovely daughter Katherine Berney for designing and drawing the 'Winking Bard' cover, and Rory McCarthy for technological wizardry. I thank the many fellow Oxfordians whose interest in the authorship question and enthusiasm for the unorthodox view have brightened the journey—including Hank Whittemore, Bill Boyle, Jan Scheffer, Alex McNeil, Nina Green, Bob Prechter, Lori di Liddo, and John Shahan. Bill and the Forever Press were essential players in putting this book together. I am greatly indebted to (and in awe of) the authors of a number of books—the Magnificent Seven—starting with John Thomas Looney (*'Shakespeare' Identified*. . .), and including Eva Turner Clark (*Hidden Allusions in Shakespeare's Plays*), Dorothy and Charlton Ogburn Sr. (*This Star of England*), Charlton Ogburn Jr. (*The Mysterious William Shakespeare*), Mark Anderson (*'Shakespeare' By Another Name*), Hank Whittemore (*The Monument*), and Charles Beauclerk (*Shakespeare's Lost Kingdom*).

I thank my wife Carole for proofing and fact-checking the manuscript. It follows, of course, that she is responsible for any typos or factual errors you may find herein.

Confidential Video Bard

1

A Midsummer Night's Dream

In the late 1970s and the early 1980s the British Broadcasting Corporation produced a series of videos comprising the complete set of plays commonly attributed to Shakespeare. These productions featured strong professional casts from the top and middle ranks of the British theatre, and experienced directors. The complete series is usually available at the larger suburban libraries. I have found that watching these videos is an excellent way of studying the Shakespeare canon, particularly for the less frequently performed plays, such as *Cymbeline* and *The Winter's Tale*.

For the more popular plays, videos of commercial productions are frequently available. This makes it possible to compare several versions, which is even more instructive. One thing it shows you is that Shakespeare's plays are so subtle and all-encompassing that no single production can be definitive—there are always other interpretations that work just as well. Directors are paid to make choices, but every choice precludes other, equally valid possibilities. Another lesson is that directors can make mistakes, choices that vitiate the potential of the text. And actors too can be creators, sustaining a powerful character throughout a long play, or infusing a cameo role with such insight that it shines like a jewel.

This essay (hopefully the first of a series) will explore and compare five video versions of *A Midsummer Night's Dream*. I will start by stating my biases: (1) Given the budgets and special effects available to film-makers, I don't think there's any reason we can't expect a realistic ass's head for Bottom; for me, this is essential for getting the scenes with Titania to work. (2) The enchantments should take place at night. This requirement should seem obvious from the title of the play, but some directors choose to ignore it.

Reinhardt-Dieterle, 1935. The first production we will consider is the 1935 black-and-white version directed by Max Reinhardt and William Dieterle. Reinhardt was an Austrian who gained a huge reputation in Europe in the early 1900s, largely on the basis of spectacular productions of *Dream*. The movie is based on his stage production, performed in Los Angeles in 1934. Dieterle was a German who had come to Hollywood in 1930 and directed many films there, including *The Hunchback of Notre Dame* (with Charles Laughton) and *Portrait of Jennie*. He was largely responsible for the actual filming of *Dream*. Warner Brothers, delighted to be involved in such a high-prestige project, showered stars upon the directors—Mickey Rooney (Puck), Olivia de Havilland (Hermia), Dick Powell (Lysander), etc. James Cagney was the reigning star of the studio and was given his choice of roles. After studying the script, he chose Bottom. He chose wisely.

Having done so many productions of *Dream*, Reinhardt understood how it worked, and that understanding shows in the film. The events in the Enchanted Forest are preceded and followed by fairy ballets that provide clarifying transitions. The fairies' closeness to Nature is emphasized by the wildlife wandering through the forest—deer, elk, even a bear (although Helena's line, "I am as ugly as a bear," is cut). The director of photography has taken care that events in the forest seem to take place at night, though we can see the action clearly. Mendelssohn's music is used effectively throughout, sometimes apparently played by an onscreen gnome band. Oberon's abduction of the changeling is explicitly shown—again, a clarifying touch.

The casting works. Cagney conveys Bottom's exuberance. Joe E. Brown is quietly hilarious as Flute, and the Athenian couples play broadly enough to justify their rhymed couplets. Rooney's Puck is made up as a child satyr, with stubby horns protruding from a mop of hair. He was eleven years old when the film was made, and had enough charm to make his overacting acceptable, except for his annoying laughter. In fact, annoying laughter is the chief flaw in this version of *Dream*—Hugh Herbert's Snout giggles constantly, and Bottom laughs overlong when he awakes from his 'dream', as do the Athenian couples.

BBC, 1981. The BBC version was produced in 1981 by Jonathan Miller, and directed by Elijah Moshinsky. It opens promisingly with Nigel Davenport projecting rock-solid authority as Theseus. Helen Mirren is lovely as Titania, but we run into trouble with the male fairies. Peter McEnery's Oberon is given stringy shoulder-length hair. Every time he leans over Titania to administer a potion, greasy strands of hair sweep across her face, and I shudder. Puck (Phil Daniels) is bare from the waist up, but wears lace cuffs and a dingy ruff. He has been outfitted with enhanced canines, so he looks like Adam Sandler playing Dracula. All his lines are given with a lower-class British accent. I cringed every time he came onscreen.

If Oberon has too much hair, Bottom has too little—they shaved Brian Glover's head, so he looks like a plebeian Yul Brynner. This is presumably to increase the contrast when he is transformed, allowing them to save the expense of building an ass's head. What they give him is two fuzzy ears and some buck teeth—the effect is more Easter Bunny than Donkey. With this handicap the seduction scene with Titania falls flat, although I did chuckle when he is scratched to climax by Cobweb and Mustardseed.

One strong point of this production is that it *looked* good. The action in the woods clearly takes place at night. The dialog is largely uncut (in the Reinhardt version, about half of it is missing). As with the other BBC productions, if you want to see what Shakespeare wrote, this is a good place to go. But for the same reason, parts of it drag—the camera wants to go places, but the people are standing around talking. Take the performance of 'Pyramus and Thisbe' at the end: I have seen stage productions of *Dream* where people were helpless with laughter at the slapstick mishaps of the Mechanicals, but in this version they simply give an inept performance of a foolish play.

Michael Hoffman, 1999. A commercial version of *Dream* was released to theatres in 1999; it was given short shrift by critics and didn't do much business. It must have been a labor of love for Michael Hoffman, who adapted the screenplay, coproduced, and directed it. Hoffman, apparently inspired by the successes of Zeffirelli (*Romeo and Juliet*) and Branagh (*Much Ado About Nothing*) has transposed the action from Athens/England to sunny Italy. For me, that's part of the problem: Oberon's line "Ill-met by moonlight, proud Titania" is delivered in a sun-drenched forest glade. In fact most of the fairy scenes seem to have been photographed in full sunlight.

The cast is star-studded, but the casting doesn't always work. The gorgeous and talented Michelle Pfeiffer seems oddly vacant as Titania. Rupert Everett (Oberon) *murmurs* all his lines—if you haven't memorized the text you won't understand a word he says. Sophie Marceau's Hippolyta is indistinguishable from Anna Friel's Hermia. As Theseus, David Strathairn seems to be giving us his impression of Fred ("Won't you be my neighbor?") Rogers. Kevin Kline's Bottom was widely praised by the critics, but for me, he is one of the main problems with this production. Kline and Hoffman have changed his character: he's not Bottom the Weaver, he's Bottom the Boulevardier, lounging at a sidewalk café, sipping cappuccino, flirting with the ladies. When he speaks, his malapropisms, coming from one who looks so suave, are not funny but embarrassing. And he has a *wife* who goes through the town square looking for him. A wife is like Chekhov's gun– – if you see her in the first act she should be used in the last. One would think Bottom's affair with Titania would change his relationship with his wife in some way, but the wife simply disappears. And finally, Hoffman shirks the ass's head. Kline gets the Easter Bunny treatment, with big fuzzy ears and three day's worth of stubble. Perhaps Kline's contract specified that his face be recognizable at all times, but it kills a line like "methinks I am marvelous hairy about the face."

The above is the bad news. Now for the good news—there are some gems in this production. Hoffman has apparently studied the Reinhardt-Dieterle film, for Stanley Tucci's Puck is Mickey Rooney's Puck aged by 40 years, the balding head adorned by stubby horns, the youthful exuberance replaced by amused resignation. Reinhardt's gnome band has morphed into a deliberate reference to the *Star Wars* cantina scene, and our introduction to Puck ("How now, spirit, whither wander you?") is brilliantly reimagined as a pickup in a singles bar. Tucci is the soul of this production, and makes it well worth seeing.

There were two other performances that stood out for me. One was Roger Rees as Peter Quince, who disappeared so completely into the character that I didn't recognize him until the closing credits, in spite of my familiarity with his work in *Nicholas Nickleby* and the sitcom *Cheers*. The other was the Philostrate of John Sessions, who combined unctuousness, servility and embarrassment so deftly that a small part became large.

Peter Hall, 1968. After viewing the preceding three videos, checked out from various suburban libraries, I received a catalog from a mail-order video company that advertised a 1968 version of *Dream* by the Royal Shakespeare company for $15. I paid my money and got the video. It was well worth it. The video, directed by Peter Hall, is apparently based on a stage production by the RSC, for the actors are supremely comfortable with their lines. Of all the productions considered here, this one is surely the best-spoken.

Hall has assembled an all-star cast. The women in particular are wonderful. Hermia is played by 23-year-old Helen Mirren, 13 years younger than when she did Titania in the BBC version. Diana Rigg, who gained fame in *The Avengers* (a 1960s TV series) plays Helena very effectively and attractively (although both she and Mirren are lumbered with awkward miniskirts). Judi Dench has a costume less dated—it consists solely of a few strategically placed ivy leaves. Her Titania is the most vivid and impassioned of any considered here. As Hippolyta, Barbara Jefford, in a black leather minidress and buskins, is every inch an Amazon queen.

Oberon and Puck are played by Ian Richardson and Ian Holm. Richardson is probably best known for his portrayal of the murderous politician Francis Urquhart in the 1990 BBC production *House of Cards*, which is essentially a modernization of *Richard III*. Holm has played a number of roles, including Polonius in the Zeffirelli *Hamlet* (1990) and the title role in the 1998 version of *Lear*. In this *Dream* (to remind us that they are fairies) their faces are painted green and their mouths bright red—they look rather like frogs who have been sucking Christmas candy. Although Holm tries to make his Puck playful by flapping his tongue and snapping his mouth, both he and Richardson have shrewd, hard-edged personas, and the longer scenes they share can be oppressive.

This production has a well-crafted ass's head, and Paul Rogers is fine as Bottom. His scene with Cobweb and Mustardseed is genuinely amusing.

The Opera, 1981. Some libraries have a video of Benjamin Britten's operatic version of *Dream*, composed in 1960. Opera is so different from spoken drama that I would not have included it in this account had I not noticed that this production—from the 1981 Glyndebourne Festival—was directed by Peter Hall.

The libretto was adapted from the play by Britten and Peter

Pears, and is in three acts of about 50 minutes each. The first two acts are set in the moonlit forest, very effectively represented by the set. The opera opens with a chorus of fairies (young boys with wings) who introduce Puck. He is charmingly played by Damien Nash, as young as Mickey Rooney in the Reinhardt film, but without the annoying laugh. We then have the quarrel between Oberon and Tytania (Britten's spelling), followed in the usual fashion by the rehearsals of the Mechanicals and the quarrels of the Athenian couples. This abridgement works well, emphasizing the unity of time and place. The third act has two scenes—the first in the forest at dawn, when Tytania is relieved of her enchantment; the second in the ducal palace, when we meet Theseus and Hippolyta for the first time, find that the lovers are reconciled, and watch the performance of 'Pyramus and Thisbe'.

Hall must have been satisfied with his choice of Mechanicals in his 1968 production, since they have the same look about them in the opera. Curt Applegreen is particularly good—perhaps the most lovable Bottom in the videos reviewed here. In this version, 'Pyramus and Thisbe' is the highlight of the show, and the reason is that Britten the composer suddenly cuts loose and starts having fun, introducing gavottes and waltzes, parodying operatic conventions, and letting the trombone roar like a lion. Britten is no doubt a great composer, but you don't find many tunes to whistle in the first 2½ acts.

Britten wrote the part of Oberon to be sung by a countertenor, a male singer who uses falsetto to sing in the female range. In this production, the part is taken by James Bowman. As an actor he's stiff and immobile and his face rarely betrays any emotion, quite a contrast with Ian Richardson's quick, ferrety Oberon in Hall's 1968 version (I suspect when you're casting countertenors the choice may not be wide). As I watched, I became increasingly annoyed—aside from the Munchkin hairdo, there was something offputting about the bland, oval face, the scruffy little goatee, the prissy, upturned mustaches. I felt like I'd seen that face before, but I couldn't put my finger on it. Then suddenly in the final scene it came to me: Bowman had been made up to look like the bust of Shakspere in the Stratford chapel!

Originally published in the Shakespeare Oxford Newsletter 37.1 (Spring 2001)

Confidential Video Bard

2

Love's Labor's Lost: the BBC *vs.* Branagh

The first of this series of essays comparing versions of Shakespeare's plays on video appeared in the Spring 2001 issue of the Shakespeare Oxford Newsletter. It dealt with *A Midsummer Night's Dream*, a play so popular that five different versions were available for comparison. In the case of *Love's Labor's Lost*, the competition is less fierce—there are only two versions, and one is a musical adaptation retaining less than half of the spoken dialog.

Elijah Moshinsky was one of the more reliable directors to work on the series of Shakespeare plays filmed by the BBC from 1978 to 1985. He directed one of the productions of *Dream* I reviewed in the last essay; in fact it was one I liked least, due largely to what I thought were misguided interpretations of Puck and Oberon. With this 1984 version of *Love's Labor's Lost*, however, he redeems himself completely—it's a beautiful piece of work.

For me the high points of this production were the appearances of the fantastical Spaniard Don Armado and his servant Moth, played by David Warner and John Kane. Their first scene ("Boy, what sign is it when a man of great spirit grows melancholy?") opens with Armado practicing the bassoon. The following dialog immediately establishes their characters—the master dreamy, self-absorbed, the servant intellectually superior and slightly condescending (rather in the manner of Jeeves and Wooster, the creations of a later British writer).

Love's Labor's Lost is well represented in Ruth Loyd Miller's edition of Eva Turner Clark's book, *Hidden Allusions in Shakespeare's Plays*. Miller contributes a lengthy introduction to Clark's chapter, and the two pieces together occupy 127 pages. Clark furnishes a historical counterpart for every character in the play—Elizabethan audiences must have

7

felt like they were watching a newsreel. The historical Berowne was the Marechal de Biron, but in the play he represents Oxford himself (Maria refers to him using the code-word "madcap"). Clark's choice for Don Armado is Don John of Austria, the half-brother of Philip of Spain whose armada had defeated the Turkish fleet at Lepanto in 1571. The elder Ogburns, more sensitive than Clark to personal references in the plays, suggest in *This Star of England* that Armado is also an Oxford figure, a Hispanified version of the 'Italianate Englishman.' In Armado's inflated rhetoric, Oxford is spoofing his own love of words. Watching the BBC video tends to confirm this suggestion; the two men conduct parallel romances (Berowne with Rosaline, Armado with the peasant girl Jaquenetta), and they are the only characters allowed to address the audience directly.

It is clear that Rosaline is the Dark Lady. Berowne describes her as "A whitely wanton with a velvet brow/With two pitch-balls stuck in her face for eyes/Ay, and by heaven, one that will do the deed/though Argus were her eunuch and her guard" (this is the authorial voice breaking through, since in the play Rosaline is innocent of the slightest impropriety). The Ogburns identify her with Anne Vavasor.

Who then is Jaquenetta? The fact that she is a peasant surely disqualifies her from being a duplicate of the courtly Vavasor. On the historical level, Clark identifies her with Mary Stuart, since Don John at one point was plotting to marry the Scottish queen (Clark points out that if Mary had been male she would have been named James, and Jaquenetta is the corresponding French diminutive). But there must be more to it than that—her lowly status is even more inappropriate for Mary Stuart than it is for Anne Vavasor. Even her admirer Armado comments on it: "I do affect the very ground (which is base) where her shoe (which is baser) guided by her foot (which is basest) doth tread." When an author as fond of name-clues as Oxford hits a note so insistently, I get suspicious. In the Shakespeare Oxford Newsletter for Fall 2000, Stephanie Hughes made the case for a relationship between Oxford and Emilia Bassano, a member of a family of Jewish musicians who had moved to the English court from Venice. Does Jaquenetta represent Emilia Bassano? Has Oxford provided his Mediterranean alter ego with his Italian sweetheart?

I think the question is important because Jaquenetta is so important to the play: its strange ending is precipitated by

Shakespeare Confidential

Costard's announcement (in the middle of the masque of the Nine Worthies) that she is pregnant by Armado. Preparations for a duel between Armado and Costard are interrupted by the arrival of Mercade with his message of death, which quenches the frivolous spirit which characterized the play to this point. The courtly lovers say goodbye, then Armado reenters and introduces two songs that close the play. The first is sung by Ver (Spring)—"The cuckoo then on every tree/ Mocks married men . . ." The second is sung by Hiems (Winter, Hiver)—"While greasy Joan doth keel the pot." ['Joan,' like 'Jill,' is a stock term for a peasant wench; Berowne too seems to have them on his mind: "Some men must love my lady, and some Joan (3.1); "When shall you see me write a thing in rhyme, or groan for Joan" (4.3); "Our wooing doth not end like an old play: Jack hath not Jill" (5.2).] Armado has the last line of the play: "You that way; we this way." Or is it a stage direction?

The second version of *Love's Labor's Lost* is the play joyously reimagined by Kenneth Branagh as a Hollywood musical; Branagh produced, directed, and stars as Berowne. He uses the device of a *faux* newsreel to set the scene, which is Europe on the brink of World War II. The newsreels—grainy b/w with an occasional frame skipped—are wonderfully done; the gossipy tone of the narrator is pitch-perfect, and the commentary allows the viewer to stay on top of the story in spite of massive cuts in the text. The device is more than a gimmick, as it provides the historical context that the Elizabethan audience got from their familiarity with names that a modern audience doesn't recognize. Sprinkled throughout the film are nine worthy songs from the 1930s by writers like Porter, Berlin and the Gershwins, plus a song from 1946 ('There's No Business Like Show Business') which serves as the climax of the festivities before the arrival of Mercade. Just as the play is stuffed with references to other literary works, the film is crammed with movie allusions (*Casablanca*, *The English Patient*, and *The Wizard of Oz*, to name three out of more than a dozen).

The cast is uniformly excellent. Nathan Lane plays Costard as a veteran vaudeville performer, and is hilarious. Timothy Spall's Armado is an interesting contrast to David Warner's portrait in the BBC video—with his lines drastically cut he's forced to give us a sketch, but it's a funny one. Richard Clifford is suave and charming as Boyet, the Princess's *aide-de-camp* (when the ladies enter on boats, Boyet is riding beside them on a bicycle, a bit of business perhaps inspired by the Princess addressing him as "our best-moving fair solicitor"). Rosaline is played by the gorgeous Natascha McElhone, and Jaquenetta by the equally gorgeous Stefania Rocca. In fact, not only are they equally gorgeous, they look a lot alike, as if Branagh were telling us he recognizes that Berowne and Armado are two sides of the same coin.

Branagh's film ends with a three-minute newsreel version of World War II in which the lovers prove that they are worthy of their ladies (the only casualty is Boyet). Although Branagh cuts the scene where Costard announces Jaquenetta's pregnancy, he includes the pregnancy itself. A brief clip in the newsreel shows Armado and Moth in a detention camp with a barely recognizable Jaquenetta standing outside the barbed wire holding an infant. A later clip shows them in the midst of a victory celebration, the infant now a toddler. Branagh agrees the pregnancy is important, but he makes you look for it.

I erred when I titled this piece 'BBC vs. Branagh.' These two versions are not competitive, they're complementary—they illuminate each other. See them both.

Originally published in Shakespeare Matters 1.1 (Fall 2001)

3

Love's Labor's Lost: Who Is Jaquenetta?

Since the previous paper was written, I have continued to think that Jaquenetta is an important character. She is the only female in the play to be fought over (by Costard and Don Armado) and the only female to conceive a life within the play's frame—the announcement of which is immediately followed by the appearance of Mercade, the Messenger of Death. While the lords and ladies play word games, Jaquenetta reminds us of fundamental realities. So I kept my eye out for historical figures that might shed some light on Jaquenetta, and eventually found two of them. They are discussed below.

Jaquenete Vautrollier. In 1558 the Huguenot printer Thomas Vautrollier and his wife Jaqueline (usually called Jaquenete) fled France to avoid religious persecution. He set up shop in London and became quite successful. In 1579 he hired a teen-aged apprentice named Richard Field who had grown up in Stratford-on-Avon, not far from the Shaksper family. Vautrollier died in 1587. Two years later, the 28-year old Field married Jaquenete, who had been running the print shop. She was old enough to be his mother, and it is speculated that the shop was advised to have an English front man to deflect a possible Catholic backlash against the Protestant propaganda the firm had been printing.

The Field-Vautrollier firm is notable for having introduced the name 'William Shakespeare' to the literary world—it printed *Venus and Adonis* in 1593 and *The Rape of Lucrece* in 1594. The printed texts of these poems are unusually accurate, and it has been suggested that Oxford personally supervised the printing. Perhaps Field recalled the name of his former Stratford neighbor and suggested it to Oxford as a possible pen name.

However, I can find nothing in the life of Jaquenete Vautrollier that suggests the sought-after wench of *Love's*

Labor's Lost. The timing is off—the play was written in late 1578 or early 1579, and the poems were printed 15 years later.

Jacquetta of Luxembourg was born in 1416. Seventeen years later she became the second wife of John, Duke of Bedford, then 44, and the brother of Henry V, King of England. They lived in Rouen, where John commanded the English forces fighting the French. He died in 1435, and Jacquetta was commanded to join the English court. A personable young captain named Richard Woodville was assigned to accompany her, and a short time later it was found that Richard and Jacquetta had secretly married.

Figure 1 - The Milkmaid, by Johannes Vermeer,

Their first-born child was a daughter, whom they named Elizabeth. She grew up to be a beauty, and at 15, she married a young knight, Sir John Grey of Groby. She bore John two sons, but he died in 1461. John had fought for the wrong side in the Wars of the Roses, and his land was to be confiscated, but when his charming widow approached the victorious Edward IV to plead for her property, the king was so taken with her that he made her his queen.

The royal couple had a fruitful marriage—she gave him 3 sons and 7 daughters. The first child, Elizabeth of York, arrived in 1466, and like her mother, grew up to be a beauty. In 1483, the exiled Henry Tudor, building political support for his planned overthrow of Richard III, promised to marry her if his campaign was successful. Henry defeated Richard in the battle of Bosworth Field and thus became Henry VII. He married Elizabeth in 1486.

Their first son, Arthur, was born that same year. He made a very promising Prince of Wales, but he died in 1502, which made Henry, the second son, heir to the throne. He was crowned Henry VIII on the death of his father in 1509. Some years later he married Anne Boleyn, and in 1533 they had a daughter, who on 15 January 1559 was crowned Elizabeth I, Queen of England.

Thus Jacquetta of Luxembourg is Queen Elizabeth's great-great-grandmother.

The Irresistible Charm of the Dairymaid. So we have a link between Jacquetta-Jaquenetta and Queen Elizabeth. The elder Ogburns[1] intuited this; in analyzing *Love's Labor's Lost*, they wrote that

> Jaquenetta seems to be a comedic presentation of the Queen, whom Oxford was obliged to court in a clandestine manner. Cleopatra-Elizabeth will one day admit that she is
>
>> No more but e'en a woman, and commanded
>> By such poor passion as the maid that milks
>> And does the meanest chores.[2]

In Scene 1.2, Constable Dull says of Jaquenetta, "For this damsel, I must keep her at the park; she is allowed for the dey-woman . . ." (that is, she is approved to serve as dairy-woman). So both Cleopatra-Elizabeth and Jaquenetta are seen as dairymaids—the former in her imagination, the latter in her occupation.[3]

Is Elizabeth associated with a milkmaid elsewhere in the plays? Yes—in Scene 3.1 of *Two Gentlemen of Verona*, the comic character Launce describes his girlfriend:

> . . . I am in love, but a team of horse shall not pluck that from me; nor who 'tis I love; and yet 'tis a woman; but what woman I will not tell myself; and yet 'tis a milkmaid . . .

The connection to Elizabeth is established by a *hairs/heirs* pun when Speed joins the scene and says (among other things) "She hath more hair than wit, and more faults than hairs, and more wealth than faults." Elizabeth did indeed have more faults than heirs.

There is in fact a robust literary tradition of celebrating the erotic appeal of the milkmaid. Representative examples are given below.

(1) *Adam Bede* by George Eliot,[4] 1859. The main female character is milkmaid Hetty Sorrel. "Hetty's was a spring-tide beauty; it was the beauty of frisking things, round-limbed, gambolling, circumventing you with a false air of innocence . . ."

(2)   *Patience*, a comic opera, libretto by William S. Gilbert, 1881. "The man loves—wildly loves! . . . His weird fancy has lighted, for the nonce, on Patience, the village milkmaid. . . . But yesterday I caught him in her dairy, eating fresh butter with a tablespoon."

(3)   *The Romantic Adventures of a Milkmaid*, Thomas Hardy, 1883. The title character is Margaret Tucker. "Her face was of the hereditary type among families down in these parts: sweet in expression, perfect in hue, and somewhat irregular in feature. Her eyes were of a liquid brown. . . . She was the 'Margery' who had been told not to 'bide about long on the road.' "

(4)   *The Producers*, a film by Mel Brooks, 1967. The character played by Estelle Winwood, known only as 'Hold Me, Touch Me', joins producer Max Bialystock in his office and suggests a role-playing exercise: "I'll be the innocent little milkmaid, and you be the naughty stable boy."

Who Impregnated Jaquenetta? Costard and Don Armado both participate in the 'Masque of the Nine Worthies', Costard as Pompey and Armado as Hector, the hero of Troy. Costard interrupts Armado's presentation to announce Jaquenetta's pregnancy (5.2.672-7):

> Fellow Hector, she is gone; she is two months on her way.. . . Faith, unless you play the honest Troyan, the poor wench is cast away. She's quick; the child brags in her belly already. 'Tis yours.

So Costard claims that Armado is responsible for Jaquenetta's pregnancy. Is he telling the truth? In his arraignment before the King (1.1.281-315), Costard has shown that he is slippery with words and intent on evading responsibility. He is part of Jaquenetta's world and has the advantage of familiarity, while Armado is a stranger, a foreigner. Costard seems strangely knowledgeable about the details of the pregnancy. And one of the two songs that end the play sings of the cuckoo, who "mocks married men."

I believe that Costard has played the naughty stable boy.

End Notes

1. Dorothy and Charlton Ogburn, *This Star of England*, p. 198

2. *Antony and Cleopatra* 4.13.73-5
3. Costard provides another Elizabeth-clue when he says of Jaquenetta, "This was no damsel neither, sir, she was a virgin" (1.1.292). His following line—"I deny her virginity"—must have gotten a huge laugh in court performances.
4. A small group of mentally unstable researchers has proposed that 'George Eliot' is the *nom de plume* of a woman named Mary Ann Evans. This is a transparent attempt to push a subversive feminist agenda.

Confidential Video Bard

4

As You Like It: 1936, 1978 and 1983

In 1896 William Gilbert was working on the libretto of his last collaboration with Arthur Sullivan, *The Grand Duke*, a comic opera set in the fictional German duchy of Hesse-Halbpfennig. One of the characters is Julia Jellicoe, an English actress. Gilbert wanted her accent to contrast with the speech of the inhabitants of 'Hesse-Halbpfennig,' so in his topsy-turvy way he gave the role to Ilka von Palmay, a Hungarian actress with a strong German accent (the rest of the cast, of course, spoke impeccable English). The 1936 film version of *As You Like It* is reminiscent of *The Grand Duke* in that the lead role is played by an actress with a German accent while the rest of the cast speaks flawless English, although in this case there is no explanation for the discrepancy (however, one character comments on it: in Scene 3.2, Orlando says to Rosalind "Your accent is something finer than you could purchase in so removed a dwelling").

The actress playing Rosalind is Elisabeth Bergner, whose fame was so great in 1936 that her name came before the title; today she comes across as dime-store Dietrich. The decision to cast her is less puzzling when you learn that the picture was produced by Paul Czinner, an Austrian director who happened to be her husband. While one may fault his judgment in selecting a female lead, his production team is amazing: the adaptation was by J. M. Barrie (*Peter Pan*), the music was by William Walton (who later composed an opera based on *Troilus and Cressida*) and the editor was David Lean, who went on to direct *Bridge on the River Kwai*, *Lawrence of Arabia*, and *Dr. Zhivago*.

Orlando is played by Laurence Olivier, then 29 and already a veteran, having done 10 previous films (his next film was to be *Fire Over England*, a tale of the Spanish Armada in which he played opposite his future wife, Vivien Leigh). This was his

Shakespeare Confidential

first Shakespearean film, and with his hooded eyes and black hair he gives a vaguely sinister impression, evoking a young version of his Richard III. In his bout with Charles the Wrestler (Lionel Braham, 58 years old, with the rippling physique of the Pillsbury Doughboy), Charles is definitely the underdog.

It is axiomatic among cinema buffs that the 'look' of a historical film is determined more by the period in which it was made than by the period in which it is supposedly set. That is definitely the case here, where the whipped-cream castles could have been left over from the 1935 *Midsummer Night's Dream*. Touchstone's costume again reminds us of Gilbert & Sullivan—he looks like he's straight from a D'Oyly Carte production of *Yeomen of the Guard*. Fashion note for *Thomas of Woodstock* fans: the fop Le Beau is wearing "Polonian shoes with peaks a hand full long, tied to the knees with chains . . ." so that "the chain doth, as it were, so toeify the knee and so kneeify the toe that between both it makes a most methodical coherence, or coherent method." (*Woodstock* 2.3; 3.2)

The second half of the film is hard to enjoy, partly because of the poor quality of the print and partly because Bergner is trying too hard to pour on the star power. There's no attempt whatever to make her disguise credible—she's still in full glamour make-up—lipstick, eye shadow, rouge—the whole nine yards. Rather than a Ganymede, she comes across as a Teutonic Ally McBeal. Her self-involved performance doesn't give Olivier anything to act against, so he mostly sits around looking moody. The only enjoyable scene in the second half comes from a surprising source—William the yokel. As was argued convincingly by Alex McNeil at the 1999 SOS conference, the character is Oxford's stand-in for Shaksper of Stratford. In this production he's played by Peter Bull, later to gain cinematic immortality as Alexi, the stolid Russian ambassador in Kubrick's *Doctor Strangelove*. His bland, rustic exterior seems to be hiding a shrewd animal cunning, which makes me think that perhaps this talented actor came close to the historical truth.

The BBC Shakespeare videos made from 1978 through 1980 all open with an introduction showing travelogue shots of Windsor Castle, Venice, Stratford-on-Avon (with the bizarre, spidery signature of its favorite son at the bottom of the frame), the Parthenon, and the Tower of London, all accompanied by a lackluster fanfare attributed to the aforementioned William

Walton (I privately refer to this as "the cheesy intro"). Jonathan Miller took over as artistic director of the enterprise around 1980, so I give him credit for changing the introduction to the dignified calligraphy over 16th century music used for the remainder of the series. The BBC production of *As You Like It* stems from 1978, and so opens with the travelogue. It was directed by Basil Coleman.

Writing in 1957, critic John Russell Brown commented on *As You Like It*:

> . . . the play's generosity and confidence spring chiefly from the characterization of Rosalind. She insures that Shakespeare's ideal of love's order is not presented as a cold theorem; in her person, love's doubts and faith, love's obedience and freedom, coexist in delightful animation.

The "delightful animation" of the BBC version is provided in full measure by Helen Mirren, a treasure of the British stage. Her performance as Rosalind goes straight to the heart, and is the chief reason to see this production. Orlando is played by Brian Stirner, who looks like Dana Carvey with a Dick Smothers mustache. Stirner is slight of build, so when he confronts Charles the Wrestler, played by tall, buff David Prowse (who was the body of Darth Vader in *Star Wars*), he's definitely the underdog. Orlando wins the match by means of an unconventional (and unconvincing) cannonball move. Jaques is played by Richard Pasco; I can't fault him as an actor—he has a character—but it's a character I can't stand: arrogant, self-involved, self-pitying. When Orlando says to him (3.2) "I am glad of your departure," I cry 'Amen!' (The 1936 production solves the Jaques problem by cutting most of his lines.) The Silvius and Phebe of Maynard Williams and Victoria Plunknett are finely drawn; Williams in particular has an innocent earnestness that is appealing.

Searching the catalog one day, I discovered that the Natick library had a video of a Canadian production of *As You Like It* from 1983. Intrigued, I made the 30-mile trip to check it out. It was well worth it—the video was based on a Stratford Festival stage production filled with fire, pacing and humor, more enjoyable in almost every way than the two versions that preceded it. The acting was fine. Andrew Gillies was a 'Goldilocks' Orlando, not predatory (like Olivier), nor wimpish (like Stirner), but just right. Roberta Maxwell was both touching and amusing as Rosalind. In Lewis Gordon's Touchstone we at last got a fool who had some smell of professionalism about him; he first appeared in clown makeup, and was equipped with tools of the trade, such as a hand puppet and bulb horn.

The artistic director of the Stratford production was John Hirsch, and he succeeded wonderfully in giving it a point of view. It opened with Dickensian urchins ironically singing "In spring time" on a bitterly cold winter's night. The fascist nature of Duke Frederick's regime is established immediately as the beggars are cleared off by the police, just prior to Orlando's entrance. Graeme Campbell's Frederick, with his flat face, black eyebrows, meringue of white hair, and curiously metallic voice is a memorable villain. His henchmen are dressed in bemedalled black uniforms, and when Oliver is dragged in for questioning, the blood on his face and his shirt tells you that the interrogation methods used were not gentle. This is comedy with a dark side.

The Video Bard's Conjecture: *When several video versions of a Shakespeare comedy are available, the most entertaining version will be based on a stage production.*

One can speculate on the reasons for this. One of them is certainly the nature of the preparation for a stage play compared with that for a filmed production. The play is an event, presented as a whole in real time; filmed productions occur as a process, accumulated shot by shot, scene by scene over several (or many) days. Stage actors are oriented toward working as an ensemble, working with fellow actors during the rehearsal period, and *with the audience* during the performance period.

I also suggest that a stage play, with live actors and an audience, is watched with a different *mental model* than a video. The viewer is aware that the actors are trying to please the audience, and that the audience is responding, ideally with pleasure and appreciation, but possibly with boredom or hostility—the actors and audience are joined in a feedback loop, involved in a human transaction. When watching a video, the viewer is of course *intellectually* aware that she is watching actors performing, but the subconscious mental model is different— at some level every story seen on a flat screen tends to be interpreted as a documentary. With the mental model for a live play, the criterion for success is 'Have these actors achieved a rhythm of speeches, actions and ideas that pleases the audience?' For a filmed piece, the criterion is 'Do I believe in the reality of what's being shown?' Thus an actor in a filmed play has a different set of tools than a stage actor: a closeup can reveal extremely subtle emotions expressed with the eyes alone (unreadable in a stage performance), but if the rhythm of the lines calls for boisterous or exaggerated behavior, the effect may be 'stagy' and unconvincing.

The director of the Stratford production reviewed above is apparently aware of this effect, and takes pains to show us that we are at a live theatrical event—trumpets invite us into the theatre, the camera pans over the rows of fellow audience members, etc. He coaxes us into choosing the appropriate mental model, so that when Touchstone emphasizes a bawdy line with a honk from his horn, or when Audrey seats herself immodestly, we react with laughter rather than embarrassment or disbelief. No wonder the Touchstone in the BBC production is so pallid and forgettable—he's surrounded by real trees and real buildings, so he has to be 'real' (that is, 'normal'), and all he can do is recite his lines. But Shakespeare was writing for the *stage*, for the live-audience experience—he meant for the lines to be delivered by a larger-than-life character, and when they are not, they lose their savor.

It will be interesting to see if *the Video Bard's Conjecture* holds up as we explore further productions in the Shakespearean canon.

Originally published in *Shakespeare Matters* 1.3 (Spring 2001)

Confidential Video Bard

5
Midsummer Night's Dream Revisited

The Spring 2001 issue of the *Shakespeare Oxford Newsletter* carried the first *Video Bard* column, in which I reviewed five productions of *Midsummer Night's Dream*, including a 1968 version based on the Royal Shakespeare Company's production, directed by Peter Hall. Some time after this column came out, I received an e-mail from *Shakespeare Fellowship* member Christopher Paul, pointing out that I had missed a more recent version of *Dream* which was his personal favorite. I was able to find it in a local video outlet. It is dated 1996, and is again based on a production by the Royal Shakespeare Company, this time under the direction of Adrian Noble.

In the last issue of *Shakespeare Matters* I reviewed three videos of *As You Like It*, and commented on the difficulties of finding a visual style appropriate for the presentation of Shakespearean plays on video. The plays were written for the stage, where the palpable presence of living actors (and their interaction with the audience) is an essential part of the experience. If they are adapted for video simply by photographing actors in realistic surroundings (as so many of the BBC versions do) the plays can seem talky and unconvincing, the heightened language inappropriate and abnormal.

I agree with Christopher Paul that the Adrian Noble production is the best *Dream* of the lot—it's the only one I've seen that seems *magical*. This version follows a 1994 stage production, so the actors have thoroughly mastered the rhythms and nuances of their lines, and Noble has reworked the material extensively for video presentation. I believe he was consciously aware of the problems mentioned above, so I am going to describe his treatment in some detail.

The camera is floating above a cloudscape; far below, one sees a lighted window. We cut to the window and glide into the room. It is a child's room; as the camera pans we see toys—a teddy bear, a miniature theatre, a rabbit figure, a clown. We pan to the Boy, asleep, with his arm across an illustrated edition of *Midsummer Night's Dream*.

Cut to the Boy walking down a long, narrow hall, passing a statue of a faun. His way is blocked by a pair of large doors. He puts his eye to the keyhole and we see Theseus talking to Hippolyta: "Now, fair Hippolyta, our nuptual hour draws on apace . . . " The play proper has begun.

First point: the director has made it clear that this is the Boy's dream, that the things we see will be governed by the laws of dreams, not by the everyday laws of cause and effect (for example, we don't see the Boy open the doors and hide under the table—he simply *is* under the table). Second point: the Boy is a surrogate audience; in every scene there are insert shots of the Boy's reaction—amusement, puzzlement, sympathy, fear. Our reactions to scenes are governed (to some extent) not by their credibility, but by their effect on the Boy.

At the end of the scene between Lysander, Hermia and Helena (1.1), Helena runs out of the room. The Boy follows her, and finds himself falling through a black void (we get a clip of the Boy in bed calling "Mommy!"). The black void gradually defines itself as a tube, and the Boy lands with a *thump* in a potbellied stove located in a crude shack. It is raining outside, and the Mechanicals enter, shaking out their umbrellas, accompanied by a rustic gavotte on the trombone.

At the conclusion of 1.2 the Mechanicals leave. An umbrella ascends above the clouds, then descends. The handle is grasped—we see it is Puck, floating in the air, the umbrella a parachute. A neighboring umbrella appears, bearing a Fairy; she and Puck do an abridged version of 2.1 ("How now, spirit, whither wander you?"). On "She never had so sweet a changeling," the Boy watches as Puck plucks a drop from the umbrella and inflates it to a large bubble, in which is seen the turbaned face of the changeling (it is, of course, the Boy's face). On the Fairy's line ("And here my mistress. Would that he were gone"), the Boy blows a stream of bubbles into a miniature theatre. As they descend we see that each bubble contains a fairy, the largest bearing Titania (a reference to the arrival of

Shakespeare Confidential

Glinda the Good in *The Wizard of Oz*; this will not be the last reference to that magical film).

The scene is now a stage, stretching to infinity, with hanging colored lights suggesting both foliage and stars. Titania accuses Oberon of dallying with Hippolyta (". . . the bouncing Amazon, your buskin'd mistress, and your warrior love . . ."), to which he replies "I know of thy love for Theseus" (thus the text hints that Titania and Hippolyta are interchangeable, as are Oberon and Theseus). When Oberon snarls "I'll make her render up her page to me" the Boy gasps, strengthening the identification of the Boy as changeling.

Oberon's speech, "I know a bank where the wild thyme blows," is delivered with his face (and Puck's) thrust into the front of a miniature theatre, while the Boy looks in from the back. All three appear to be normal size, in contrast to the bubble-borne entrance of Titania and the fairy band, when they were all small enough to fit inside the toy stage. When Oberon mentions a "sweet Athenian lady," the Boy moves a miniature female figure forward onto the stage. On Puck's line, "Fear not my lord! Your servant shall do so," Puck and Oberon grasp umbrella handles and are wafted skyward; the camera pulls back to show they are suspended by marionette strings which the Boy is lifting—another dazzling change of scale.

The action has moved from a realistic representation of a boy's bedroom to a mostly realistic 18th century drawing room to a semi-realistic shack, and finally has transcended reality altogether by showing only stages—miniature and infinite. The director has seized every opportunity to show us that what we are seeing is not real, but magical.

In the last newsletter, the Video Bard made a conjecture: *When several video versions of a Shakespeare comedy are available, the most entertaining version will be based on a stage production.* The video reviewed here provides further support for this conjecture. In addition, we discussed the necessity of guiding the viewer away from "normal," realistic expectations to a mental model appropriate for the stage. The director of this production, as discussed above, has done that most brilliantly.

Doubling. It is fairly common for the actors playing Oberon and Titania to double as Theseus and Hippolyta, as they do in this production. Less common is having the actor playing Puck

(Oberon's assistant) double as Philostrate (Theseus's assistant); both parts are played here by Barry Lynch with sly knowingness. An even bolder stroke is having the Mechanicals (Snout, Starveling, Quince and Flute) double as the Fairies (Moth, Cobweb, Mustardseed and Peaseblossom), reminding us that in *The Wizard of Oz*, the Kansas Mechanicals (Hunk, Hickory and Zeke) reappear in Oz as the Scarecrow, the Tin Woodman, and the Cowardly Lion (Snug the Joiner appears in lion costume in this *Dream* sequence).

Personnel. Alex Jennings displays a laser-like intensity as Oberon/Theseus, and Lindsay Duncan is serenely voluptuous as Titania/Hippolyta (she won a Tony for her work in *Private Lives*). We commented above on the textual hint that these personæ are blurred; the actors support this by playing the two roles in exactly the same way, leading to a little joke at the end: after the performance of 'Pyramus and Thisbe' Hippolyta congratulates the players; when she comes to Bottom there is a start of mutual recognition (though of course it was Bottom and Titania who had the roll in the hay). Desmond Barrit is the most lovable Bottom of any production I've seen. The Boy is sympathetically played by Osheen Jones.

The Director. Adrian Noble recently resigned as Artistic Director of the Royal Shakespeare Company, possibly over controversy associated with his proposal that the existing Shakespeare theatre at Stratford-upon-Avon be torn down (how's that for symbolizing the Paradigm Shift?). I have barely scratched the surface in describing the fantastic weave of Shakespearean text, cultural references and beautiful images in this amazing video. Noble is one of our most imaginative directors—he is a national treasure, and after his resignation will surely land on his feet. But will the Royal Shakespeare Company?

Originally published in *Shakespeare Matters* 1.4 (Summer 2002)

6
Titus Andronicus: Jane Howell and Julie Taymor

A writer for the Boston Globe once wrote a column advancing the proposition that, as currently used, the adverb "arguably" meant "not." The example he gave was "*Titus Andronicus* is arguably Shakespeare's greatest play."

Titus Andronicus is the play in which Titus's daughter, Lavinia, is raped and mutilated by the sons of the Empress Tamora. In revenge, Titus kills the sons and bakes their remains into a pudding, which he serves to the Empress. While it is probably not Shakespeare's greatest play, I believe the Grand Guignol aspects of the plot have caused it to be underrated—at its best it deals with the great themes treated in later, more respectable plays: Roman politics, madness (real or feigned), motiveless malignancy, interracial coupling, crushing losses, father-daughter relations, and revenge (justified or unjustified). And as usual, the players are the brief abstracts and chronicles of the time—the play is rich in references to Elizabethan events and personalities, though not all of these references are clear or consistent.

The Howell version. The BBC video was produced in 1985, and directed by Jane Howell. It opens with the camera contemplating a skull. We then see the face of a bespectacled young teen-ager whom we will later find is Young Lucius, the grandson of Titus Andronicus. The scene then opens up to show lines of masked, armored warriors. We are in a crypt, awaiting the ceremonial interment of those who fell defending Rome against the invading Goths.

The first words spoken are the Captain's welcome to the victorious Titus: "Romans make way!" Scene 1.1 continues through Titus's speech ("Kind Rome, that hath thus lovingly reserv'd . . ."), then shifts to a public square where Saturninus and Bassanius each appeal to the crowd to be named emperor. In the text, the political speeches begin the play; Howell's transposition of scenes is an unusually bold move for the BBC series, which tends to be quite conservative in its treatment of the plays.

Elizabethan subtext. Eva Turner Clark dates the play to 1576, regarding it as Oxford's reaction to 'the Spanish Fury,' the rape of Antwerp by the Spanish army in that year. She identifies the emperor Saturninus as Philip of Spain, Tamora as Mary, Queen of Scots, and the arch-villain, Aaron the Moor, as Charles Arundel, a Catholic traitor who was denounced by Oxford, and who denounced him in return. This may all be true, but I believe there are other levels. As played by Eileen Atkins, Tamora looks a lot like portraits of Elizabeth. Who was Elizabeth's illicit lover? The dark-complected Robert Dudley, whom she had created Earl of Leicester, and whom she nicknamed 'her Moor'. It has long been accepted that in the play *Hamlet*, Claudius represents Leicester. In his mother's chamber, Hamlet compares his father with Claudius: "Could you on this fair mountain leave to feed, and batten on this moor?" For years Leicester had hopes of marrying Elizabeth, thus becoming king. How, then, would Aaron's first speech (2.1) have sounded to courtiers?

> *Then, Aaron, arm thy heart and fit thy thoughts,*
> *To mount aloft with thy imperial mistress,*
> *And mount her pitch, whom thou in triumph long*
> *Hast prisoner held, fettered in amorous chains . . .*
> *Away with slavish weeds and servile thoughts!*
> *I will be bright, and shine in pearl and gold,*
> *To wait upon this new-made empress.*
> *To wait, said I? To wanton with this queen . . .*

Leicester was famous for his ornate clothing. And Elizabeth always assigned him apartments adjoining her own.

But Aaron is not only Leicester. For those willing to consider the hypothesis that Henry Wriothesley, 3rd Earl of Southampton, was Oxford's son by Elizabeth, Aaron is Oxford as well. In 4.2, a nurse enters, carrying a child Tamora has just given birth to, whose color reveals that Aaron is the father. Instructed to destroy the child to avoid scandal, Aaron (who has hitherto been evil incarnate) defends his son with his sword, and praises him in terms reminiscent of the Sonnets ("*Sweet blowse, you are a beauteous blossom sure*"). He defies Tamora's older sons:

Shakespeare Confidential

> Stay, murderous villains, will you kill your brother?
> Now, by the burning tapers of the sky,
> That shone so brightly when this boy was got,
> He dies upon my scimitar's sharp point,
> That touches this my first-born son and heir!

Fran Gidley has suggested that "the burning tapers" is a reference to the supernova which first appeared in November 1572, and which some have identified as "yond same star that's westward from the pole," mentioned in the first scene of *Hamlet*. Wriothesley is thought to have been born in October 1573, so presumably he was "got" in January 1573, when the supernova was only two months old, and still fresh in everyone's mind.

The author chose well when he named his villain Aaron. The biblical Aaron, Moses' brother, was a high priest who created a calf of gold, leading his tribe down the path of idolatry. Aaron the Moor is also associated with gold: he buries a bag of it in the forest to produce as 'proof' when he later levels false accusations.

The Taymor Version. Julie Taymor has become known for her theatre work, culminating in her imaginative staging of Disney's *The Lion King* on Broadway. *Titus*, released in 2000, is her first movie. The first half hour is brilliantly conceived. The camera discovers a boy in a kitchen, his head covered with a paper-bag mask. The TV emits sounds of cartoon conflict while the boy hurls toy soldiers against each other and squirts them with catsup. A wall of the kitchen explodes, and a burly thug runs in, picks up the boy, and carries him down a long flight of stairs. They emerge into an open area which is evidently the center of the Coliseum, and the crowd roars as the thug lifts the boy triumphantly into the air. Armored figures march robotically onto the field—are they Roman soldiers, or are they the boy's action figures grown large? Titus appears, crusted with the dust of battle, and speaks the first words of the film, "*Hail, Rome, victorious in thy mourning weeds!*"

This opening is extremely effective in its sociocultural implications, and in establishing the nonrealistic atmosphere required, as noted in the discussion of Adrian Noble's version of *Midsummer Night's Dream* in our previous column. In fact, the two opening sequences could be described in the same way: *a young boy in a modern domestic setting is taken through a long hallway and experiences dramatic events in an ambiguous era*. Wait a minute—it's *the same boy!* In both films, the boy is played by Osheen Jones, Britain's answer to Macaulay Culkin. Julie Taymor has evidently been studying the work of Adrian Noble, and has found it good. And in transposing the opening scenes of the play proper, Taymor shows she has been studying the work of Jane Howell as well.

Taymor does a masterful job of mixing eras—lumbering tanks and snarling motorcycles accompany the armored soldiers—suggesting the unchanging primal nature of the militaristic impulse. The contest between Saturninus and Bassanius for the crown is wittily staged as a 1930s political campaign—the candidates harangue the crowds through loudspeakers mounted on sleek convertibles. But after Saturninus becomes emperor and chooses Tamora as his bride the movie descends into cliché—your standard Roman orgy, with cocktails, jazz band, and lots of leering. A few minutes after that, Taymor inserts a shot which is appalling in its heavy-handedness: Titus and Tamora, separated by flames, glaring at each other from opposite sides of the screen, while the severed limbs and torso of Tamora's sacrificed son gyrate between them. A similar *faux pas* occurs almost halfway through the film. Titus's plea to the Roman judges ("*Be pitiful to my condemned sons*") is movingly filmed as being addressed to a crowd of citizens hurrying heedlessly past him; but the mood is broken by a silly sequence involving an angel hovering around a sacrificial lamb with the face of another of Titus's sons.

The Actors. Jessica Lange, an established Hollywood star, plays Tamora in the Taymor production. She is effective, but tends to be overwhelmed by the elaborate costumes and hair-dos provided, and perhaps takes the play too seriously—she doesn't seem to be having much *fun*. Eileen Atkins, on the other hand, is having a wonderful time—with her kohl-rimmed eyes and lop-sided wolfish grin she completely inhabits the part of the Empress, and is one of the reasons for watching the BBC production. Of the two Aarons, the BBC's Hugh Quarshie may seem overmatched by the older, stronger Harry Lennix, but he brings a fresh charm and ready smile to the role that makes his presence welcome, and underlines the comedic aspects of the play. Alan Cumming plays Saturninus as a selfish, spoiled, degenerate, androgynous brat—exactly the kind of emperor we've seen in every sword-and-sandal epic Hollywood ever churned out (maybe for Taymor that's the joke). I much prefer Brian Protheroe's performance in Howell's version—someone who's in over his head, and is easily led by his vengeful wife.

Of course, the crown jewel in any production of this play is the title role. Trevor Peacock has been one of the mainstays of the BBC Shakespeare series, performing roles as diverse as Talbot in *1 Henry VI*, a bawd in *Pericles*, and Feste in *Twelfth Night*. He gives us a gravel-voiced, blue-collar Titus who may not be the brightest bulb on the tree, but who gets the job done. Anthony Hopkins, however, is one of the world's greatest actors, who in *Titus* is at the height of his powers. And by a sly twist of fate, he is forever associated in the public mind with the cannibalistic Hannibal Lecter in *Silence of the Lambs*. So when he says "I'll play the cook," and, clad in chef's whites, serves the Empress the remains of her sons, the moment is delicious.

Originally published in *Shakespeare Matters* 2.1 (Fall 2002)

Confidential Video Bard

7

Three *Lears*: Hordern, Holm, and Olivier

Hordern. Jonathan Miller is a British director who was trained as a physician, then entered show business as one-fourth of a troupe performing a collection of irreverent skits called *Beyond the Fringe* (the other members were Alan Bennett, Dudley Moore, and Peter Cook). In 1979 he became executive producer of the BBC's ongoing video productions of the Shakespeare plays, and in 1982 he directed their version of *King Lear*.

I don't know if Miller has a curl in the middle of his forehead, but when he's good (*Taming of the Shrew*) he's very good, and when he's bad, he's horrid. Unfortunately, the latter is the case with *Lear*.

The problems begin with his casting Michael Hordern in the title role. Hordern has had a long movie career (he played Senex in the film version of *A Funny Thing Happened on the Way to the Forum*) and has been a frequent performer in the BBC films. The problem is his appearance. With a lined, puffy face and receding hair and chin, he looks like a disgruntled grocer. When you see him saying lines like "Come not between the dragon and his wrath" or "Ay, every inch a king," cognitive dissonance sets in. Senex, yes—Lear, no.

Another problem is that Miller has a pet theory about the Fool. He writes in his memoir, *Subsequent Performances*, "I have never been tempted to see the Fool as anything other than an old man, Lear's contemporary, and a broken-down rather insufferable clown. He comes closer to Lear than anyone and this is not because he is a young, charming, soft, capering goat but due to his age and performance, which is rather like an old music-hall comic . . ." Miller seems to believe that there are only two choices possible when casting the Fool—a broken-down clown or a young capering goat. My own perspective on the Fool comes from association with several productions of

Shakespeare Confidential

Gilbert & Sullivan's *Yeomen of the Guard*, whose central character is a professional jester. Much of the dialog and several of the songs in *Yeomen* deal with the difficulties of being a professional comic, emphasizing the training, talent and discipline required (this, of course, is true of music-hall comics as well). In line with his Fool theory, Miller selected an actor (Frank Middlemass) who looks like Hordern's twin brother. His profession is indicated by grimy smudges of greasepaint on his face; other than that, there is no trace of training or talent—he comes off as simply annoying. It's a remake of *Grumpy Old Men*.

Holm. A more recent version of *King Lear* was shown on PBS stations in 1998 and is available as a video. Directed by Richard Eyre and starring Ian Holm, it is based on a stage production by the Royal National Theatre. Holm came to prominence in 1966, playing the menacing pimp Lennie in Pinter's *The Homecoming*. In 1968 he played Puck in Peter Hall's production of *Midsummer Night's Dream*, the video of which was reviewed in the Shakespeare Oxford Newsletter for Spring 2001 (see our p. 5). Edginess and menace come easily to Holm, so it is natural that he should fall into the Anger Trap—that is, if you're playing Lear and you start out angry, you've got nothing but anger to play until you go mad.

It's tempting to describe this production as *Lear 101*, suitable for beginners. You know Regan is up to no good because she's bleached her hair. You know Edmund's the bad guy because he wears black leather, has beady eyes and an Alcatraz haircut. You *don't* know it from his wonderful "Thou, Nature, art my goddess" speech because that has been cut, with parts of it redistributed as voice-overs in other scenes.

Eyre apparently subscribes to Miller's Fool theory, as he has cast an older actor (Michael Bryant) who, with his white beard and peaked cap looks like a lawn ornament, a garden gnome come to life. However, there is a rapport between him and Holm; one can believe that their relationship is long-lived—the acting rescues the directorial concept. In fact, that is true of the whole production: in spite of some mistaken choices, the talent of the actors saves it. The "sharper than a serpent's tooth" scene between Lear and Goneril (Barbara Flynn), for example, is heart-wrenching.

Olivier. The Laurence Olivier version, produced for television and directed by Michael Elliott, was released in 1983. If the Eyre-Holm version is *Lear 101*, this is the master class—instead of "good" characters and "bad" characters, we have nuanced, three-dimensional human beings. This is made evident in the very first scene, between Gloucester, Kent and Edmund. The latter is played by Robert Lindsay, a frequent performer in the BBC series who can do either "good" (Benedick) or "bad" (Iachimo in *Cymbeline*). Gloucester is played by Leo McKern (*Rumpole of the Bailey*). When I saw Gloucester, with his potato face and cunning, pig-like eyes telling Kent (in effect) 'This is my bastard son—it was lots of fun screwing his mother,' I gasped at his callousness, and started to understand where Edmund was coming from.

Olivier is far too canny to fall into the Anger Trap. His Lear is initially all sweetness and solicitude. He smacks his lips in pleasurable anticipation of Cordelia's expression of her love for him. When she is asked "What can you say to draw a third more opulent than your sisters'?" and says "Nothing," most Lears bark out "Nothing will come of nothing" as a rebuke. Olivier says it in a gentle, wheedling tone, as if he were explaining the rules of the game to a child. His anger when Cordelia refuses to play the game is initially tentative until Kent jumps in: "What wouldst thou do, old man?" Then it explodes. This is the first version of *Lear* I've seen where the opening scene is convincing and moving, rather than simply establishing the premise for the rest of the action.

Even aside from Olivier, the cast is packed with great actors. Diana Rigg moves with feline grace and brings out a subtle comic side to Regan; her delivery of "He hath ever but slenderly known himself" is alone worth the price of admission. And in John Hurt we at last have a Fool with the smack of professionalism about him (Hurt achieved cinematic immortality by giving thoracic birth to a monster in the 1979 film *Alien*). Hurt miraculously avoids giving us either a broken-down clown or a capering young goat, but gives us instead a sensitive human being, deeply attached to Lear, who indeed "hath much pined away." Hurt does with the Fool's chiding what Olivier did with "Nothing will come of nothing" in the preceding scene; he makes it seem more like affectionate teaching than a rebuke.

Shakespeare Confidential

What struck me after watching this *Lear* was the extent to which the "good" characters precipitate the catastrophes that befall them (they don't *deserve* these catastrophes, but as Clint Eastwood observes in *Unforgiven*, "*Deserve*'s got nothin' to do with it"). Gloucester's callousness and credulity motivate and enable Edmund's villainy; Kent's outspokenness and impetuousness lead to his banishment and imprisonment in the stocks; Cordelia's devotion to verbal integrity rivals Isabella's fierce defense of her chastity in *Measure for Measure*. And, of course, Lear himself is the prime example.

Part of the enormous power of Shakespeare's plays is their resonance with the life of their creator, Edward de Vere. And part of the emotion with which this great version of *Lear* is charged comes from its resonance with the life of Laurence Olivier. He had been theatrical royalty for half a century when this film was made, initially (with John Gielgud and Ralph Richardson) one of the princes, and eventually king of the great Shakespearean roles. Now in the video he is seventy-six, frail, in poor health. He lived six years longer, increasingly feeble, but this was his last great role, his farewell to the world of Shakespeare. And he is still every inch a king.

Originally published in Shakespeare Matters *2.3 (Spring 2003).*

Confidential Video Bard

8

Taming of the Shrew: Zeffirelli and Miller

The Taming of the Shrew (1967) was stage director Franco Zeffirelli's first film. Starring what was then the world's most famous couple, Richard Burton and Elizabeth Taylor, it came on the heels of their disastrous (but well-publicized) version of *Cleopatra*.

The first 10 minutes of the film are a delight. We follow Lucentio (Michael York, in his film debut) and Tranio (Alfred Lynch) through the hills of Lombardy into Padua, which is bursting with medieval life. Zeffirelli displays the talent for suffusing the film with the look and feel of the Italian setting that he used to such good effect in his version of *Romeo and Juliet*, released the following year. But after the first 10 minutes, the overacting begins. Michael Hordern, as Baptista, bumbles and stumbles, rolls his eyes and purses his lips (attentive readers will recall that Hordern was not my favorite Lear). Victor Spinetti, who was droll as the neurotic technician in the Beatles movies *Hard Day's Night* and *Help*, plays Hortensio with a mincing manner and a Doris Day wig, calling so much attention to his efforts to be funny that he isn't. I have the feeling that Zeffirelli, drawing on his stage experience, encouraged everyone to play broadly, with the result that Hordern and Spinetti gave stage performances, while York and Lynch miraculously escaped. As did Cyril Cusack, whose sly Grumio is always amusing.

Richard Burton's characterization of Petruchio is opaque to me. In half the scenes he is a brawling, drunken lout, while in the other half he seems to be a reasonable man using rational methods to pursue achievable goals. I can't connect the dots, so ultimately I don't find the performance satisfying. As Kate, Elizabeth Taylor just exists—she's an icon rather than an actress.

Shakespeare Confidential

The film is always marvelous to look at—Zeffirelli has a fine eye for integrating architecture, fabrics, costumes and lighting so that every frame is visually satisfying. The screenwriters have trimmed about half the dialog, sometimes replacing it with interpolated scenes not in the original text, such as Kate's tumble into the river on the way to Verona, or the wedding itself, which occurs offstage in the original. And I have come to appreciate the final 20 minutes of the film, which documents the last stage of Kate's conversion. As Kate and Petruchio are about to enter Lucentio's house for the wedding feast, he stops her and says "Kiss me, Kate." She says "What, here in the street?" He asks if she is ashamed of him; she replies "No, God forbid, but ashamed to kiss." Finally, she relents and gives him a platonic peck on the nose. Petruchio looks disgruntled, but they proceed to the banquet. The turning point comes when Kate, watching children roughhousing between the tables, melts perceptibly (maybe Taylor is an actress after all). Apparently she at last sees herself in a domestic union ruled by cooperation rather than confrontation, and so is able to rise to the challenge of the obedience wager, and during her speech to the froward wives she discovers the pleasure of using socially accepted means to continue to beat up on Bianca. Petruchio again says "Kiss me, Kate," and she responds with genuine intensity.

In my last column I castigated BBC director Jonathan Miller for giving Michael Hordern the title role in his production of *Lear*. In this column I offer enthusiastic praise for his decision to cast Monty Python alumnus John Cleese as Petruchio in his production of *Shrew* (1980). Cleese has mastered the art of making the dialog sound like he just thought of it, so his Petruchio is natural, immediate, and convincing—as intelligent as Cleese himself, and surprisingly gentle. Sarah Badel's Kate is a worthy opponent; their wooing scene (2.1.182) is hilarious. In this exchange, the playwright achieves a bawd rate approaching unity—that is, almost every line contains a salacious *double entendre* (the corresponding scene in the Zeffirelli production falls flat because most of the lines have been cut, and what remains is overwhelmed by slapstick struggles).

Miller has written that his approach to a production is sometimes determined by a single line of text, in the same way that a paleontologist reconstructs the entire body of an extinct animal from an isolated fragment. I believe that his treatment of the final third of *Shrew* was inspired by Vincentio's reference to Kate as "my merry mistress" (4.5.53). Petruchio and Kate are traveling back to Padua, and he has got her reluctantly to agree that the object shining in the sky is the "moon, or sun, or what you please." An old man (Vincentio) approaches them on the road; Petruchio addresses him as "fair lovely maid" and bids Kate "embrace her for her beauty's sake." By now Kate has gotten into to spirit of the thing and goes over the top: "Young budding virgin, fair, fresh, and sweet . . . Happy the parents of so fair a child! Happier the man whom favorable stars allot thee for his lovely bedfellow!" Then when Petruchio, deadpan, corrects her—"Why, how now, Kate, I hope thou art not mad. This is a man, old, wrinkled, faded, withered"—the absurdity of the scene overwhelms her, and she collapses, shrieking with laughter. It's a wonderful moment, and it's the turning point for this Kate—hanging out with Petruchio is a lot more fun than throwing stools at Bianca. So when he asks for a kiss before they enter the banquet, she responds passionately, and he murmurs "Is this not well?"

Stephen Moorer's Pacific Repertory Theatre will be performing their version of *Shrew* during the Shakespeare Fellowship's fall conference in Carmel, 9-12 October 2003. We have seen that the arc of Kate's metamorphosis varies from production to production; it will be interesting to see how Moorer stages it.

Several years ago I was in a production of *Kiss Me, Kate*, the great Cole Porter musical which opened on Broadway in 1948. The most effective scenes in the show were the ones lifted directly from *Shrew*—they had a zest and sparkle that far outshone the by-the-numbers foolery of the scenes forming the contemporary plot. But now when I watch *Shrew* as a straight play, certain lines ("I've come to wive it wealthily in Padua," "Where is the life that late I led?") seem flat and empty when spoken, as if crying out to be sung. Why not do a show that combines the best of both worlds: a stripped-down version of *Shrew* that incorporates Porter's wonderful songs? If there's anybody out there with a lot of money, please contact me, and I'll start work on the script right away. The working title is *Kiss Me, Shrew*.

Originally published in *Shakespeare Matters* 2.4 (Summer 2003).

Confidential Video Bard

9

Taming of the Shrew Revisited, plus other Carmel performances

Apparently I am considered an easy mark by mail-order video dealers, since every week the postman brings me several catalogs, usually hawking something like the complete *œuvre* of Doris Day and Rock Hudson. However, late last summer I got a catalog offering a video of a 1976 stage performance of *Taming of the Shrew* by San Francisco's American Conservatory Theatre, directed by William Ball. Since I had just reviewed two versions of *Shrew* for *Shakespeare Matters* (Summer 2003) I was intrigued. Yielding to temptation (my usual response), I ordered the video. It turned out to be a jewel.

The production is explicitly based on the Italian *commedia dell'arte* style—the company enters dressed in white clown suits and wearing black masks with projecting beak-like noses. They take places on each side of the stage, and acting as a chorus, accompany the action with music, percussion, and group responses (they sigh when Bianca appears, cheer whenever 'Padua' is mentioned). The acting of the principals is bawdy, broad and mannered. Marc Singer is a good-natured Petruchio with a strapping physique. Kate is played by Fredi Olster, a classic beauty in the Raquel Welch tradition. Rick Hamilton sustains a sly Tranio, and Raye Birk, with bulging eyes, a goatish beard and a running gag involving noxious breath, is hilarious as Gremio, the *senex* figure. Slapstick abounds—the wooing scene ("Good morrow, Kate") is staged as a TV wrestling smackdown. It would be easy to dismiss this production as vulgar, silly nonsense. The first time I watched it I laughed a lot, but didn't see the artistry. On later viewings I came to appreciate the rich and detailed reactions that each of the actors had to the others' speeches. In spite of the exaggeration, recognizable human beings were interacting emotionally in clearly specified ways. This production was so clear and so funny that it convinced me that Oxford came back from his Italian tour determined to try his hand at *commedia dell'arte.*

The *Shrew* presented by Stephen Moorer's Pacific Repertory Theatre in Carmel (during the Fellowship conference in October) was directed by Mark Shilstone-Laurent, who may have been familiar with the video discussed above, since his production was in much the same style. One of its great strengths was the masterful Petruchio of Kevin Black—he had the audience in the palm of his hand from the moment he swaggered onto the stage. Emily Jordan as Kate was small but fierce. Her tendency to go over the top was fine in *Shrew*, but sometimes distracting in *Henry VI*, in which she played Queen Margaret. *Shrew* was staged in the magical Forest Theatre. During the performance a luminous full moon gradually rose behind the trees, reaching maximum visibility just in time for Petruchio's line "Good Lord, how bright and goodly shines the moon!" This got a big laugh, as did many other lines and bits of business. One of the rewards of being in the audience was watching just how involved the many teenagers were—whooping when the lovers kissed, and responding with genuine amusement to a play more than 400 years old.

In a previous column (see p. 19) I discussed the distinct *mental models* with which a viewer responds to a filmed production or an actual stage performance of a given play, suggesting that the viewer subconsciously thinks of the film as a *documentary*, for which the judgmental criterion is *believability*, while a staged performance is judged by other criteria—skill of the performers, rhythm, interweaving of ideas and actions, etc. It may be useful to summarize this distinction by imagining a continuum—call it the *documentary/commedia* continuum—on which a given production may be placed. (I am using 'documentary' as a shorthand term for the style of presenting a fictional narrative which depends on the *suspension of disbelief* to achieve its effect.) As the nomenclature implies, film is the medium *par excellence* for documentary presentations, while a stage and live performers (actual or implied) are necessary for the *commedia* effect. But the position of a given performance on the continuum depends on the material as well as the medium. The stage plays of Ibsen or Arthur Miller, for example, would be clustered around the documentary end, while films such as the Warner Bros. cartoons or the Marx Brothers movies are the modern versions of *commedia*. For *Shrew*, the BBC video starring John Cleese (see p. 35-6) is about as close as you can get to the documentary end of the scale, while the ACT version discussed here defines the *commedia* end. The remarkable thing is that both are so successful.

During the conference, Roger Stritmatter gave a paper on the Induction Scene that opens the Folio text of *Shrew*, in which a vagrant, Christopher Sly, is made to think he is lord of the castle; the play proper is then presented as entertainment for him. Roger pointed out that the Induction Scene is a miniature version of the authorship scam, in which an illiterate yokel is represented as the 'lord' of the greatest plays ever written. It is noteworthy that in none of the productions of *Shrew* discussed here or earlier is the Induction Scene used. A little thought suggests why. If you use the Induction Scene, you inexorably place the rest of the play on the *commedia* end of the continuum—these are actors, seeking to entertain, rather than representations of real people. In the film versions (Zeffirelli, BBC), the director does not want to do that—he wants you to *believe* what the actors are doing. How then do we explain the absence of the Induction Scene in the two stage versions we have discussed? The answer is that in these productions, **the** Induction Scene is replaced by ***an*** induction scene. The ACT version starts with the masked, costumed actors taking the stage in a stylized manner, dancing wildly, and then taking a group bow, establishing the presentational nature of what is to follow. The PRT performance began with a solo juggling act (appropriately, performed by a Christopher) which, again, prepared the audience to expect *commedia*-type performances. Quod erat demonstrandum.

1, 2 Henry VI. Much of the matter of these plays concerns the illicit love affair between the Duke of Suffolk and Queen Margaret (the wife of Henry VI), and the political antagonism between Suffolk and Cardinal Beaufort. In a paper given before the performances, Barbara Burris enhanced our appreciation of the plays by pointing out the parallels between Suffolk, Margaret and Beaufort, and the historical figures Leicester, Elizabeth and Burghley.

Stephen Moorer has mastered the art of presenting Shakespeare's history plays in exciting, compelling ways. He stages them in the intimate Circle Theatre, where the audience is close enough to grasp every nuance of gesture and expression, and he uses the many entrances to weave scenes together in a cinematic rush. And not least, he has assembled a company of superb actors. Fresh from his star turn as Petruchio, Kevin Black proved a stalwart member of the ensemble in the principal role of Suffolk. David Mendelsohn, heroic as the Black Prince in the 2001 production of *Edward III*, assumed a completely different persona as the devout, indecisive Henry. Travis Brazil did yeoman duty in four ensemble roles, capping them with a fifth as a demonically energetic Jack Cade, ironically brought low by a mild-mannered gardener with a large pair of shears. The gardener was played as a lovable eccentric by our old friend, Kevin Black. Speaking of old friends, the cast included two veterans of the 1976 ACT *Shrew*: Rick (Tranio) Hamilton, here playing a Duke of York determined to reach the throne, and Fredi (Kate) Olster, now Dame Eleanor Cobham, whose interest in sorcery proves so unfortunate. The wheel has come full circle.

Originally published in *Shakespeare Matters* 3.2 (Winter 2004)

Confidential Video Bard

10

The Merchant of Venice: 2004 and 1980

Imagine that a Shakespeare play goes unfilmed until the BBC productions, and then decades later is remade as a gorgeous, internationally-financed movie with famous stars. Now imagine it again.

The first time, it was *Titus Andronicus*, done by the BBC in 1985, then redone by Julie Taymor in 2000, with Anthony Hopkins in the title role (see p. 25-9). This time it's *The Merchant of Venice*. An excellent version by the BBC came out in 1980, then Michael Radford's lush production was released in the waning days of 2004—just in time to be eligible for the next round of Academy Awards (alas, in vain). Radford is a relative newcomer to the world of film. He is perhaps best known for *Il Postino* (1994), a romantic comedy also set in Italy. His *Merchant* was filmed on location in Venice and Luxembourg, and like Zeffirelli's *Romeo and Juliet* (1968) and Branagh's *Much Ado About Nothing* (1993), immerses us in the sights, sounds, and smells of Renaissance Italy. It contains two towering performances by seasoned male stars. Al Pacino's turn as Shylock is the more noticeable one—all the critics have praised it—but Jeremy Irons as Antonio is equally subtle and profound.

The film opens with some text explaining the legal status of Jews in 16th-century Venice, and then gives us a wordless crowd scene illustrating the hostile treatment of Jews in which we see Antonio contemptuously spitting on Shylock. The scene shifts to an interior with Antonio and friends, and the first line of the film is the same as that of the play: Antonio says "In sooth I know not why I am so sad." Irons does indeed look sad—every molecule in his face sags.

The negotiation for Antonio's borrowing the money from Shylock (1.3) is brilliantly staged. The scene opens with a goat being slaughtered in the marketplace. During the ensuing dialog between Bassanio and Shylock (then joined by Antonio) the anonymous butcher hacks a pound of flesh off the carcass and wraps it up for the Jew. This scene makes bloodily explicit what otherwise would be merely an abstract possibility.

Joseph Fiennes had the title role in *Shakespeare in Love* (1998) and played Leicester in *Elizabeth* (1998), which perhaps explains why I don't like him much. I was wishing for someone different to play Bassanio, and then it occurred to me that perhaps the director intended for the character to be borderline unlikeable. Both the text and the film make it clear that Bassanio is a spendthrift whose sole business enterprise is his plan to marry an heiress. Fiennes' 'Shakespeare' was a loser who spent most of the film dithering over 'Romeo and the Pirate's Daughter,' and his 'Leicester' was a weasel who spent most of the film professing love for Elizabeth while banging the court beauties (in this, at least, the film was historically accurate). Joseph Fiennes is apparently the poster boy for flawed studliness.

Lynn Collins is lovely as Portia, and effective in the trial scene as the young legal expert Balthasar. To make the disguise more believable, the director has given her some stubbly facial hair, which seems to be modeled on what we see in the Droeshout portrait. Zuleikha Robinson plays Shylock's daughter Jessica with the collagen-engorged lips so characteristic of 16th-century Jewish virgins.

My nominee for Most Enjoyable Performance in a Minor Role: David Harewood as the Prince of Morocco. He's black as coal and merry as a cricket, and he's surrounded by a posse of homeys who hum and chuckle appreciatively at his every *bon mot*.

The BBC video is a very different experience from the movie. To see Radford's film is to be transported through time and space to 16th-century Venice; to watch the BBC version is to see a group of accomplished actors perform Shakespeare's play. One notable difference is that the BBC retains all the dialog, while Radford cuts at least two-thirds of it. Another difference is the characterization of Shylock. Pacino inhabits the role and makes it tragic; the BBC's Warren Mitchell gives us a lively Shylock with a garment-district accent and a ready laugh. It's a comic performance that sometimes works better than the tragic one—for example when Mitchell as Shylock gleefully proposes the "merry bond" (1.3.139) one can almost believe

Antonio's acceptance. And Mitchell can turn on the tragedy when required, as when Tubal reports his daughter's spending (3.1), or at the end of the courtroom scene (4.1).

Gemma Jones is an excellent actress—she had the lead in the BBC's 1978 series *The Duchess of Duke Street*—but in this production she seems a little weird. In her first scene, with long blonde curls and a wedding-cake dress, she looks (and sounds) like Glinda the Good from *The Wizard of Oz* (1939). I find John Nettle (Bassanio) to be more likeable than Joseph Fiennes, and Leslee Udwin is touching as Jessica. John Franklyn-Robbins, in the title role, is noble and affecting, without neglecting the darker currents in the character.

Oxford's offstage cameo. I call your attention to Scene 1.2, in which Nerissa is asking Portia how she likes the various suitors.

Nerissa:	What say you then to Falconbridge, the young baron of England?
Portia:	You know I say nothing to him, for he understands not me, nor I him. He hath neither Latin, French, nor Italian; and you will come into the court and swear that I have a poor pennyworth in the English. He is a proper man's picture, but alas! who can converse with a dumb-show? How oddly he is suited! I think he bought his doublet in Italy, his round hose in France, his bonnet in Germany, and his behavior everywhere.

'Falconbridge' is the family name of Philip the Bastard, the hero of *King John*, and next to Hamlet perhaps the clearest authorial voice in the canon. The names 'Falconbridge' and 'Oxenford' are precisely parallel in construction: an animal (two syllables) followed by a means of crossing a river (one syllable).[1] Latin, French and Italian are the foreign languages in which Oxford was most fluent; the indication that Portia's offstage suitor can't speak them I take to be 'allusion by negation' (just as the admonition 'Don't think of a purple elephant' invariably evokes the mental image of a grape-hued pachyderm). I take "Who can converse with a dumb-show" to be another such sly allusion—Oxford was a voluble and witty talker, the very opposite of a pantomime artist. We then switch to a positive allusion: France, Germany and Italy were countries that Oxford visited during his grand tour of 1575-6. He could hardly have been known as 'the Italianate earl' without a wardrobe of Italian doublets, and it's generally agreed that Oxford is the figure caricatured by Barnabe Riche as "riding towards me on a footcloth nag, apparelled in a French ruff, a French cloak, a French hose . . ." And finally we have Portia's surmise that "he bought . . . his behavior eVery-where." Alfred Hitchcock made a practice of including a brief anonymous appearance in each of the films of which he was the *auteur*. I believe Portia's description of her offstage English suitor to be Oxford's equivalent of Hitchcock's prank. As a wise person once said, "The advantage of being an Oxfordian is that you get the jokes."

Significance of names. In reading the play I came across a situation that puzzled me. *Balthasar* is the servant Portia sends to Bellario to implement her impersonation of a judge. It is also the name she adopts as that judge. I don't think of Shakespeare as being a lazy writer—why would he use the same name twice?

The Book of *Daniel* recounts that when King Nebuchadnezzar conquered the Israelites, he caused a group of youths to be sent to Babylon. Among these was Daniel, who as a captive was renamed **BELTESHAZZAR**. The king had an ominous dream which proved opaque to all the wise men of his kingdom, but Daniel was able to interpret it. "Then the king made Daniel a great man, and gave him many great gifts, and made him ruler over the whole province of Babylon, and chief of the governors over all the wise men of Babylon" (*Daniel* 2.48). As governor, Daniel gained a reputation as a wise and upright judge.

Some time later, Nebuchadnezzar was succeeded by his son, Belshazzar. The young king fell into impious ways. He gave a great feast at which wine was served in the holy vessels of the Israelites. A disembodied hand appeared and wrote a cryptic message on the wall of the palace. Daniel, the expert interpreter, was brought in, and the message was declared to be "You have been tried in the scales and found wanting." "And that night was Belshazzar the king of the Chaldeans slain" (*Daniel* 5.30).

Various authorities state that *Balthasar*, the name used by our author for both the servant and the assumed judge, is a modified form of **BELSHAZZAR**, the Chaldean king. But this name differs by only one Hebrew letter (tet, ט) from **BELTESHAZZAR**, the name given Daniel as a captive. Some scholars speculate that 'ט' is a particle meaning 'servant of,' so that the modified form *Balthasar* could apply both to the servant and the person served, illuminating Shakespeare's use of the same name for the servant and the disguised Portia. Also illuminated is Shylock's cry of "A Daniel come to judgment! Yea, a Daniel!" when the Portia upholds the validity of his bond (4.1.221)—in assuming the name *Balthasar* Portia has literally become a Daniel. And note too how the image of being 'tried in the scales' resonates with the courtroom scene in the play.

Scholars have speculated on the origin of the name *Shylock*, which is found nowhere else in literature. Eva Turner Clark[2] has theorized that it comes from the last name of Michael Lock, who misrepresented the value of ore returned by Martin Frobisher, thus causing Oxford to invest £3000 in a disastrous enterprise, together with the slang meaning of 'shy,' which the *Oxford English Dictionary* gives as "of questionable character, disreputable, 'shady'." Ian Wilson speculates that the name comes from the Hebrew **SHALAKH** (שלך), "generally translated as cormorant, a particularly apposite choice for *The Merchant of Venice*'s voracious Jew, though from whom Shakespeare might have learnt this particular piece of Hebrew is one of his many mysteries." [3] Allan Bloom suggests that the name comes from a character mentioned in *Genesis* 11.12-15.[4] The name is rendered *Salah* in the King James version; in the original Hebrew it's שלח, where the first letter (shin) can be pronounced *sh*, and the final letter (khet) is a gutteral, like the 'ch' in German: thus **SHALACH**.[5] *Genesis* 11.14 states that "*Salah* lived thirty years and begat *Eber*." The distinction between *b* and *v* is labile between languages (e.g. English *even* and German *eben*) and within Hebrew: the first consonant in the Hebrew alphabet, ב, is named bet or vet, and is pronounced *b* or *v*.[6] The translators of the King James Bible chose to render ב as *b*. If we choose the alternative rendition, *v*, the verse, roughly translated, becomes '*Shylock* was *Ever*'s father.' Perceptive Oxfordians (Mildred Sexton, for one) have long regarded Shylock as a Burghley figure—Burghley being William Cecil, Lord Burghley, who was E. Vere's guardian and father-in-law. Either this is an outrageous coincidence, or it sheds further light on the author's choice of the name. I'm beginning to believe there are no arbitrary names in Shakespeare.

Originally published in *Shakespeare Matters* 4.2 (Winter 2005).

End Notes

1. W. S. Gilbert used this method of allusion in writing his 1881 comic opera *Patience*. The character based on poet Algernon Swinburne was called Reginald Bunthorne.' In both cases the last name is an animal followed by a feature of the landscape (brook, thicket) both monosyllabic.

2. Eva Turner Clark, *Hidden Allusions in Shakespeare's Plays*, Kennikat Press, New York, 1974, pp. 335-6.

3. Ian Wilson, *Shakespeare: The Evidence*, St. Martin's Griffin, New York, 1993, 215. How these Stratfordians love their mysteries! There is no mystery about how Oxford could have learned Hebrew: his confidential steward was Israel Anez, or Ames, a member of a prominent Jewish family (Clark, p. 347). *Note added 18 July 2009*: Nina Green says this family was not Jewish.

4. Allan Bloom, *Shakespeare's Politics*, Basic Books, New York, 1964, 33.

5. Hebrew words are read from right to left. Most of the letters are consonants; vowels are usually indicated by diacritical marks, omitted here.

6. *Encyclopedia Americana*, Grolier, Danbury CT, 2003, vol. 14, 34. I thank Rabbi Jonathan Kraus of Temple Beth El in Belmont, Massachusetts, for help with the Hebrew language.

11
The Legend of the Round Earthers

A long time ago in a land far away, there arose a civilization that spanned an entire continent. This civilization was very powerful and technologically advanced, but in some ways it was naïve. For example, most of its citizens believed the Earth was flat. Great universities had distinguished professors of Geography, and these professors would write books. Every year a book would be published by one of them explaining why Flatness was inevitable, or democratic, or just plain ordained by God.

Eventually a group of citizens began to have doubts about the flatness of the Earth. "The Sun is round," they said, "the Moon is round—might not the Earth be round too?" The professors of Geography scoffed at this idea. "The Sun and Moon are in the *sky*," they said, "that's why they're round. Get your feet back on the ground!" But one of the doubters thought of an experiment: he set up a pole of a standard height and measured the length of its shadow exactly at noon. He then traveled several hundred miles north and did exactly the same thing. The lengths of the shadows differed, just as they would on the surface of a sphere, and the experimenter, who was from a town called Waco, was able to calculate that the circumference of the Earth was around 25,000 miles. The professors of Geography jeered at this result, calling it "the Shadow Theory," or (deliberately mispronouncing the experimenter's town of origin), "the Whacko Theory." Several of them wrote books explaining in great detail why the Round-Earth theory was wrong. One of the most popular of these books was written by a professor named Jephtha Fairoaks; it was entitled *Flatness: the Documentary Facts*.

Many of the citizens who believed in a round Earth began exploring the consequences of this theory, with exciting results.

"Look," said one of them, "when a ship sails toward the horizon, the hull disappears first, then the sails, just as you'd expect for a curved Earth." Another noted that hitherto inexplicable lunar eclipses could be explained if a spherical Earth was occasionally interposed between the Sun and the Moon. These citizens formed an association to sponsor meetings and publications that would help them tell each other what they had learned about Roundness Theory. And each day, some of them learned something new, and they were happy, although some of them were bothered by the scorn directed at them by the professors of Geography and other Flat-Earth believers.

Then one day one of the Round-Earthers said "I have an idea! Let's sponsor a splendid feast! It will be in a luxurious place, and we'll have food and drink, and musicians and mummers, and many Flat-Earthers will come and see what fine fellows we are, and then they too will believe in a Round Earth." And so it came to pass that a splendid feast was held, with musicians and mummers and bounteous food and drink, and indeed, many Flat-Earthers came to the feast, and several of them said "What fine fellows these Round-Earthers are." But none of them changed their minds, and the professors of Geography were more scornful than ever. The association of Round-Earthers was saddled with an enormous debt from the feast, and they said "Oh, Lord! If only everybody realized that the Earth is round!"

The years went by with little change. Until a night exactly 100 years after the original experiment that established the roundness of the Earth, when a gigantic monolith mysteriously appeared on a hill just outside the little town of Waco. Some experts described it as a cube, while others said it had more the shape of a brick, but whatever it was, the object was silently emitting psychomagnetic waves that subtly affected neuronal belief structures in the human brain. Within 100 hours everyone in the empire realized that the Earth was indeed round. The professors of Geography said they had known it all along, and they quickly began writing books explaining why Roundness was inevitable, or democratic, or just plain ordained by God. The fastest writer was Professor Jephtha Fairoaks, and his book came out first, so subsequent books by other professors referred to him as "the father of modern Geography," or "the brilliant originator of Roundness Theory." And more and more books were published, and they all referred to Professor Fairoaks and to each other, but none of them referred to books and papers by the experimenter from Waco and his followers. The original Round-Earthers were completely ignored, and this made them sad. There didn't seem to be much use in exploring Round-Earth theory when so many professors were doing it. They even missed the scorn the professors used to fling at them. They stopped coming to association meetings, or contributing to its publications, and the association just faded away, except for reunions held every 10 years, when the original Round-Earthers would get together, drink too much, and reminisce about being called names like "promulgators of pernicious doctrine," "loopy lemmings," and "the sub-scientific equivalent of the sub-religious Scientologists." Then they would sigh, and have another drink.

Moral No. 1. Be careful what you wish for.

Moral No. 2. Recognize a Golden Age when you're in it.

This parable was read at the Shakespeare Oxford Society conference held in Newton, Massachusetts, 11-14 November 1999, and subsequently published in the Shakespeare Oxford Newsletter *35.3 (Fall 1999). The "splendid feast" is a reference to the 1998 SOS conference in San Francisco, which was indeed sumptuous, and went way, way over budget.*

12
Mathematical Models of Stratfordian Persistence

The year 1593 saw the publication of the first work attributed to "William Shake-speare," the narrative poem *Venus and Adonis*. Subsequent years saw other publications with this attribution: another poem, a number of plays, a collection of sonnets, and finally, in 1623, a large volume entitled *Mr. William Shakespeares Comedies, Histories, & Tragedies* appeared, containing thirty-six plays. This collection, usually referred to as the First Folio, contained introductory material eulogizing the deceased author, but provided remarkably little biographical information. Ben Jonson addresses the author as "Sweet Swan of Avon!" and Leonard Digges refers to "thy Stratford Moniment." These references have been interpreted to mean that the author was William Shaksper, a native of the village of Stratford-on-Avon. This interpretation, bolstered by further events, such as the appearance of Nicholas Rowe's biography (1709) and David Garrick's Stratford Festival (1769), became the orthodox belief.

The first major public challenge to belief in the Stratfordian Shakespeare occurred in 1856 with the publication of Delia Bacon's book, *The Philosophy of the Plays of Shakespeare Unfolded*. Bacon argued that the plays had been written by a group of Elizabethan courtiers including Francis Bacon (no relation), Walter Raleigh, and Edmund Spenser, an assertion that in public debate soon took on the simpler form, "Bacon wrote Shakespeare." This debate stirred up interest in the authorship question, and several other candidates were proposed, e.g. Christopher Marlowe, the Earl of Derby, and the Earl of Rutland. The paucity of evidence for the Stratfordian attribution was authoritatively summarized in George Greenwood's book *The Shakespeare*

Problem Restated (1908), a work which inspired Mark Twain's essay "Is Shakespeare Dead?" (1911). Both Greenwood and Twain are careful to point out that they are not claiming that Bacon was the author; rather that it was impossible that it could be the Stratford man.

The modern phase of the authorship question began in 1920 with the publication of a book by John Thomas Looney, *"Shakespeare" Identified*. Looney was an English schoolmaster who had taught Shakespeare's plays for many years and had grown skeptical of the traditional attribution. He embarked on a systematic search for the identity of the true author, armed with a set of characteristics (e.g., "A member of the higher aristocracy . . . Loose and improvident in money matters . . .") gleaned from Looney's study of the plays.

Looney's special insight was that an author writing Shakespeare's works pseudonymously would not have had time for a second career; thus he looked for someone who was relatively unknown, rather than a famous figure like Bacon or Raleigh. He started out by scanning an anthology of Elizabethan poetry, looking for contributors who wrote in the meter used in *Venus and Adonis*. He found a candidate in Edward de Vere, Seventeenth Earl of Oxford, and further research showed that the set of required characteristics Looney had derived fit Oxford like a glove. He summarized his research in his book, which is still a thrilling account of a major discovery, beautifully written, cogently argued, and utterly compelling.

The subject I will examine here is the response to this book of the academic community, loosely defined as the ensemble of all professors teaching English literature in four-year degree-granting colleges, or in associated graduate studies. In accordance with current usage, those who are firmly committed to the view that Shaksper of Stratford was the author of Shakespeare's works will be termed Stratfordians, while those convinced by Looney's arguments will be designated Oxfordians. A further category comprises those who believe that Oxford wrote the works, but find it politically disadvantageous to admit it, the crypto-Oxfordians. (As the term implies, the identities of crypto-Oxfordians are hidden, but I have my own favorite candidates, including Helen Vendler, author of *The Art of*

Shakespeare's Sonnets, whose insistence that Shakespeare writes with the voice of a "fictive speaker" forestalls discussion of any possible autobiographical elements, and Louis Marder, who is surely aware that printed etchings reverse the original image.) To simplify the discussion, we will assume that all academics belong to one of these categories, so

$$P = P_{St} + P_{Ox} + P_{cOx}$$

where P is the population of academics, and the subscripted quantities correspond to the categories defined above. For further simplification, the variable we will be dealing with is

$$p = P_{St}/P$$

the fraction of the population composed of committed Stratfordians. Specifically, we will examine possible models of the time evolution of the Stratfordian population, p(t).

Figure 2 illustrates a possible model for academic behavior: we assume that prior to the appearance of Looney's book, the population is entirely Stratfordian (p = 1). Then in 1920, professors start reading about the Oxfordian hypothesis, and realize that it solves many nagging questions raised by the Stratfordian attribution,

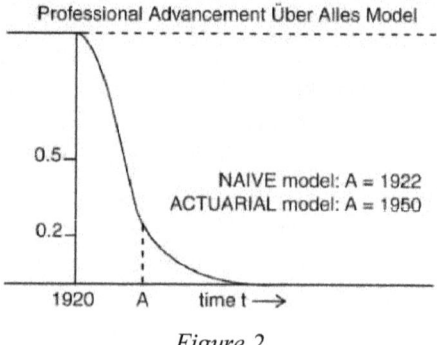

Figure 2

and that in addition, it makes possible a depth and coherence of understanding of the works that was previously unattainable. The Stratfordian population then drops rapidly, so that after about a year, p has declined to about 0.20. This model obviously does not account for the observed facts, so it must be termed the *Naive Model* of academic behavior. A more realistic model (the *Actuarial Model*) might be devised from the following scenario: we assume that the senior faculty (say 50 years old in 1920) guard the gates of orthodoxy while 20-year-old grad students read Looney on the sly. In about 30 years (~1950) the former grad students are the senior faculty, and the Oxfordian attribution has become orthodox. Again, this model fails to account for the fact that English departments are still (apparently) overwhelmingly Stratfordian.

A much more successful scheme is the *Professional Advancement Über Alles Model*, which assumes that the promotion of a young Shakespeare scholar depends on his or her writing a book that is well received by the Old Guard. Since the Old Guard is Stratfordian, the successful book will be written from a Stratfordian viewpoint, even if the authorship question is not explicitly discussed. Over time, as the successful young author him/herself becomes a member of the Old Guard, it will of course be impossible to disown the earlier work, so the Stratfordian orthodoxy is stable and self-perpetuating for all time, as indicated by the dashed horizontal line $p(t) = 1.0$ at the top of Fig. 2.

While the above model is, sadly, the most accurate one considered so far, there are indications that it is unduly pessimistic: at the time of writing I am aware of at least two English departments (Concordia University in Portland, Oregon, and the US Air Force Academy in Colorado Springs) headed by Oxfordian scholars, and the de Vere Studies Conference, organized at Concordia University by Dr. Daniel Wright, is about to have its fourth annual meeting. So $p(t)$ must be diminishing, at however glacial a pace. We therefore propose a Modified Professional Advancement Model. Again, we assume that the academic population consists of Stratfordians, Oxfordians, and crypto-Oxfordians, that $p(t)$ is the fraction of committed Stratfordians, and that the time variable t is the number of years after 1920. We assume that $p(0) = 1.0$ (that is, in 1920, all academics were Stratfordians). We then assume there is a gradual decay in $p(t)$ (that is, some academics become Oxfordians or crypto-Oxfordians) until $p(t) = 0.5$. That represents the point at which Oxfordians and crypto-Oxfordians are as numerous as Stratfordians, and there is thus little reason for hiding one's Oxfordian proclivities. It is therefore a critical point, initiating a change of phase in the system (analogous to a warming ice crystal when temperature $T(t)$ reaches 0^0 Centigrade).

The *Modified Professional Advancement Model* is capable of yielding quantitative results if a suitable function is chosen to describe the decay of p(t). The function that comes immediately to mind is the exponential function,

p(t) = exp(-rt)

where the notation "exp" indicates that the constant e (= 2.718...) is to be raised to the power represented by the quantity in parenthesis (this function is widely used to represent a number of physical processes, including radioactive decay). As noted above, t is the time in years since 1920; r is a rate constant which we will call the "academic rationality index," a quantity which can range from 1 to 0. If r = 1 we get complete conversion to the Oxfordian attribution within a few months, thus reproducing the *Naive Model* illustrated in Fig. 2. If r = 0 the rate of Stratfordian decay is zero, reproducing the simple *Professional Advancement Model* (the dashed horizontal line in Fig. 2). Since the former model is too optimistic and the latter is too pessimistic, we know that the value of r which best fits the actual situation is less than 1 and greater than 0. If we knew the value of p(t) for any given time, we could solve for r and use that value to predict the year in which p(t) would reach the critical value of 0.5. Unfortunately, estimating p(t) requires

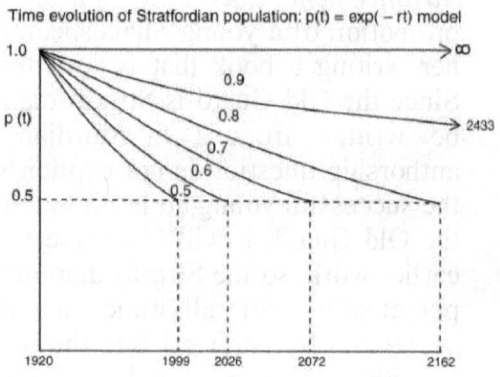

Figure 3

Time Evolution of Stratfordian Population
p(t) = exp(-rt) model

p (1999)	r	t$^{1/2}$	Y$^{1/2}$	ΔY
0.9	0.00135	513	2433	434
0.8	0.00286	242	2162	163
0.7	0.00479	152	2072	73
0.6	0.00665	106	2026	27
0.55	0.00767	90	2010	11
0.5	0.00889	79	1999	0

Table 1

knowing the population of crypto-Oxfordians, P_{cOx}, and no experimental method for determining this number has yet been devised (by the definition of a crypto-Oxfordian, questions about authorial orientation will not be answered candidly). The best we can do is assume a series of values of p for the year 1999, solve for r, then calculate the critical year in which p(t) = 0.5. The results for a series of these calculations are shown in Table 1 and plotted in Figure 3 (both on p. 54).

Table 1, for example, shows that if p(t) in 1999 were 0.7, it would reach 0.5 by the year 2072, 73 years from 1999, a discouraging prediction, since the author does not expect to be around in 2072.

As mentioned above, the exponential function is used for modeling the process of radioactive decay. One of the physical features of this process is that the radioactive nuclei do not interact with each other; the probability that any given nucleus will decay in any given period of time is entirely

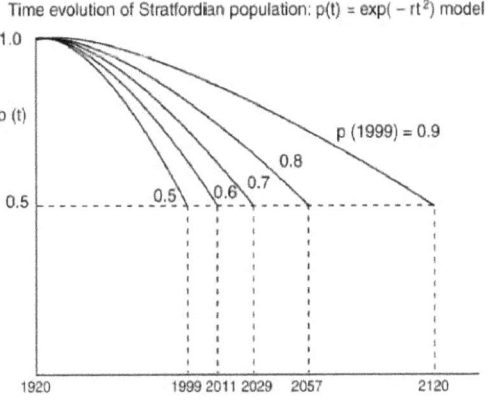

Figure 4

Time Evolution of Stratfordian Population
p(t) = exp(-rt) model

p (1999)	r	t½	Y½	ΔY
1	0	∞	∞	∞
0.9	0.000 0173	200	2120	121
0.8	0.000 0367	137	2057	58
0.7	0.000 0586	109	2029	30
0.6	0.000 0840	91	2011	12
0.5	0.000 1111	79	1999	0

Table 2

independent of what the other nuclei are doing, and from this standpoint, a sample of radioactive material can be regarded as a collection of non-interacting particles. It may be that the simple exponential function is inadequate to describe English departments, where there is at least the possibility that members might interact. This possibility could be accounted for mathematically by increasing the time dependence of the function used to describe the decay. This can be done most simply by raising t in the exponent to a higher power:

$$p(t) = \exp(-rt^2)$$

The results of using this function to solve for a series of values of r using assumed values for p are shown in Table 2 and plotted in Figure 4 (both on p. 55). Examination of Fig. 4 shows us what we should have recognized immediately, that $\exp(-rt^2)$ is a Gaussian function, widely used in population studies. Table 2 shows us that the Gaussian function is more optimistic than the simple exponential: if p(t) is 0.7 in 1999, it is predicted to reach the critical value of 0.5 in 2029, when some of us may still be around.

Switching from $\exp(-rt)$ to $\exp(-rt^2)$ changes the dimension of the academic rationality index r from $(\text{years})^{-1}$ to $(\text{years})^{-2}$. Note the extraordinarily small values of r in Table 2: if p(t) is 0.7 in 1999, r is 0.000 0586 (equivalent to 58.6 microberneys, where a berney is taken as the standard unit of rationality).

In one sense this has been an empty exercise: we don't know the current value of p, we're not sure that the dynamics are Gaussian, we're not even sure that 0.5 is the critical value of p (perhaps the power of senior faculty is such that p must fall to 0.4 or 0.3 before a paradigm shift occurs). However, for some people, it is satisfying to have constructed a mathematical model, even if it is a fuzzy one; the parameters have been defined, even if their exact values are not known. Certainly efforts could be made to get a firmer estimate of p; perhaps a crypto-Oxfordian hotline could be established to gather anecdotal evidence. It may be that one value of this study is to clarify the time perspective. I first read Charlton Ogburn's great book, *The Mysterious William Shakespeare*, in 1986, and it seemed to me that the case he made for Oxford's authorship was obvious and irrefutable. If I had been told then that thirteen years later the orthodox view would still be firmly established, I would have been astonished. The Gaussian model tells us that even if the current academic population is 30 per cent Oxfordian and crypto-Oxfordian, it will be another 30 years before that view prevails. We should be prepared for a long haul.

AFTERWORD. On 22 April 2007, William Niederkorn of *The New York Times* reported that, "In an Education Life survey of American professors of Shakespeare, 82 percent said there was no good reason to question whether William Shakespeare of Stratford-on-Avon was the principal author of the poems and plays . . . " Taking the variable p as 0.82, we calculate a rationality index of 26.2 microberneys and a critical point ($p = 0.5$) 163 years from 1920, i. e. 2083. That seems about right.

Originally published in *The Oxfordian* (Vol. 2, 1999)

13

Six Reasons Why Stratfordian 'Scholarship' Is So Bad

1. The overriding reason is, of course, they have the wrong guy. Imagine for a moment that the works of Samuel Langhorne Clemens were commonly attributed to Marcus P. Twayne of Duluth, Minnesota. How many insightful papers on *Tom Sawyer* and *Huckleberry Finn* would you expect to see? The orthodox scholars would say things like "*Twayne must have acquired his intimate knowledge of Southern customs by talking with travelers at the Partygirl Tavern.*"

2. Orthodox scholars have an agenda, which is to defend the Stratfordian attribution. They dare not initiate research which might lead to results tending to undermine the legend of the lad from Stratford. When Stanley Wells and Paul Edmondson bring out a book like *Shakespeare Beyond Doubt*, it isn't because they have new insights to share—it's because they're protecting the lucrative flow of tourists who come to see the 'birthplace'.

3. Stratfordians are required to disparage Edward de Vere. "*You think that violent, villainous fool wrote these wonderful plays and poems? You must be crazy!*"

4. Stratfordians are required to disparage William Shakespeare (the putative author). This may seem counter-intuitive, but it serves to lighten the burden of explaining the astonishing erudition found in the works. "*Sure he made mistakes—you can't take a boat from Verona to Milan, and Bohemia doesn't have a seacoast— but whaddaya expect? He's just a kid from a rural village.*"

5. The main (only?) piece of evidence for Stratford Will: *"His name is on the plays!"* Thus orthodox scholars are forbidden to explore the possibility that works that have survived anonymously (*The Spanish Tragedy, Thomas of Woodstock*) are by the author of *Hamlet*.

6. Stratfordians acknowledge that *Julius Caesar* is about Julius Caesar and that *Henry V* is about Henry V, but they cannot admit seeing historical figures under other names, such as Henry VII as Posthumus in *Cymbeline*, or Leicester as the villain in *Titus Andronicus, Hamlet*, and many more. With this restriction they miss a host of historical parallels—and a lot of juicy court gossip. Ironically, it was Robert Cecil's fear of being identified with another hunchback—the character Richard III—that made him blackmail Oxford into suppressing his identity as author, so that people would not be tempted to associate characters in the plays with political figures. Stratfordians are obeying Cecil's *diktat* over 400 years after it was made.

Sir Walter Scott as Paleo-Oxfordian, Part 1

14

Kenilworth

Kenilworth is a novel by Sir Walter Scott, published in 1821. The plot concerns the efforts of the arrogant and ambitious Robert Dudley, Earl of Leicester, to ingratiate himself with Queen Elizabeth while keeping secret his earlier marriage to Amy Robsart. Scott plays fast and loose with the historical chronology: the action supposedly takes place in the summer of 1575, while the historical Amy Robsart died in 1560.

I was reading the novel to get Scott's take on Leicester when I came across a startling passage. Leicester is bustling through the court, greeting followers and exuding bonhomie, when he spots a familiar face:

> Ha, Will Shakespeare—wild Will!—thou hast given my nephew, Philip Sidney, love-powder—he cannot sleep without thy Venus and Adonis under his pillow!—we will have thee hanged for the veriest wizard in Europe. Hark thee, mad wag, I have not forgotten thy matter of the patent, and of the bears.[1]

"The veriest wizard in Europe." As an Oxfordian, I could scarcely miss the name-clue *veriest*, referring to Edward de Vere. Coincidence? Perhaps. How about *wizard*? Could it refer to Henry Howard's accusation that de Vere was a sorcerer and the owner of a book of prophecies? And why *Europe*? Surely Leicester would have said "the veriest wizard in England," unless Scott was trying to point to someone who was known as "the Italianate Englishman," who had traveled extensively in France, Germany, Italy and Sicily, and who spoke colloquial French and Italian.

There are other clues. Philip Sidney was indeed Leicester's nephew, but his name is associated with de Vere's because of the tennis quarrel. And Leicester calls Shakespeare a "mad wag," which, like "madcap," is used in the plays to designate characters (Philip the Bastard, Feste, Prince Hal) identified with Oxford. And 128 pages later, Oxford himself puts in a cameo appearance. The Queen has been told that Amy is the wife of

Varney, Leicester's henchman, and has commanded her to appear at court. Varney appears with certificates testifying that Amy is too sick to travel. Elizabeth asks if the certificates can be authenticated, and Varney replies "So please your Majesty, my young Lord of Oxford, who is here in your presence, knows Master Anthony Forster's hand and his character." The novel goes on to describe Oxford as a "a young unthrift whom Forster had more than once accommodated with loans at usurious interest," and reports that he "verified the certificate."

What did Scott know, and how did he know it? Scott was writing 100 years before the publication of Looney's *Shakespeare Identified*; was there a confidential tradition of Shakespearean identity that reached from the 17th century to the 19th? We know there is such a tradition somewhere in the bowels of the British government—the bust in the Stratford chapel was altered to look more authorial around 1749,[2] and more recently someone has quietly been persuading historians to eliminate references to Henry Wriothesley and Henry de Vere.[3]

Elsewhere I have developed evidence that Herman Melville's last work, *Billy Budd*, is his homage to Edward de Vere as the author of Shakespeare's works.[4] Did Melville tap into a confidential tradition, or did he anticipate Looney by researching 16th-century poets, casting his conclusion in the form of a *roman à clef* rather than a literary detective story? Melville's grandfather claimed that the family was descended from titled Scottish nobility. The ambassador to the Elizabethan court when Mary Stuart reigned in Scotland was Sir James Melville. Further research is necessary to verify the details, but I believe that both Scott and Melville were paleo-Oxfordians; that is, those who knew the truth about Shakespearean authorship before Looney published *Shakespeare Identified*. There may be more of them.

I no longer fear that the Paradigm Shift will leave us with nothing to do. The fun is just beginning.

Originally published in the *Shakespeare Oxford Newsletter* 36.3 (Fall 2000)

End Notes

1. Scott is apparently referring to a scene from a play produced by students at St. John's College, Cambridge, ca. 1600, *The Returne from Parnassus I*. The character *Ingenioso* has quoted *Venus and Adonis* to another character, *Gullio*, who replies:

    > . . . Let this duncified worlde esteeme of Spencer and Chaucer, I'le worship sweet Mr. Shakspeare, and to honoure him will lay his Venus and Adonis under my pillowe, as wee reade of one (I do not well remember his name, but I am sure he was a kinge) slept with Homer under his bed's head. [W. D. Macray, ed. *Parnassus: Three Elizabethan Comedies* (Clarendon, 1886).]

    Scott here exhibits his customary insouciance with historical dates, since Sidney died in the Netherlands in 1586, and *Venus and Adonis* was not published until 1593.

2. Richard Whalen, 'The Stratfod Bust: a Monumental Fraud', *The Oxfordian* VIII, (2005), 7-24.

3. Peter W. Dickson, "Are British scholars erasing two heroic earls from Jacobean history to protect the Shakespeare industry?" *Shakespeare Oxford Newsletter* 35.1 (Spring 1999), 8-9, 24.

4. See '*Billy Budd* and *The Monument*,' p. 182-95, this volume.

Sir Walter Scott as Paleo-Oxfordian, Part 2

15

The Abbot

A few years ago I read *Kenilworth*, Sir Walter Scott's 1821 novel about the Earl of Leicester's attempts to persuade Queen Elizabeth to marry him, and the associated murder of his wife, Amy Robsart. Verbal clues in the novel led me to believe that Scott was aware of Edward de Vere's authorship of the Shakespeare canon a hundred years before the publication of Looney's *Shakespeare Identified*. Richard Whalen[1] has made the case for such knowledge on the part of Charles Dibdin (a composer in David Garrick's circle ca. 1769) and Robert Plumer Ward (like Scott, a 19th-century novelist). Thus there appears to have been an ongoing community of literary figures who knew the identity of the Bard and referred to it cryptically in their writings. I term these people *paleo-Oxfordians*.

Another of Scott's novels, *The Abbot* (1820), offers a fictional treatment of historical events of 1567-68 in Scotland—the imprisonment of Mary, Queen of Scots, in a castle on the island of Lochleven, her forced abdication, and her subsequent escape. In spite of the title, the protagonist of the novel is Roland Græme, an orphan adopted as a page by Lady Avenel. Græme eventually joins the suite of Mary Stuart and aids in her escape. I believe that Scott intended the knowing reader to associate Græme with Edward de Vere, for reasons given below.

(1) *High Rank.* In spite of his apparently humble origin, perceptive observers detect evidence of nobility. The domestic, Lilias, muses

> He must, she thought, be born of gentle blood; it were shame to think otherwise of a form so noble and features so fair; the very wildness in which he occasionally indulged, his contempt of danger and impatience of restraint, had in them something noble: assuredly, the child was born of high rank. [28][2]

A few pages later, she exclaims

> . . . he speaks as if he were the son of an earl! [70]

Of course, at the end of the novel it is revealed that he *is* in fact the son of a nobleman, the Baron Julian Avenel.

(2) *Association with Falconry.* Beginning with Chapter 4, much is made of young Roland's friendship with Adam Woodcock, Avenel's falconer. They argue about whether to feed the eyases washed or unwashed meat; hawking terms and metaphors permeate much of the dialog.

(3) *Catholic Leanings.* Wingate, the castle steward, notes

> I have often noticed that the boy had strange observances which savoured of Popery, and that he was very jealous to conceal them [78]

In fact, the battle between Catholicism and the Reformed Church for Græme's allegiance is one of the major themes of the book.

The above traits constitute three of the criteria adduced by Looney (p. 103, Miller edition) in seeking the identity of the Bard: No. 2. A member of the higher aristocracy; No. 5. A follower of sport (including falconry); No. 9. Of probable Catholic leanings, but touched with skepticism.

(4) *Word-clues.* On page 55, Wingate says of Græme ". . . but the youth is a fair youth . . ." It takes but the buzz of a vocal cord to change 'fair' to 'vair,' the contemporary pronunciation of 'Vere.' On page 271, Adam Woodcock tells him " . . . thou hadst been the *veriest* crack-hemp of a page that *ever* wore feather in thy bonnet," providing two references to the Vere family name (emphasis added). Another word-clue is 'madcap,' a term characteristically used in the Shakespeare plays (along with the equivalent, 'mad wag') to describe

characters such as Prince Hal, Philip the Bastard, and Feste, who are extensions of the author. 'Madcap' is applied to Roland Græme at least five times [139, 187, 225, 230, 466]. No other character is referred to in this way.

(5) *Græme's Age.* In the main part of the novel, Græme's age is given as 18 [231, 398]. Since the events described take place in 1567, he must have been born in 1549. This is within a year of Edward de Vere's birth, even with the possible ambiguity of whether he was the son of John de Vere or of Thomas Seymour.

(6) *The Ceremony of the Ewer.* After Græme has been installed as a page in Mary Stuart's retinue at Lochleven, he serves dinner to her ladies-in-waiting.

> When he observed that they had finished eating, he hastened to offer to the elder lady the silver ewer, basin, and napkin, with the ceremony and gravity which he would have used towards Mary herself. [356]

As explained in Vol. II of the Miller edition of Looney (p. 106–117), the Office of the Ewrie was a hereditary function of the Earls of Oxford. The duties consisted of serving a newly-crowned monarch at the banquet following the coronation in exactly the manner described above. Note that Scott is careful to introduce the word 'ceremony' into his description of what was ostensibly a rather mundane event, and to indicate that it normally would have involved the Queen.

For the most part, the references associating Græme with Oxford are nonfunctional—icing on the cake, or caviar for the knowing—not affecting the plot or intended to reflect actual events in de Vere's life. There is one possible exception to this view. The climactic set-piece of the novel is the battle between forces loyal to Mary and those supporting the Protestant Lords (historically this took place at Langside on 13 May 1568; Scott places it at Crookstone); Mary's forces were seeking to depose Moray, the Regent, and return Scotland to the Church of Rome.

It is during this battle that Roland (now surnamed Avenel) first experiences combat, and is transformed from a page to a knight. A year and a half after the Battle of Langside there was an uprising in England, instigated by the Catholic earls of the North with the object of deposing Elizabeth and replacing her with Mary, thus returning England to the Church of Rome. This rebellion was suppressed by Elizabeth's forces, led by Thomas Radcliffe, Earl of Sussex. He was accompanied by his 19-year-old protégé Edward de Vere, who thus gained his first experience of combat.

About two-thirds of the way through the novel, Roland is sent on an errand from Lochleven to a village on the shore. The villagers are celebrating May Day, and the festivities include a performance by a group of traveling players. Scott's account includes the following remarkable sentence:

> . . . Amid all these, and more acceptable than almost the whole put together, was the all-licensed fool, the Gracioso of the Spanish drama, who, with his cap fashioned into the resemblance of a coxcomb, and his bauble, a truncheon terminated by a carved figure, wearing a fool's cap, in his hand, went, came, and returned, mingling in every scene of the piece, and interrupting the business, without having any share himself in the action, and ever and anon transferring his gibes from the actors on the stage to the audience who sate around, prompt to applaud the whole. [415]

This sentence is remarkable for at least two reasons: (a) it contains 17 commas, more than any sentence I can remember encountering before, and (b) almost everything it mentions is inappropriate to the scene it purports to describe. In *Lear* (1.4.201), Goneril refers to her father's jester as his "all-licensed fool." This term is appropriate for a court, where the reigning authority may give a jester permission to deal with sensitive topics, but it makes no sense applied to traveling players performing on a village green. Who does the licensing? It appears to have been included simply to point us in the direction of the Shakespeare plays. "Truncheon" is an odd word in this context—an archaic meaning is "the shaft of a spear." Webster's dictionary defines "gracioso" as "a sportive and comic character in Spanish comedy," that is, a madcap. Scott apparently uses the Spanish word (capitalized) to imply that this madcap is a noble, habitually addressed as "your Grace." The Gracioso is described as "mingling in every scene of the piece, and interrupting the business, without having any share himself in the action." This is not what an actor does, it's what a *director* does during the rehearsal process—and can we doubt that Oxford himself directed the plays he wrote? Then there's "ever and anon transferring his gibes from the actors on the stage to the audience . . . ." How do you do that? Does the Fool listen to each actor's lines, then run to the edge of the stage and repeat them to the audience? A play staged that way would be booed rather than applauded. Scott is describing what the *author* does, "ever and anon," providing the gibes that the actors then deliver to the audience. Even the word "stage" is inappropriate, as Scott has previously established that the performance takes place on a plot of greensward. I can only conclude that Scott is giving the mature Oxford—actor, director and playwright—a cameo appearance, perhaps to balance the use of the young Oxford as a model for Roland.

Figure 5 - Edward de Vere, 17th Earl of Oxford

Scott was writing almost two hundred years after publication of the First Folio, and fifty years after David Garrick's Stratford Jubilee mythologized the Lad from Stratford. How did he learn the truth? One of Scott's biographers[3] writes

> Indeed, his literary art was based on memory: he learned about the recent past by listening eagerly to the memories of survivors of distant adventures, and his most fruitful approach to history was through a chain of recollection.[3]

And later,

> It was Scott's friend and former schoolfellow Adam Ferguson who first introduced him to the society of those whom Scott later called 'the most distinguished literati of the old time who still remained, with such young persons as were thought worthy to approach their circle and listen to their conversation'.

So evidently there were circles of "distinguished literati" within which the secret of the Bard's identity was passed from generation to generation. These were the people that Scott expected would understand and appreciate his oblique references to Oxford as Shakespeare, the audience for whom he wove these references into the fabric of his story. The significance of Scott's knowledge of Oxford is not so much that Scott knew it, but that a community of literati knew it. As we think about the history of the authorship question, it is important to be aware of these clandestine groups. The study of paleo-Oxfordian communities and populations would seem to be a fruitful field for further investigation.

Previously published in Shakespeare Matters 3.1 (Fall 2003)

End Notes

1. Richard Whalen, *Shakespeare Oxford Society Newsletter* 31.4 (Autumn 1995), 12
2. Page numbers in square brackets refer to the Houghton Mifflin edition of 1913.
3. David Daiches, *Sir Walter Scott and His World* (Viking, New York, 1971), 19.

Sir Walter Scott as Paleo-Oxfordian, Part 3

16

The Monastery

I have argued on two previous occasions that a close reading of novels by Sir Walter Scott (*Kenilworth, The Abbot*) suggests that Scott was aware that the works of Shakespeare were actually written by Edward de Vere, 17th Earl of Oxford, and moreover, that Scott was familiar with many of the details of de Vere's life. Since Scott was writing one hundred years before the publication of Looney's book, *Shakespeare Identified*, I have dubbed Scott a 'paleo-Oxfordian.' Response to these essays from the community of Oxfordians interested in Scott's works has been so enthusiastic that I have been encouraged to delve into yet another of the Waverley novels.

The Monastery (1820) is the prequel to *The Abbot* (also from 1820). It follows the fortunes of two brothers, Halbert and Edward Glendinning. Halbert's interests are chiefly hunting and the use of arms; Edward's nature is contemplative and spiritual—indeed, he becomes the eponymous cleric of the sequel. The plot is moved along from time to time by a ghost called 'the White Lady,' a contrivance to which many of Scott's readers objected (*The Monastery* was not one of his more successful novels).

One of my motives in undertaking another Scott novel was to see if I could find one which did *not* contain a character resembling Edward de Vere—a control, so to speak, to make sure I was not reading things into the novels that weren't there. For the first week or so I thought *The Monastery* was it. Then on page 171 Sir Piercie Shafton, the Euphuist, is introduced. Mysie, the miller's daughter, describes him thus:

> "I think this rider be not of our country. He has a crimson velvet bonnet, and long brown hair falling down under it, and a beard on his upper lip, and his chin clean and close shaved, save a small patch on the point of it . . ."

I don't know about you, but the image I get on reading this description bears a strong resemblance to the Welbeck portrait of Oxford in a foppish mode (see the Welbeck on p. 67).

More clues follow:

> ... the etiquette of the times did not permit Sir Piercie Shafton to pick his teeth, or to yawn, or to gabble like the beggar whose tongue (as he says) was cut out by the Turks [p. 174] [1]

The reference to tooth-picking reminds us of the Bastard's speech in *King John* (1.1.190) in which he pictures himself as a courtier: "Now your traveler,/He and his toothpick at my worship's mess,/And when my knightly stomach is suffic'd,/Why then I suck my teeth and catechize . ." And 'Turk' was Elizabeth's nickname for Oxford.[2]

When Sir Piercie Shafton first makes his appearance in the novel he is accompanied by Christie of the Clinthill, a thuggish henchman of the lawless Baron Julian Avenel. On approaching the Glendinning dwelling, Christie calls out to a servant

> "Ha! Art thou there old Truepenny?" [171]

This is virtually identical to Hamlet's line as he addresses his father's ghost (1.5.150). It has been pointed out[3] that 'Truepenny' is a direct reference to Oxford's father, who was the son of a Vere (True) and a Trussel (part of the mechanism used in stamping pennies). At the end of the chapter, Christie is regaling the servants with tales of his wild exploits

> ... and Tibb Tacket, rejoiced to find herself once more in the company of a jack-man, listened to his tales, like Desdemona to Othello's, with undisguised delight. [185]

So the section of the narrative introducing Sir Piercie Shafton begins and ends with a specific allusion to one of the Shakespeare plays.

Sir Piercie is an enthusiastic follower of the school of Euphuism:

> "Ah, that I had with me my Anatomy of Wit—that all-to-be unparalleled volume—that quintessence of human wit—that treasury of quaint invention—that exquisitely-pleasant-to-read, and inevitably-necessary-to-be-remembered manual of all that is worthy to be known—which indoctrines the rude in civility, the dull in intellectuality, the heavy in jocosity, the blunt in gentility, the vulgar in nobility, and all of them in that unutterable perfection of human utterance, that eloquence which no other eloquence is sufficient to praise, that art which, when we call it by its own name of Euphuism, we bestow on it its richest panegyric."[4] [179]

He is referred to many times in the text as "the Euphuist." The ostensible implication of the definite article is that, of the characters being discussed, he is the only one devoted to the practice of Euphuism. It can also be taken to mean that Sir Piercie is intended to be identified with the central figure of Euphuism (in the same way that 'the Christ' is the central figure of Christianity, or that 'the Dane' is the ruler of Denmark). Who is the central figure of Euphuism? The orthodox answer is that it's John Lyly, secretary to the Earl of Oxford, who is taken to be the author of *Euphues: His England* and *The Anatomy of Wit*. However, Brame and Popova, using linguistic techniques, have concluded that "The fingerprint evidence shows that de Vere did write the plays ascribed to his former secretary Lyly . . ."[5] Warren Dickinson, an independent scholar, concurs: "This nobleman who nursed *The Anatomy of Wit* with great love must certainly have been Lord Oxford." [6] However, Sir Piercie, like Oxford, is not restricted to the Euphuistic style.

> . . . Sir Piercie . . . replying without trope or figure, in that plain English which nobody could speak better when he had a mind. [186]

Slighter clues abound almost without limit.

> [Sir Piercie] broke forth into a soliloquy. "What foul fiend sent this wench hither? . . . But patienza, Piercie Shafton . . . " [197]

The word 'soliloquy' inevitably reminds us of Hamlet. The phrase 'foul fiend' recalls Edgar's speeches in *Lear* (3.4.61 *et seq*). And why use the Italian word for 'patience' if not to remind us of Oxford, "the Italianate Englishman"? Later, Sir Piercie reminisces:

> " . . . —quitting the tiltyard, where I was ever ready among my compeers to splinter a lance . . . —exchanging the lighted halls, wherein I used nimbly to pace the swift coranto, or to move with a loftier grace in the stately galliard . . ." [208]

Ogburn quotes an account of Oxford's triumph at jousting in the court tournament of May 1571: "The challengers . . . all did very valiantly, but the chief honour was given to the Earl of Oxford."[7] Mention of "the stately galliard" echoes Sir Toby Belch's line in *Twelfth Night* (1.3.120), "What is thy excellence in a galliard, knight?" More directly, we are reminded that Oxford himself was one of the best dancers in the Elizabethan court.[8] Later, in the second volume, there is further mention of Sir Piercie's excellence in a galliard (and other forms of music), together with his predilection for sonnets.

> Then she could hear him resume his walk through the room, and, as if his spirits had been somewhat relieved and elevated by the survey of his wardrobe, she could distinguish that at one turn he half recited a sonnet, at another half whistled a galliard, and at the third hummed a saraband. [2:150]

Again like Oxford,[9] Sir Piercie has been having financial troubles.

> " . . . my estate, I wot not how, hath of late been somewhat insufficient to maintain the expense of those braveries wherewith it is incumbent on us, who are chosen and selected spirits . . . to distinguish ourselves from the vulgar." [212-3]

Oxford himself makes a cameo appearance in one of Sir Piercie's nostalgic reminiscences about the idyllic life he led in Elizabeth's court.

> " . . . it was my envied lot to lead the winning party at that wondrous match at ballon, made betwixt the divine Astrophel (our matchless Sidney), and the right honourable my very good lord of Oxford."[10] [2:52]

Presumably Scott intends to remind the reader of the tennis-court quarrel involving Oxford and Sir Philip Sidney, though of course Oxford and Sidney did not play each other, but argued about the use of the court. Perhaps the incident is an invention of Sir Piercie's, since at the end of the novel it is revealed that he is not everything he claims to be. But *ballon* is not the only exercise at which Sir Piercie is adept; Scott himself testifies that

> The English knight was master of all the mystery of the *stoccata, imbrocata, punto-reverso, incartata*, and so forth, which the Italian masters of defence had lately introduced into general practice.[11] [2:54]

And Sir Piercie, like Oxford, is eager to put his skills to the test in actual combat.

> "In a word, I am willing to head all who will follow me, and offer such opposition as manhood and mortality may permit . . . and be assured, Piercie Shafton will measure his length, being five feet ten inches, on the ground as he stands, rather than give two yards in retreat, according to the usual motion in which we retrograde." [2:286]

It is unusual to see the word "retrograde" in a nonastronomical context. The only other example I can think of is Claudius's speech to Hamlet (1.2.112): "For your intent in going back to school in Wittenberg, it is most retrograde to our desire . . ."

Shakespeare Confidential

At one point Sir Piercie lists some of the "braveries" by which he distinguishes himself from the vulgar.

> "... my rich crimson silk doublet, slashed out and lined with cloth of gold, which I wore at the last revels, with baldric and trimmings to correspond—also two pair black silk slops, with hanging garters of carnation silk—also the flesh-coloured silken doublet, with the trimmings of fur, in which I danced the salvage man at the Gray's-Inn mummery ..." [215]

Ogburn[12] lists some of Oxford's youthful expenditures for clothing: "... one doublet of cambric, one of fine canvas, and one of black satin... four yards of velvet and four others of satin, for to guard and border a Spanish cape ... one velvet hat and one taffeta hat: two velvet caps, a scarf, two pairs of garters with silver at the ends, a plume of feathers for a hat, and another hat band." Ogburn also has something to say about Edward de Vere and Gray's Inn: "At seventeen, in 1567, Edward was admitted to Gray's Inn, there to acquire the legal knowledge that would impress so many in the plays." Ogburn describes "masques" and "revels" performed by the students at Gray's Inn, and adds "If we know our man, he lent a hand in the writing and production of those masques and acted in them, taking the first steps to making himself 'a motley to the view'."

Question 1. *Did Scott knowingly use historical figures as prototypes for his fictional characters?* The answer is *yes*. In his notes at the end of the second volume, Scott writes

> JULIAN AVENEL. If it were necessary to name a prototype for this brutal, licentious, and cruel Border chief, in an age which showed but too many such, the Laird of Black Ormiston might be selected for that purpose. He was a friend and confidant of Bothwell, and an agent in Henry Darnley's murder. At his last stage he was, like other great offenders, a seeming penitent...[2:315]

Question 2. *Can the parallelisms between Sir Piercie and Oxford described above be attributed to chance, or do they require that Scott have had Oxford specifically in mind?* We summarize the similarities and clues (in the order listed above) as follows: *appearance/ toothpick, Turk/ 'Truepenny' quote/ Desdemona-Othello/ Euphuism/ skill in plain English/ speaks Italian/ good jouster/ good dancer/ knows sonnets/ good musician/ financial troubles/ plays ball with Oxford and Sidney/ good fencer/ aspires to military leadership/ fancy* *dresser/performer at Gray's Inn*. Let us assume the null hypothesis—that is, that Scott was interested only in creating a generic foppish courtier and did not have Oxford specifically in mind. Then he might well have chosen *appearance, Euphuism, good dancer, knows sonnets, good musician, financial troubles,* and *fancy dresser* to characterize his creation. This accounts for seven of the 17 attributes and clues we listed. It seems clear that Scott intended Sir Piercie to be a comic character, but some of the remaining attributes are at odds with such an intent—for example, a comic character is not usually one who is a *good jouster*, a *good fencer*, or one who *aspires to military leadership* (these are, however, known attributes of Edward de Vere). The jousting is particularly difficult to reconcile with the null hypothesis—it required enormous amounts of money to acquire the armor, the war horse and other accoutrements. At the end of the novel, it is revealed that Sir Piercie is the grandson of a tailor, and would have no estates to draw on for an expensive pastime like jousting. It plays no part in the plot. Apparently Scott has given his courtier an attribute that undermines the character's believability for no good reason, except (possibly) to enhance his resemblance to Edward de Vere.

So far we have examined 10 of the 17 attributes and clues, and have found that seven are consistent with the null hypothesis while three mitigate against it. Let us admit that the toothpick-Turk quote, the Desdemona-Othello reference, and the game of *ballon* with Oxford and Sidney, while suggestive, do not rise to the level of evidence. We have four items left to examine. (1) *Skill in plain English*. Who other than Oxford/Shakespeare could be described as speaking English better than any other? (2) *Speaks Italian*. This attribute is revealed by one word, "*patienza*," spoken by Sir Piercie to himself. No doubt there were a number of Elizabethan courtiers who could read Italian, or speak it occasionally, but how many habitually *thought* in Italian? To me, this is a clear reference to de Vere, the 'Italianate Englishman.' (3) Christie of the Clinthill's quote of the 'Truepenny' line from *Hamlet*. What function does this serve? Christie cannot be knowingly quoting from *Hamlet* (a) because the character is illiterate, and (b) the setting of the novel is the early 1560s, and 1583 is the earliest date anyone has suggested for the writing of *Hamlet* (though it must be admitted that Scott the writer gives avoidance of anachronism a remarkably low priority). And remember that

'Truepenny' is not just a line from *Hamlet*, but a codeword incorporating two Vere family names. The only explanation I can think of is that Scott is blowing a fanfare for the *cognoscenti*, signaling that after 171 pages he is ready to introduce his Oxford character. (4) *The Gray's Inn performance.* This casually-mentioned detail is one of astonishing specificity, and it comes like a bolt from the blue. How many foppish courtiers went to law school? (Well, Oxford did, and he went to Gray's Inn.) Nowhere in the novel is Sir Piercie's legal training required, mentioned, or even hinted at. And he performed in a dramatic production! Surely the probability of a novelist imbuing a courtier from central casting with these specific attributes is vanishingly small. As far as I'm concerned, the null hypothesis is dead as a doornail.[13, 14]

Later. I have found my control sample. Scott's novel *The Fortunes of Nigel* (1822), though it has a sprinkling of Shakespeare quotes, is (as far as I can determine) completely free of Oxford-identified characters.

This paper first appeared in *Shakespeare Matters* 4.1 (Fall 2004)

End Notes

1. Pagination follows the 1893 edition of Dana Estes & Co., Boston. This edition consists of two volumes bound as one; page 123 in Volume 2 will be written as 2:123.
2. Paul Altrocchi, " 'My Turk': Why the Nickname?" *Shakespeare Matters* 3.3 (Spring 2004) 22-24. See also *SM* 3.4, p. 2.
3. Stephanie Caruana, *Shakespeare Oxford Society Newsletter* 29.3A, Summer 1993.
4. You will be astonished to learn that the critics found Sir Piercie to be as objectionable as the spectral White Lady.
5. Michael Brame and Galina Popova, *Shakespeare's Fingerprints* (Adonis, 2002), 405.
6. Warren Dickinson, *The Wonderful Shakespeare Mystery* (Omni, 2001), 231.
7. Charlton Ogburn, *The Mysterious William Shakespeare* (EPM Publications, 1984), 479.

8. Ogburn, 473, 598. *The Dictionary of National Biography* (Oxford, 1921) in its entry for *Edward de Vere* (Vol. XX, pp. 225-9) quotes a letter from Gilbert Talbot to his father (11 May 1573): "My Lord of Oxford is lately grown into great credit, for the queen's Majesty delighteth more in his personage, and his dancing and valiantness, than any other."

9. DNB, *loc. cit.* : " . . . Oxford's continued extravagance involved him in pecuniary difficulties."

10. The Oxford English Dictionary defines *ballon* (obs., rare) as "a little ball or packe." It defines *balloon* (alt. spelling *ballon*) as "the game played with this ball." The citation for *balloon* is "The winning party at that wondrous match at *ballon*."

11. Compare Mercutio's line in *Romeo and Juliet* (2.4.25): "Ah, the immortal *passado*, the *punto reverso*, the *hay!*"

12. Ogburn, 453-4.

13. *2 Henry VI*, 4.10.40

14. Those who attended the 2003 Shakespeare Fellowship Conference in Carmel will recall that one can prove anything using anagrams.However, I cannot resist pointing out that a perfect anagram for SIR PIERCIE SHAFTON is IRONIC SHAFTSPIERE. 'Shaftspiere' is at least as close to 'Shakespeare' as 'Shake-scene,' which our orthodox brethren without exception construe as a reference to the Bard.

17

In Search of Rosencrantz and Guildenstern

Usurping powers start wars and plot assassinations while two minor characters participate without affecting or even understanding the historic events taking place. Rosencrantz and Guildenstern thus seem to embody the situation of the average citizen in today's world, and for some have become the most poignant figures in *Hamlet*. They are 20th-century characters trapped in a 16th-century play, a quality Tom Stoppard took as the basis for his 1967 play, *Rosencrantz and Guildenstern Are Dead*.

Oxfordian scholars have long recognized that most of the characters in *Hamlet* can be linked to real-life historical characters: Polonius with Burghley, Gertrude with Elizabeth, Claudius with Leicester, and so forth. Eva Turner Clark provides a list of such identifications, but omits the ill-fated Danish courtiers.[1] Is it possible to find their real-life equivalents? There should be plenty of candidates, since the families Rosenkrantz and Gyldenstierne (to use the Danish spellings) were among the most powerful in Denmark, and had many members in government and court circles. More immediately, how did the author of *Hamlet* learn of these real-life Danish names? Some Stratfordian scholars have speculated about this. Their suggested scenarios are discussed below.

Scenario 1: the Tycho Connection. In 1938 the indefatigable orthodox scholar Leslie Hotson published a book entitled *I, William Shakespeare, Do Appoint Thomas Russell, Esquire*. This sounds like a quote from Shakespeare's will, but as the indefatigable heterodox scholar Richard Whalen points out,[2] it is not. Hotson identified a Thomas Russell of Strensham as one of the overseers of the will of William Shakspere of Stratford, the man to whom the works of Shakespeare are commonly attributed. He further determined that Russell's stepson was Leonard Digges (1588-1635), whose verse "To the Memorie of the deceased Authour Maister W. Shakespeare" is in the preface to the First Folio and contains the phrase "thy Stratford Moniment," one of the foundation stones of the Stratfordian attribution. On the basis of this connection, Hotson posits a close friendship between Leonard Digges and Shakspere, although (as Whalen points out) there is no documentary evidence that they were acquainted, and Digges was 24 years younger than the Stratford man.

Leonard Digges' father was Thomas Digges (c. 1546-1595). As Peter Usher has emphasized,[3] the elder Digges was a mathematician and astronomer of enormous stature in the scientific world of the 16th century. Digges published works advocating the revolutionary Copernican theory of the cosmos, and was the first to envision an infinitely large universe filled with stars. Hotson cites a letter (December 1590) from the Danish astronomer Tycho Brahe to the English scholar and antiquary Thomas Savile in which Tycho desires to be remembered to the astrologer Dr. John Dee and to "the most noble and most learned mathematician Thomas Digges," whom he heartily wishes well.

Figure 6 - Tycho Brahe, Epistolæ

In a postscript Tycho writes "I included four copies of my portrait recently engraved in copper at Amsterdam."[4] This portrait is presumably similar to the one included as the frontispiece to Tycho's collected letters, *Epistolæ,* published in 1596 (Fig. 1).[5] It shows Tycho framed by an arch supported by columns. The structure bears the names and arms of his ancestors (paternal ancestors on the left, maternal ancestors on the right). The portrait shows the name ROSENKRANS on the left side of the arch and GVLDENSTEREN on the bottom of the left column. Hotson concludes "There is little doubt that from 1590 Digges had a copy of his learned friend's portrait, bearing the names *Rosenkrans* and *Guldensteren*, at his house in Heminges's parish. Perhaps Shakespeare saw them there."

Hotson's scenario was accepted by A. J. Meadows in *The High Firmament* (1969), a lucid history of astronomical thought. Meadows writes

> Thomas Digges was the leading English mathematician of his time. His father, Leonard Digges, was a friend of John Dee (both had an equal interest in astronomy and astrology) and he, himself, had been Dee's pupil. Thomas' younger son, also called Leonard, was a friend of Shakespeare, and wrote one of the prefatory verses to the first folio. When Shakespeare was in London he lived close to the Digges' house and may have been acquainted with Thomas Digges. Certainly this would explain a reference in Hamlet where the names, Rosencrantz and Guildenstern, happen to be the names of two ancestors of the Danish astronomer, Tycho Brahe. Shakespeare could have learnt of this from Digges, who was the leading English correspondent of Tycho Brahe, and would therefore probably have been acquainted with his ancestry (of which Tycho was proud).

There are several statements here that could be challenged, but the most interesting development is that Hotson's conjectured friendship between Leonard Digges and Shakspere (which Whalen's observations render highly improbable) has now been elevated to established fact. Meadows is still relatively cautious when it comes to drawing the final link ("Shakespeare could have learnt of this from Digges . . ."), but the caution has given way to virtual certainty by May 1981, when astronomer Owen Gingerich (in the periodical *Sky and Telescope*) writes

> Tycho, from his Uraniborg palace on Hven, could easily look northward across the strait to the Elsinore castle, the setting of *Hamlet*. Shakespeare may well have seen Digges' copy of the *Epistolae*. In any event, the coincidence with the names Rosencrantz and Guildenstern in the play is so striking that we may be reasonably sure that Tycho's portrait was one of the sources for *Hamlet*'s cast of characters.

Hotson's hypothesized chain of transmission for the Tycho portrait is quite extended: [Tycho→Savile→T. Digges→L. Digges→Shakespeare]. By claiming that the elder Digges was Tycho's leading English correspondent, Meadows eliminates Savile from the chain, and by ignoring Leonard he shortens the chain further to [Tycho→T. Digges→Shakespeare], but loses specificity in that he no longer identifies the source of the portrait. Gingerich speaks of "Digges' copy of the *Epistolae*": unfortunately Digges died in 1595 and publication of the *Epistolæ* didn't take place until 1596. So unless new documents come to light, Savile must be included in the chain, and Shakespeare must have seen Tycho's portrait between 1590 (when it was printed) and 1593 (when Savile died) if this scenario is to be historically accurate.

These three authors are all Stratfordians—that is, they believe that Shakespeare, the author of *Hamlet*, was in fact Will Shakspere of Stratford. An alternative view is that 'Shakespeare' was the pen name of Edward de Vere, 17th Earl of Oxford (1550-1604).[6] The above scenarios can easily be adapted to the Oxfordian view by assuming that Digges knew de Vere. This is less far-fetched than Hotson's hypothesized friendship between Shakspere and Leonard Digges. Thomas Digges and de Vere were within four years of being the same age, rather than separated by a 24-year interval. Digges was well-connected at the Elizabethan court, and de Vere was one of its foremost courtiers. Moreover, there was a close connection between Digges and William Cecil, Lord Burghley. Digges' book on the "new star" of 1572 (now known as *Tycho's supernova*) was dedicated to Burghley, and found an honored place in his extensive library. De Vere grew up in the Burghley household and eventually married Burghley's daughter Anne. He had unrestricted access to Burghley's library.

Authorship aside, there is an unsatisfying facet to the theory that the Danish courtiers' names were chosen from Tycho's portrait. It seems arbitrary. Did the author look at the portrait and exclaim 'Rosencrantz and Guildenstern! The very names I need for the characters in my new play!' There are 14 distinct names on the structure surrounding Tycho. Why 'Rosencrantz and Guildenstern'? Why not 'Markeman and Rosenspar'? Why not 'Axellsøn and Stormvase'? A defender of the Tycho connection would say 'Shakespeare had his own reasons. He liked the imagery—"Rosy Wreath" and "Golden Star"—and if he had chosen "Axellsøn and Stormvase" we'd be wondering why he hadn't chosen "Rosencrantz and Guildenstern".' Maybe so. But it still seems arbitrary.

Another difficulty with the above scenarios is that the author of *Hamlet* displays a deeper and more detailed knowledge of Danish customs than can be accounted for by supposing he lifted his Danish names from a portrait of Tycho. One example of this is the very fact that that he names Wittenberg as the university which Hamlet and his two friends attend. Wittenberg was the nearly universal choice among Danish nobility. Thoren writes

> [Anders] Vedel was already in Wittenberg . . . Many other Danish students were there too. They habitually came in such numbers, in fact, that Danish kings paid regular pensions to Wittenberg professors to ensure that their subjects would be well received. One modern scholar described the university as the postgraduate school of the University of Copenhagen in that era.[7]

Another example is the author's awareness of Danish drinking habits. Ferguson quotes an example from Tycho himself:

> A letter from Tycho to Bartholomew Schultz—evidently written at the dining table—reported that he and his companions were drinking "one mug after the other, filled to the brim" and exclaimed that such drinking "to the very dregs" was a learned art in itself . . . "We dedicate these toasts to you to the sound of trumpets, recorders and lutes . . . " he told Schultz.[8]

It is impossible for me to read this description without thinking of Scene 1.3 in *Hamlet*:

[A flourish of trumpets . . .]

Horatio: What does this mean, my lord?

Hamlet: The King doth wake tonight, and takes his rouse,
Keeps wassail, and the swagg'ring up-spring reels;
And as he drains his drafts of Rhenish down,
The kettle-drum and the trumpet thus bray out
The triumph of his pledge.

Scenario 2: the Willoughby Connection. Peregrine Bertie (1555-1601), later known as Lord Willoughby d'Eresby, married Oxford's sister, Mary Vere, in 1578. In 1582 he was sent on a diplomatic mission to Denmark to award Frederik II the Order of the Garter and to negotiate for British shipping rights in the Baltic. While in Denmark he visited Tycho Brahe's astronomical castle, Uraniborg, on the island of Hven.[9]

The British Library possesses a collection of Willoughby's correspondence (Cotton MS Titus C VII). Some refer to his travels in Denmark, and among these is a list of names entitled *Noblissimi ad Generosi, Regni Daniae Inclÿti Cosiliarÿ et*

Senatores.[10] It is a list of 24 guests at a state dinner given for him during his mission. Three of the names are:

Petrius Guildenstern de Thim
Georgius Rosenkrantz de Rosenholm
Axellius Guildenstern de Lingbÿ

(Note that the Latinized spelling of Gyldenstierne as it appears here is the spelling adopted in the final version of *Hamlet*.) Brief biographies (using the Danish spelling) are given below.

Jørgen Rosenkrantz (1523 – 96) was a member of the state council (*rigsraad*), a member of the regency council that ruled Denmark during the minority of Christian IV, one of the most powerful men in the Danish government, and a patron and ally of Tycho Brahe. He finished his education at the University of Wittenberg, as did most of the Danish nobility. His ties to the family of Tycho Brahe were unusually close: after the death of his parents he was raised by an aunt who was married to the elder Axel Brahe (also a *rigsraad*). Jørgen's son, known as 'Holger the Learned,' married a daughter of the younger Axel Brahe, Tycho's brother. Holger Rosenkrantz and Tycho were close friends, and their correspondence is an important source for Tycho's biographers.

Peder and Axel Gyldenstierne (both *rigsraad*s) were sons of the elder Knud Gyldenstierne (also a *rigsraad*). Peder (1533 – 94) was raised in the warrior tradition and served 18 years as Marshal of the Realm. Axel (1542 – 1603) served for some years as viceroy of Norway. Again, there are blood ties to Tycho: Axel was a son of Tycho's mother's aunt. The two men were close friends and political allies, and one of Tycho's leading assistants, Flemløse, later served as Gyldenstierne's personal physician.

Lord Willoughby's negotiations over shipping rights would have involved the most powerful members of the Danish court, probably including the men described above. Did he go back to London and regale his brother-in-law with amusing stories of the foibles of the Danes? In any event, Oxford would have had access to the guest list mentioned above. There is no known connection between Willoughby and Shakspere of Stratford.

There are two objections to identifying Jørgen Rosenkrantz and Peder or Axel Gyldenstierne with the Danish courtiers in *Hamlet*. One is the objection raised above—the nagging sense of arbitrariness. There were 24 names on the guest list course—why choose Rosencrantz and Guildenstern? The other objection, perhaps more fundamental, is the lack of correspondence between the high positions held by these formidable men (*rigsraad*s all) and the relatively lowly status of Hamlet's two friends in the play. Jørgen, Peder and Axel were haughty nobles who held great power in the Danish court—hardly the type to be summoned hastily to renew a friendship and spy on a moody prince.

Two More Candidates. If the above candidates possess characteristics that render them unlikely as models for the courtiers in *Hamlet*, what characteristics would we find in more acceptable candidates? From reading the play, we know that the two are friends, that they travel together, and that they both attended school in Wittenberg. As we noted above, there is already a set of associations linking characters in the play with figures in Elizabeth's court, so ideal candidates for Hamlet's friends should be of approximately Hamlet's age—that is, a generation younger than Claudius (Leicester) or Gertrude (Elizabeth).

In 1941 the Danish writer Palle Rosenkrantz published a two-volume novel entitled *Rosenkrantz og Gyldenstjerne: Roman fra Renæssancetiden* ("Rosenkrantz and Gyldenstierne: A Novel from the Renaissance Era"). Although it was a work of fiction, the book featured two real-life figures as its protagonists: Frederik Rosenkrantz (1571 – 1602) and Knud Gyldenstierne (1575 – 1627). They are of the appropriate generation, both attended Wittenberg, and they traveled together to England in 1592, though apparently they were not beheaded on their arrival at the English court. Recent biographers of Tycho Brahe have mentioned them as the prototypes of the courtiers in *Hamlet*.[11]

The distinguished historian John Robert Christianson has kindly allowed us to include as appendices his biographical sketches of these two historical figures. The level of detail provided in these sketches is useful in enabling us to avoid misconceptions. For example, Ferguson states " . . . the two kinsmen were in England on a diplomatic mission in 1592 . . ."[11] The phrase "diplomatic mission" leads one to imagine an enterprise of great pith and moment, such as dealing with Lord Burghley about Baltic trade routes, or reporting to Robert Cecil about Catholic activities in Scandinavia. Referring to the information provided by Christianson, however, we find that in 1592 Rosenkrantz was 21 and Gyldenstierne 17. Rosenkrantz had just finished his tour of Italy and had not yet entered service in the Danish court. Gyldenstierne had been studying and traveling in Germany with his tutor, Bacmeister. Unless documents turn up with information to the contrary, it seems likely that the kinsmen's visit to England was simply the last leg of the Grand Tour.

Timelines. When was *Hamlet* written? The answer depends on one's authorial orientation. The play was entered in the Stationer's Register in 1602.[12] Stratfordians assume it was written about 1600. If Frederik and Knud are assumed to be the original sources for the Danish names in *Hamlet*, the timing works out well for Stratfordians—Shakspere meets them during their 1592 visit (possibly in the Mermaid Tavern), the names are filed in his capacious memory, and when he starts writing *Hamlet* in 1600, they bubble up ready to hand.

Figure 7 - *Rosencrantz and Guildenstern Are Dead.*

However, there are indications of *Hamlet*'s existence well before 1600. In particular, Thomas Nashe's preface to Robert Greene's *Menaphon* (1589) speaks of "whole *Hamlets*, I should say handfuls of tragical speeches."[13] Since Shakspere was manifestly still in Stratford in 1589 (he's named in legal proceedings) Stratfordians have decided that the play Nashe is referring to is somebody else's *Hamlet*, though there is no documentary evidence to this effect. Oxfordians, of course— embracing an older playwright, one who lived in London—have no difficulty in accepting a version of the *Hamlet* we know and love in 1589, or even earlier. Clark[14] has suggested that initial work on *Hamlet* was inspired by two events: the diplomatic mission to Denmark in 1582 carried out by Lord Willoughby

(Oxford's brother-in-law), and the death in June 1583 of Thomas Radcliffe, Earl of Sussex. Sussex had been a father figure to the young Oxford and had overseen his introduction to military action, putting down the Northern Rebellion of 1569. It was widely suspected that he had been poisoned at the behest of his political antagonist, Robert Dudley, the Earl of Leicester, who had a reputation as a poisoner rivaling the Borgias.[15] The Gertrude-Claudius parallel is suggested by the close relationship between Elizabeth and Leicester, which lasted until his death in 1588.

If *Hamlet* was started in 1583, Frederik and Knud are effectively eliminated as the sources of the Danish names (Frederik was 12, Knud 8). Also eliminated is the 1596 portrait of Tycho Brahe. We are left with the guest list brought back from Denmark by Lord Willoughby, in spite of the objections of arbitrariness and inappropriateness raised above. Apparently the playwright *did* like the imagery of 'Rosy Wreath' and 'Golden Star.' I still harbor the fantasy that sometime in 1592 Frederik and Knud met Oxford. Perhaps they dropped in on Willoughby to reminisce about when he negotiated with Uncle Jørgen and Papa Henrik, and Oxford, hearing of the presence in England of the bearers of the names he appropriated for his play, invited them to dinner.

The Cosmological Connection. In 2001 Peter Usher opened up a completely new dimension in this inexhaustible play by pointing out the existence of a cosmic allegory in *Hamlet*.[3] According to Usher, Claudius (and Elsinore) represent the Ptolemaic cosmology, in which the stationary Earth is orbited by the seven ancient planets (the Sun, the Moon, Mercury, Venus, Mars, Jupiter and Saturn). Hamlet (and Wittenberg) represent the heliocentric Copernican system, which forms the basis of our present beliefs. Rosencrantz and Guildenstern are identified with the short-lived Tychonic cosmology (a compromise proposed by Tycho in 1577), in which a stationary Earth is orbited by the Sun and Moon, while the other planets revolve around the Sun. Usher presents a number of arguments in support of his thesis, including Shakespeare's use of technical terms associated with astronomy ('opposition' and 'retrograde,' etc) and the name of the usurping king ('Claudius' appears nowhere in the source materials,[16] but is in fact Ptolemy's first name). Wittenberg had been a hotbed of heliocentrism since 1541, when the mathematician Georg Joachim von Lauchen ('Rheticus') visited Copernicus in Poland and returned to Wittenberg to teach his views. Just as the Tychonic system had little support among 16th-century astronomers, so Rosencrantz and Guildenstern are relatively minor characters in the play—their deaths occur offstage and do not lead to any confrontations—while the battle between the Ptolemaic and Copernican systems results in the climactic bloodbath of the final act, followed by the arrival of Fortinbras from Poland (the home of Copernicus). It is then that Hamlet passes the cosmological baton (" . . . the election lights on Fortinbras, he has my dying voice.")

The Tychonic cosmology was a hybrid system, combining elements of the Ptolemaic and the Copernican. In the play, Rosencrantz and Guildenstern are ambiguous figures, currying favor with both Claudius and Hamlet. Historically, England was the home of an active group of Copernicans (including Thomas Digges, his father, and others) who advanced and elaborated Copernican astronomy, administering the *coup de grâce* to the Tychonic system. In the play, Rosenkrantz and Guildenstern are sent to England and beheaded.

Once the Tycho↔R&G association is made, the penny drops and the light comes on. Thoren[17] has pointed out that while there were over a hundred noble families in 16th-century Denmark, some were more noble than others. Four families were the most noble of all—the Brahes, the Billes, the Rosenkrantzes, and the Gyldenstiernes—and their lines had so intertwined that they were essentially one big family. Tycho's father was a Brahe and his mother was a Bille; the names Rosenkrantz and Gyldenstierne simply complete the quartet. The effect is similar to writing a *roman à clef* about America in the 1960s and naming a presidential candidate 'Fitzgerald.' Everybody (in America at least) would know who you meant. Now the previously-voiced objections—arbitrariness and inappropriateness—fall away. Now it is clear there is nothing arbitrary about the choice of names—the battle of cosmologies is part of the warp and woof of the play, and the names of the Danish courtiers are as close as the author could come to saying 'Tycho' without giving up the claim that he was writing fiction. The fact that Jørgen Rosenkrantz and Peder and Axel Gyldenstierne were powerful individuals no longer bothers us, since the reference is not to them, but to a cosmological system.

Shakespeare Confidential

There is just a bit more to be said. Earlier I facetiously quoted a hypothetical defender of 'the Tycho connection' as saying that Shakespeare chose the names Rosencrantz and Guildenstern from Tycho's portrait because he liked the imagery—'Rosy Wreath' and 'Golden Star.' But Shakespeare, the master weaver, has indeed woven these names into the fabric of the play. The first act opens with a description of the appearance of the Ghost "When yond same star that's westward from the pole had made his course t'illume that part of heaven where now it burns . . ." There's our Golden Star. And it has been identified[18] as *Tycho's supernova*, which was first observed 6 November 1572. Where? In Wittenberg. The image of a Rosy Wreath suggests Ophelia, "larded all with sweet flowers." When Gertrude describes her drowning (4.7) she talks of Ophelia's "fantastic garlands" and "crownet weeds," both phrases suggesting wreaths. The reference is even more specific at Ophelia's burial (5.1), where the Doctor of Divinity protests "Yet here she is allowed her virgin crants . . ." The rare English word 'crants' does not appear in desk dictionaries, but the Oxford English Dictionary defines it as "a garland, chaplet, wreath."[19]

The Oxford Scenario. From the age of four until he was twelve, Edward de Vere lived with and was tutored by the renowned scholar Sir Thomas Smith (1513-77).[20] Smith was known to be an enthusiastic student of astrology and astronomy (Hughes writes that he had "a professional's knowledge" of these subjects). When his father died, de Vere became the ward of William Cecil, Lord Burghley. We have already noted that de Vere had unrestricted access to Cecil's extensive library, which not only had Thomas Digges's book on Tycho's supernova, but also Copernicus's seminal volume, *de Revolutionibus*.[21] Thus throughout his childhood, de Vere had the encouragement and opportunity to develop an active interest in astronomy and cosmology. His brother-in-law, Lord Willoughby, was interested enough in these topics to visit Tycho's observatory Uraniborg during his 1582 mission. From Tycho's letter to Savile (cited above) we know that Tycho was not shy about describing his work and seeking credit for it, and he probably would have been eager to explain his hybrid cosmology to the distinguished English visitor. It is easy to imagine that Willoughby's tales of his encounter with Tycho (together with a report on Danish customs, such as the ritualized drinking at banquets, the preference for sending young nobles to Wittenberg, and the political ascendancy of the four foremost families) started working in Oxford's imagination, and coalesced the next year when his mentor Sussex died, perhaps by poison. In mystery-novel terms, Oxford had the means, the motive, and the opportunity to write a *Hamlet* with a cosmological subtext well before Nashe mentioned the play in 1589. Some Oxfordian scholars believe he continued working on *Hamlet* throughout the rest of his life.

Epilogue. Those with a knowledge of Oxford's life will, on reading the biographical sketch of Frederik Rosenkrantz, have a strong sense of *déjà vu*. Both lost their fathers at an early age and then were raised by a powerful politician. Both received exemplary educations and then toured Europe, especially Italy. Both got into trouble from an affair with a lady of the court—Oxford with Anne Vavasor, Rosenkrantz with Rigborg Brockenhuus—resulting in the birth of a son. Both sons, when they reached manhood, saw military service. Both Oxford and Rosenkrantz were wounded in a duel in their early thirties: Oxford was lamed by Thomas Knyvet in 1582; Rosenkrantz died in 1602 from injuries received when he tried to separate two duelists. Although I have rejected the notion that Frederik and Knud were the original models for the Danish courtiers in *Hamlet*, I think that these and other correspondences mentioned above should qualify them as honorary, or *ex post facto* members of the play's *dramatis personæ*, along with Burghley, Elizabeth, Leicester, and, of course, Oxford. Long live Rosenkrantz and Gyldenstierne!

ACKNOWLEDGMENT: I am extremely grateful to Professor John Robert Christianson of Luther College, Decorah, Iowa, for invaluable help during the preparation of this work, and for permission to use his biographical sketches.

End Notes

1. Eva Turner Clark, *Hidden Allusions in Shakespeare's Plays*, Kennikat Press, New York, 1974, p. 637.

2. Richard Whalen, "Cross-Examining Leonard Digges on his Stratford Connections," *Shakespeare Oxford Newsletter* 37.1, Spring 2001.

3. Peter Usher, "Advances in the Hamlet Cosmic Allegory," *The Oxfordian* IV, 2001, pp 25-49.

4. Letter printed in *Tychonis Brahe Dani opera omnia*, J. L. E. Dreyer, ed., Gyldendal, Copenhagen, 1913-29, 7: 283-5.

5. Engraved by Jacques de Gheyn II (see J. R. Christianson, *On Tycho's Island* (2000), pp. 117, 286)

6. Charlton Ogburn, *The Mysterious William Shakespeare*, EPM Publications, McLean VA, 1984.

7. Victor Thoren, *The Lord of Uraniborg*, Cambridge, London, 1990, p. 22.

8. Kitty Ferguson, *Tycho and Kepler*, Walker, New York, 2002, p. 112.

9. John Robert Christianson, private communication.

10. Shakespeare Oxford Society Newsletter 29.1A, Winter 1993, p. 18.

11. Thoren, 429; Ferguson, 265n.

12. Frank Kermode in *The Riverside Shakespeare*, Houghton Mifflin, Boston, 1974, 1136.

13. E. K. Chambers, *The Elizabethan Stage*, Oxford, 1923, Vol. IV, 234.

14. Clark, p. 634 *et seq.*

15. *Leicester's Commonwealth*, Dwight C. Peck, ed., Ohio University Press, 1985.

16. The generally acknowledged sources for *Hamlet* are *Historica Danica* by Saxo Grammaticus, printed in Latin in 1514 and translated into Danish by Anders Vedel in 1575, and a free adaptation of Saxo's material by François de Belleforest, *Histoires tragiques*, published in Paris in 1576. The name of the Claudius character in the first source is 'Feng'; in the second it is 'Fengon.'

17. Thoren, 341.

18. D. W. Olson, M. S. Olson and R. L. Doescher, "The Stars of *Hamlet*," Sky and Telescope, November 1998, 68-73.

19. Alternate spellings: cranse, crance, craunce, corance. The OED offers a quote from 1890: "The 'crants' were garlands which it was usual to make of white paper, and to hang up in the church on the occasion of a young girl's funeral." In a

post-Freudian era, the symbolism seems almost embarrassingly explicit.

20. Stephanie Hopkins Hughes, "'Shakespeare's' Tutor: Sir Thomas Smith (1513-1577)," *The Oxfordian* III, 2000, 19 – 44.

21. Eddi Jolly, "'Shakespeare' and Burghley's Library: *Bibliotheca Illustris: Sive Catalogus Variorum Librorum*," *The Oxfordian* III, 2000, 3 – 18.

This paper was first published in
Shakespeare Matters 3.3 (Spring 2004)

Appendix A. Frederik Rosenkrantz

by J. R. Christianson[1]

Frederik Rosenkrantz of Rosenvold and Stjernholm was baptized 2 September 1571 in Skanderborg Castle chapel, died 18 August 1602 in Wessely, Moravia, and was buried in Týn Church in Prague, where Tycho Brahe was also buried. He was a son of state councilor Holger Rosenkrantz (1517 – 75) and Karen Gyldenstierne (1544 – 1613). His father died when he was a child, and his uncle, state councilor Jørgen Rosenkrantz (1523 – 96), was appointed his ward.

Rosenkrantz received an excellent education, first in Ribe School, where he lived in the household of Tycho Brahe's friend, Peder Hegelund (Bishop of Ribe 1595 – 1614), and then abroad with Hans Poulsen Resen as his preceptor.[2] They studied in Rostock 1584-86 and Wittenberg 1586-89. During a short trip home to Denmark in 1589, they sailed out to the island of Hven and spent two days as guests of Tycho Brahe at Uraniborg, where Anders Sørensen Vedel was also visiting at the time. During 1589-91, Rosenkrantz and Resen studied in Padua and Siena and also visited other parts of Italy, including Rome, Sicily, and even Malta.[3]

Rosenkrantz was in England in 1592, but not with Resen. The Danish biographical dictionary simply noted that he traveled with Knud Gyldenstierne.[4]

After completing his education abroad, Rosenkrantz entered the service of the Danish court in 1593. In the years 1595-99, he held the fief of Giske in Norway.[5] In the spring of 1599, Rosenkrantz advanced to the fief of Lundenæs in Denmark. He was brilliant, charming, learned, and polished, and had prospects of a splendid career as a courtier when he threw it all overboard in 1598 by seducing Rigborg Brockenhuus (1579 – 1641), a maiden-in-waiting in the court of Queen Anna Catherine. Rigborg bore him a son in 1599. Because this took place in court between two courtiers, it was a grave offence to the laws governing conduct at court. Rigborg Brockenhuus lost all rights of inheritance and was walled into a room in her father's castle at Egeskov until after his death in 1604.

Frederik Rosenkrantz fled to Hamburg but was brought back to Denmark and sentenced by a court of his peers to the loss of honor and two fingers, which would have deprived him of his name, property, and all future prospects. However, the sentence was commuted to exile when he agreed to travel to Hungary and fight against the Ottoman Turks. On the way, he visited Tycho Brahe in Prague. He regained his honor on the field of battle, but his petition to return to Denmark was denied by King Christian IV. Rosenkrantz died from wounds suffered while attempting to break up a duel.

His son with Rigborg Brockenhuus was eventually granted the name and arms of Rosenkrantz and fought in the battle of Lutter am Barenberg in 1626, where he was taken prisoner by the imperials but later released. He died in 1634.

1. © 2003 by J. R. Christianson. All rights reserved.
2. Resen was Bishop of Roskilde 1615-38, and later a Gnesio-Lutheran foe of Tycho Brahe's circle.
3. These years of study abroad are described in detail in Bjørn Kornerup, *Biskop Hans Poulsen Resen*, (Copenhagen: G. E. C. Gad, 1928-68), **1**: 60-132.
4. *Dansk biografisk leksikon* 1982, **12**: 335.
5. The kings of Denmark also ruled Norway, Iceland, and Schleswig-Holstein.

Appendix B: Knud Gyldenstierne

by J. R. Christianson[6]

Knud Henriksen Gyldenstierne of Aagaard was born on the ancestral estate of Aagaard in Jutland on 31 July 1575 and died in Bergen, Norway, in 1627. His father, Admiral Henrik Gyldenstierne (1540 – 92), had first been married to Tycho Brahe's eldest sister, and after her death to Mette Rud, who was the mother of Knud.

In 1584, Knud Gyldenstierne entered the noble academy at Sorø, where he studied until he and his cousin, Corfitz Rud, (1573 – 1630), traveled abroad in 1589 with Johan Bacmeister as their preceptor. They studied in Zürich in 1589, Strasbourg 1590-91, Rostock 1591, and Wittenberg at some time during these years. Then the two cousins parted. Knud Gyldenstierne visited Scotland and England in 1592, while Corfitz Rud continued his studies abroad from 1592-97 in Padua, Bologna, Siena, Malta, Spain, and France, visiting England and Holland on his way home to Denmark.[7]

Upon returning to Denmark, Knud Gyldenstierne served at the Danish court until 1598, when he assumed the management of his inherited estates. He married a noblewoman, Sophie Lindenow, in 1608, and served with distinction as standard bearer in the Kalmar War with Sweden (1611-13).

He was named governor of the fief of Vestervig Cloister in Jutland in 1612-18. He accompanied King Christian IV on a journey to Germany during these years, together with his own squires in the royal livery. He and another nobleman, Otto Skeel, were sent on a mission to Muscovy as royal Danish couriers, where they were held hostage for a time.[8]

From 1618 until his death in 1627, Knud Gyldenstierne held the important command of Bergenhus Castle in Norway. He ruled Bergen, the largest city in Norway, and an immense surrounding fief, and had frequent opportunity to deal with the Scottish merchants who were numerous in the thriving port city. His widow, Sophie Lindenow, governed Bergenhus fief during the year of grace after his death.[9]

6. © 2003 by J. R. Christianson. All rights reserved.

7. Vello Helk, *Dansk-norske studierejser fra reformationen til enevælden 1536-1660* (Odense: Odense Universitets-forlag, 1987), 229, 336.

8. H. A. Riis-Olesen, "De kongelige lensmænd på Vestervig Kloster," *Historisk årbog for Thy og Mors* 1971:28-43, at http://www.thistedmuseum.dk.

9. Kr. Erlsev, *Danmark-Norges Len og Lensmænd 1596-1660* (Copenhagen: Hoffensberg & Trap, 1885), 42, 43, 79.

The Spanish Tragedy, Part 1

18

Who Wrote *The Spanish Tragedy*?

The Spanish Tragedy was one of the most popular and important plays of the Elizabethan era. If you ask an academic who wrote it, the reply will be "*Thomas Kyd, of course*," and it will be given in a voice ringing with authority and certitude.

But it may not be quite that simple. In their introduction to the play, Brooke and Paradise note that

> The early editions of *The Spanish Tragedy* are all anonymous, and none of the theatrical notices of the play mentions Kyd. We owe our knowledge of his authorship to Thomas Heywood, who quotes three lines (IV.i.86-88) in his *Apology for Actors*, 1612, with the words: "Therefore, M[aster] Kid, in his Spanish Tragedy, upon occasion thus presenting itself, thus writes." [1]

So Kyd was identified as the author by a single arcane allusion published at least two decades after the play was written.

But surely, a lot is known about his life, his education, his writing habits. Actually, no. The *Encyclopedia Britannica* tells us he was baptized 6 November 1558 in London. It then discusses *The Spanish Tragedy*, and skips to his final months. He was rooming with Christopher Marlowe in 1593 when he was arrested for atheism and questioned under torture. After this ordeal he wrote a letter to the authorities stating that the heretical material found in his apartment was Marlowe's. He died the next year. The *Britannica* states "That letter is the source for almost everything that is known about Kyd's life." Strange how elusive these Elizabethan dramatists are.

Like *Taming of the Shrew*, *The Spanish Tragedy* opens with an induction scene. The ghost of Don Andrea, a Spanish nobleman killed in a battle with the Portuguese, appears with Revenge, a spirit, and they discuss the circumstances of his death. (One is reminded of the scene (5.2) in *Titus Andronicus* in which the empress Tamora presents herself to the seemingly deranged Titus in the character of 'Revenge.') The scene shifts to the Spanish court. Balthazar, the Portuguese prince who killed Don Andrea, is led in as a captive. Two young courtiers, Horatio and Lorenzo, argue over who was responsible for his capture. Horatio is awarded the ransom, but Lorenzo is given custody of Balthazar. Horatio visits Bel-imperia, fiancée of the slain Don Andrea, and they fall in love. However, the King of Spain, who is Bel-imperia's uncle, decides to award her to Balthazar to seal the peace between Spain and Portugal. Lorenzo and Balthazar visit Bel-imperia's house and find her intimately involved with Horatio. They murder Horatio, and the rest of the play follows the efforts of Hieronimo, Horatio's father, to find the murderers and avenge his son's death. He eventually does so by staging a play within the play, in the course of which Bel-imperia stabs Balthazar, then kills herself, and Hieronimo dispatches Lorenzo and commits suicide.

It is the common wisdom that *The Spanish Tragedy* is the direct predecessor of *Hamlet*. The *Britannica* says of Kyd that "his characterization of Hieronimo in *The Spanish Tragedy* prepared the way for William Shakespeare's psychological study of Hamlet." Warren Dickinson has given a list of 12 specific parallels between the plots of the *Tragedy* and *Hamlet*, including similar use of a play within the play; spying, deception and counter-deception, and the death of almost all major characters at the end.[2] Dickinson has focused on plot parallels. Following in the footsteps of Brame and Popova,[3] we will examine similarities in word use ('fingerprints') between *The Spanish Tragedy* (ST) and the Shakespeare canon.

Names. The use of *Horatio* for a major character immediately reminds us of *Hamlet*, of course, and the fact that Horatio Vere was Oxford's cousin. An interesting contrast is that in the *Tragedy*, Horatio is the first character to be killed onstage, while in *Hamlet* he is virtually the last one left alive. The major female character is *Bel-imperia*, a name meaning 'Beautiful Empress,' which would make anyone in the Elizabethan court think immediately of the Queen. The other female character, Hieronimo's wife, is named *Isabella*, the Spanish form of 'Elizabeth.' Is the author trying to curry favor with someone? One of the minor characters is named *Jaques*, a name that Shakespeare liked so well (possibly because of its scatological undertones) that he used it for two separate characters in *As You Like It*. Another name that Shakespeare fancied was *Balthazar*. He used it in four plays, including *Comedy of Errors*, *Much*

Ado, and *Romeo and Juliet*. In *Merchant of Venice* the name is used both for one of Portia's servants and for Portia herself, disguised as a young judge.

Haggard. The frequent use of hawking imagery by Shakespeare has often been noted.

Petruchio:	Another way I have to man my haggard, To make her come, and know her keeper's call . . .
Hortensio:	I will be married to a wealthy widow Ere three days pass, which hath as long lov'd me As I have lov'd this proud disdainful haggard. *Taming of the Shrew* 4.1.193, 4.2.37
Othello:	If I do prove her haggard, Though that her jesses were my dear heart strings, I'd whistle her off, and let her down the wind To prey at fortune. *Othello* 3.3.260
Ursula:	I know her spirits are as coy and wild As haggards of the rock *Much Ado* 3.1.36
Viola:	And like the haggard, check at every feather That comes before his eye. *Twelfth Night* 3.1.62

In *The Spanish Tragedy* we find

Lorenzo:	In time the savage bull sustains the yoke, In time all haggard hawks will stoop to lure . . ST 2.1.3

The first half of this quote is also found in *Much Ado* (1.1.260):

Don Pedro:	Well, as time shall try: "In time the savage bull doth bear the yoke."

The Riverside Shakespeare explains the punctuation[4] by saying the line is an inaccurate quote from Kyd's *Spanish Tragedy*. Eva Turner Clark says the quote is from *Hekatompathia*, a collection of sonnets attributed to Thomas Watson,[5] published in 1582. Several modern Oxfordian scholars believe that 'Thomas Watson' was one of Oxford's pen names.

Tickle. The use of 'tickle' as an adjective or adverb (meaning 'easily affected; not firm or steadfast') is relatively rare.

Lucio:	I warrant it is, and thy head stands so tickle on thy shoulders That a milkmaid, if she be in love, may sigh it off. *Measure for Measure* 1.2.172
York:	Anjou and Maine are given to the French, Paris is lost, the state of Normandy Stands on a tickle point now they are gone. *2 Henry VI* 1.1.214
Lorenzo:	Now stands our fortune on a tickle point And now or never ends Lorenzo's doubts. ST 3.4.74

Coy. The use of 'coy' as a transitive verb is also rare.

Titania:	Come sit thee down upon this flow'ry bed, While I thy amiable cheeks do coy, And stick musk-roses in thy sleek smooth head, And kiss thy fair large ears, my gentle joy. *Midsummer Night's Dream* 4.1.1
King:	Brother of Castile, to the prince's love What says your daughter, Bel-Imperia?
Cyprian:	Although she coy it, as becomes her kind, And yet dissemble that she loves the prince, I doubt not, I, but she will stoop in time. ST 2.3.1

(With this example we get a hawking allusion thrown in for free!)

Soft and Fair.

Benedick:	Soft and fair, friar. Which is Beatrice? *Much Ado* 5.4.72
Hieronimo: —	Soft and fair, not so; For if I hang or kill myself, let's know Who will revenge Horatio's murder then? Nay, soft and fair! You shall not need to strive. Needs must he go that the devils drive. ST 3.12.16, 80

Shakespeare Confidential

I will be his priest. This statement is made by Suffolk in *2 Henry VI* (3.1.271) as he, Margaret, Beaufort and York plot to murder Gloucester. A footnote in the Riverside edition glosses it as "perform the last rites for him"—that is, dispatch him. It is used in exactly the same sense in the *Tragedy* (3.3.36).

> Pedringano (grappling with watchmen):
> Now by the sorrows of the souls in hell
> Who first lays hands on me, I'll be his priest.

Ifs and ands. In Scene 3.4 of *Richard III*, the protagonist gets Hastings to say that those practicing witchcraft on Richard's body deserve death. He then accuses Hastings' wife and mistress of the deed.

> Hastings: If they have done this deed, my noble lord—
>
> Richard: If? Thou protector of this damned strumpet, Talk'st thou to me of "ifs"? Thou art a traitor. Off with his head!

Dickinson[6] quotes a somewhat earlier version, *The True Tragedy of Richard the Third* (1594).

> Richard: If, villain—feedest thou me with ifs & ands ..

In the *Tragedy* (2.1.77) we find

> Lorenzo: What, villain! Ifs and ands? (offers to kill Pedringano)

From my bed. In *Midsummer Night's Dream* (3.1.129) Titania is roused from her nap by the transformed Bottom.

> Titania: What angel wakes me from my flow'ry bed?

This is surely a comic echo of the tragic scene (ST 2.5.1) in which Hieronimo hears the moans of his murdered son.

> Hieronimo: What outcries pluck me from my naked bed .

Swear on my sword. After his encounter with the Ghost, Hamlet (1.5.143) urges secrecy upon his companions.

> Hamlet: Never make known what you have seen tonight.
> Nay, but swear't.
> Upon my sword.

A similar scene (ST 2.1.87) occurs in the *Tragedy*.

> Lorenzo (offering his sword):

> Swear on this cross that what thou say'st is true
> And that thou will conceal what thou hast told.

Ambiguous replies. There are scenes both in *Hamlet* (1.2.120) and the *Tragedy* (3.14.160) in which the protagonist gives an ambiguous response which is accepted at face value by his antagonist.

Hamlet:	I shall in all my best obey you, madam.
Claudius:	Why, 'tis a loving and a fair reply.
Hieronimo:	. . . it is fit for us That we be friends: the world's suspicious, And men might think what we imagine not.
Balthazar:	Why, this is friendly done, Hieronimo.

Pocas palabras. This is a Spanish phrase: literally 'few words'—a genteel form of 'shut up'. Hieronimo uses it in the *Tragedy* (3.14.118). These two are the only words of Spanish to be found in the play. Shakespeare uses a truncated version of the phrase in *Much Ado* (3.5.17).

Dogberry:	Comparisons are odorous—*palabras*, neighbor Verges.

The phrase is also found in the Induction of *Taming of the Shrew*.

Sly:	Therefore *paucas pallabris*, let the world slide.

From the above examples I conclude that there is a remarkable overlap between the vocabularies of the author of *The Spanish Tragedy* and the author of the Shakespeare plays. The overlap is not only one of vocabulary, but extends to the dramatic imagination itself, and is so strong that I believe it indicates they were the same person.

Xenolingual passages. In 10 instances, characters suddenly break out into Latin. These passages range from two words ("Vindicta mihi"—'Vengeance is mine') to 14 lines in length. This is perhaps understandable; Latin is the language of classical allusion, and in fact several of the passages contain quotes from or allusions to works by Claudian, Virgil, Curtius, Statius and Seneca. More puzzling is the fact that on three occasions a character switches to Italian, although those who do so are supposed to be native Spaniards. Are we dealing with an author who occasionally thought in Italian? One would almost think he spent the better part of a year in Italy, conversing with the natives. (There is no record of Kyd's having visited the continent.) Another puzzling twist occurs in Scene 4.2, when Hieronimo instructs those who are to perform in his play within the play (Hieronimo, like Hamlet, writes lines for players).

> Hieronimo: Each one of us
> Must act his part in unknown languages,
> That it breed the more variety:
> As you, my lord, in Latin, I in Greek,
> You in Italian; and for because I know
> That Bel-imperia hath practis'd the French,
> In courtly French shall all her phrases be.

French, Italian, Latin and Greek are the languages in which we know Oxford to be competent. The author does not follow through with the polyglot play: a note inserted in the text reads "Gentlemen, this play of *Hieronimo* in sundry languages was thought good to be set down in English, more largely for the easier understanding to every public reader."

The author's range of knowledge. One scene in the *Tragedy* (3.13) deals with a group of petitioners who approach Hieronimo in his capacity as marshal with various legal problems. The dialog here is sprinkled with legal terms, and is quite detailed. At the end of that scene, the protagonist's knowledge of music is revealed.

> Hieronimo: And thou, and I, and she will sing a song,
> Three parts in one, but all of discords fram'd—
> Talk not of chords, but let us now be gone,
> For with a cord Horatio was slain.

T. W. Ross, editor of a modern edition of the *Tragedy*, spends three pages enthusing about the author's skillful use of the "flowers of rhetoric," by which he means devices such as apostrophe, anastrophe, anadiplosis, hyperbole, stichomythia, psychomachia, parallelism and polyptoton, all of which he finds utilized in this play. He writes "By varying the rhetorical tricks and by assigning them to appropriate characters and situations, a master playwright like Kyd could use them functionally, not simply for decoration".[7] Ross cites Sister Miriam Joseph, who has published an extensive study of these same rhetorical devices as found in the works of Shakespeare.[8]

The strange case of the 'additions'. Another puzzling circumstance is the existence of a set of 'additions' to the play. Brooke and Paradise[1] sum it up.

> On Sept. 25, 1601, and June 22, 1602, Philip Henslowe, in behalf of the Admiral's Men, made large payments to Ben Jonson for two sets of 'adicyons' to a play referred to under the title of *Jeronimo*. Critics do not see Jonson's hand, however, in the remarkable additions which appear first in the 1602 Quarto . . . They are of surprising literary quality, surpassing the original play in this respect, but are not recognizably Jonsonian and probably date from 1597, when Henslowe produced a revival of the play, which he marked as 'new'.

Kyd couldn't have written the new lines; he died in 1594. The immediate thought that comes to mind is that Oxford wrote the play when he was young, perhaps about the time of *Titus Andronicus* (which Clark[9] dates to 1576), then provided improved dialog for the revival, as suggested above. But then why was *Jonson* paid?—Oxford was in continual need of money. Oh, right—a nobleman couldn't take money for literary work. Jonson was a go-between. And Kyd was a beard.

Conclusion. So what have we found out? In Kyd we have a shadowy figure from the Elizabethan age whose life is known to us only through a handful of documents, none of which have anything to do with poetry or drama. Establishment scholars tell us that this man wrote a wildly successful play, a play requiring detailed knowledge of law, music and falconry, plus fluency in Italian and Latin, familiarity with Latin classics, and the skill in the 'arts of rhetoric' of a master playwright—a play that prefigures *Hamlet* in at least a dozen ways. Establishment scholars also tell us that the Shakespeare plays—works requiring detailed knowledge of law, music, falconry, classic literature, and the arts of rhetoric— were written by a shadowy figure from Stratford, whose life is known to us only through a handful of documents, none of which have anything to do with poetry or drama. In the immortal words of the Bard,[10] "It's déjà vu all over again." Or to put it more plainly, I believe that Edward de Vere wrote *The Spanish Tragedy*.[11]

Shakespeare Confidential

This paper was originally published in
Shakespeare Matters 4.2 (Winter 2005)

End Notes

1. Tucker Brooke and Nathaniel Paradise, *English Drama 1580-1642* (Heath, 1933), p. 130. Scene and line numbers follow this edition.
2. Warren Dickinson, *The Wonderful Shakespeare Mystery* (Omni, 2002), 309
3. Michael Brame and Galina Popova, *Shakespeare's Fingerprints* (Adonis, 2002)
4. *The Riverside Shakespeare*, G. Blakemore Evans, ed. (Houghton Mifflin, 1974) footnote, 335
5. Eva Turner Clark, *Hidden Allusions in Shakespeare's Plays* (Kennikat Press, 1974), 539
6. Dickinson, 313
7. Thomas W. Ross, ed., *The Spanish Tragedy* (Univ. California Press, 1968), 6
8. Sister Miriam Joseph, *Shakespeare's Use of the Arts of Language* (Columbia Univ. Press. 1947)
9. Clark, 47-8
10. I'm referring, of course, to the contemporary poet and philosopher, Yogi Berra.
11. I have recently learned that Dr. Daniel Wright has been studying *The Spanish Tragedy* for several years, and has reached similar conclusions.

The Spanish Tragedy, Part 2

19

Hidden Allusions in Oxford's *Spanish Tragedy*

In a previous paper[1] I suggested that *The Spanish Tragedy*—one of the most successful plays of the 16th century, commonly attributed to Thomas Kyd—had in fact been written by Edward de Vere, using a pen name other than 'Shakespeare'. If this is indeed the case, the play should share characteristics with others in the Shakespearean canon.

Eva Turner Clark[2] has shown us that each of the Shakespeare plays contains 'topicalities'—references to contemporary events, personalities, or political situations that amused knowledgeable members of the audience and added another layer of meaning to the fictitious events portrayed onstage. The ultimate example of this is *Hamlet*, with Polonius clearly recognizable as Burghley, Claudius as Leicester, Gertrude as Elizabeth, etc. In this play, the author, as Hamlet, explicitly states that "the players are the abstract and brief chronicles of the times." This does not mean, however, that there is a fixed, one-to-one correspondence between persons and events alluded to and the contents of the play. The plays are like dreams, and the allusions are fluid and shifting. In *Hamlet*, Laertes starts out resembling Thomas Cecil, Burghley's older son, but in the last act he turns poisoner, thus morphing into Leicester, and one realizes with a start that **LAERTES** is a perfect anagram for **A LESTER**.[3]

If the Shakespeare/Oxford plays are filled with topicalities, and if Oxford wrote *The Spanish Tragedy*, then we would expect that play to contain topical allusions as well. This paper is a preliminary attempt to find them.

The plot of *The Spanish Tragedy*.[4] The play opens with an induction scene: a dialog between the ghost of Andrea, a Spanish courtier killed in a battle with the Portuguese, and the spirit of Revenge. Andrea laments that he was slain by Balthazar, a Portuguese prince. Revenge assures him that as events unfold he will see Balthazar killed by Bel-imperia, who was Andrea's lover while he lived. The next scene (1.2) takes place in the Spanish court. The group onstage includes the King of Spain and Hieronimo, who is apparently a military hero, since he is Marshal of Spain. Balthazar (the Portuguese prince) is brought in—he has been captured. Horatio (Hieronimo's son) and Lorenzo (Bel-imperia's brother) argue about which of them should be credited with capturing Balthazar. Solomon-like, the King decrees that Lorenzo be awarded Balthazar's horse and weapons, while the ransom will go to Horatio. Lorenzo is given custody of Balthazar, who is to enjoy the freedom of the court.

Scene 1.3 takes place at the court of Portugal, where it is supposed that Balthazar has been killed in the course of the battle. A courtier named Villuppo accuses another, Alexandro, of using the confusion of battle as a cover to assassinate Balthazar. The ruler of Portugal sentences Alexandro to death. Scene 1.4 takes us back to Spain, where Horatio recounts the circumstances of Andrea's death to Bel-imperia. They fall in love.

In Act 2 we find that the loosely-held captive Balthazar has himself fallen in love with Bel-imperia. Lorenzo bribes her servant, Pedringano, to tell them who she favors, and the servant reveals that it is Horatio. Lorenzo and Balthazar have formed an alliance, and Lorenzo vows to remove Horatio from the scene to clear the way for Balthazar's wooing. When Horatio and Bel-imperia meet for a tryst in Hieronimo's garden, they are set upon by Lorenzo and Balthazar, and Horatio is brutally murdered. Hieronimo, sleeping nearby, is awakened by Horatio's cries. When Hieronimo finds the corpse of his son, his reason is momentarily unseated (the subtitle of the play is *Hieronimo is Mad Again*).

Lorenzo and Balthazar, fearing that Hieronimo is growing suspicious, kidnap Bel-imperia and sequester her in a room in the palace. She writes a letter to Hieronimo (using her own blood as ink)[5] naming Lorenzo and Balthazar as the murderers of his son. Hieronimo, like Hamlet, is suspicious of this information, thinking it might be a trap, but when he intercepts a letter from Pedringano to Lorenzo which confirms Bel-imperia's accusations, he plots his revenge. In the meantime, Hieronimo's wife, Isabella, unable to bear her grief, commits suicide.

In the last act Hieronimo stages a play he has written, ostensibly for the court's amusement. The play is called *The Tragedy of Soliman, the Turkish Emperor* (Suleiman the Magnificent was the Turkish ruler that Charles V struggled with for much of his career). Hieronimo's script calls for Perseda (played by Bel-imperia) to stab Soliman (played by Balthazar). The courtiers comprising the audience, of course, are expecting her to use a harmless stage prop, but she uses a real knife, killing Balthazar, and thus avenging Andrea. She then stabs herself, and Hieronimo stabs Lorenzo. After explaining his motives to the court, Hieronimo stabs Lorenzo's father, then himself. The play closes with the ghost of Andrea expressing his satisfaction with the way things turned out. Revenge has the last words:

> Then haste we down to meet thy friends and foes:
> To place thy friends in ease, the rest in woes;
> For here though death hath end their misery,
> I'll there begin their endless tragedy.

I have recounted the plot in mind-numbing detail to give us the necessary background for exploring topicalities. Let us see where it leads us.

Hieronimo. In another study[6] I suggested that there are no arbitrary names in Shakespeare. If that is also true of Oxford writing as 'Thomas Kyd' we would expect the name 'Hieronimo' to have some connection with a real-life figure. We mentioned above that since the character Hieronimo is Marshal of Spain, he should be a military hero. Is there a historical figure with a military record and an association with the name 'Hieronimo'?

It turns out there is. Charles V (of the house of Habsburg) ruled as Holy Roman Emperor from 1519 to 1556 (he was the last emperor to be crowned by a pope). One historian writes

> . . . Charles was the prototypical military hero, whose victories over the Lutherans in Germany were on a par with his triumphs over the papacy, over France and over the Turks at Vienna in 1529.[7]

His grandparents were Ferdinand and Isabella of Spain (the ones who pawned their jewels to finance Columbus's voyages). His father and mother were Philip the Handsome and Joanna the Mad (madness ran in the family: Charles's grandson Carlos was criminally insane). Charles had three legitimate children: Maria,

Juana, and a son, Philip, who succeeded to the throne of Spain as Philip II in 1556. Charles had two illegitimate children who gained political prominence: Margaret of Parma, who was governor of the Low Countries and mother of Alexander Farnese—and John, usually called Don John of Austria to emphasize the Habsburg connection. Plagued by ill health, Charles abdicated as emperor in 1556 and retired to a monastery, San Jerónimo de Yuste, where he spent the final two years of his life. 'Jerónimo' is a variant spelling of 'Hieronimo.' The monastery was administered by members of the Hieronymite order of monks.

Horatio. The prototype of this character should be known for military prowess, since Horatio unhorsed Balthazar in the battle preceding the action of the play. The other requirements are that he be a son of Charles V, and that he be murdered.

Don John of Austria led a coalition of Christian forces against the Turks in 1571, and destroyed the Turkish fleet in the bay of Lepanto. As a result he became the most celebrated military hero of that time. He was acknowledged as the son of Charles V in a public ceremony 2 February 1560.[8] The question is, was he murdered?

After Don John's triumph at Lepanto, Philip stationed him in Genoa and Messina for a couple of years, and then in 1576 made him governor-general of the Low Countries, which were in open revolt against Spain. This was not a post that Don John liked. As one historian notes,

> . . . Don John was ambitious for greater glory and for more tangible rewards. In particular, he wanted some territory of his own. The king, however, was determined that he should have none, and it became the task of Antonio Pérez to control Don John's aspirations.[9]

In fact, Don John had a very specific plan. He wanted to use the soldiers under his command to invade England, where he was assured they would be welcomed as liberators by the Catholic population. He would then rescue Mary of Scotland from her castle keep, depose Elizabeth, install Mary as queen of England, and marry her, thus becoming king.

Antonio Pérez was Philip's personal secretary and chief advisor. He handled all correspondence between Philip and Don John, and set up a network of spies to watch John's every move. At the behest of Pérez, John's personal secretary was removed and replaced by Pérez's old friend, Juan de Escobedo. The move backfired: by 1577 Escobedo had become an outspoken advocate of Don John's interests, going so far as to suggest that the Spanish government be placed in Don John's hands so that Philip could retire.[9] On 31 March 1578 Juan de Escobedo was stabbed to death in Madrid, just a few streets from the royal palace. On 1 October 1578 Don John died in the Netherlands, reportedly of typhoid fever.

During Philip's reign, three deaths occurred which have provoked prolonged debate about Philip's involvement: the death of Don Carlos (Philip's son and heir) in July 1568, and the deaths of Escobedo and Don John, mentioned above. One of Don John's biographers, Charles Petrie, has the following to say about the death of Don Carlos:

> ... [Philip] had Don Carlos arrested on January 19th ... From that moment he was dead to the world, which saw him no more, and on July 25th, 1568, he died: there is not a shred of evidence that he was murdered on his father's orders, as Philip's detractors have maintained.[10]

You don't have to be one of Philip's detractors to recognize that if Philip ordered the death of Carlos, it was because he had to. Always strange, Carlos had suffered a head injury in a fall down a stairway that turned him into a homicidal maniac. Allowing him to succeed to the throne of Spain would have been catastrophic: Philip understood how dangerous it would be for a nation if its leader was divorced from reality.

Regarding Philip's role in the assassination of Escobedo, one biographer, at least, is forthright.

> Escobedo had been murdered at the king's command, and the deed had been arranged by Antonio Pérez. Although whole books have been written denying Philip's complicity in the murder, there seems to be little doubt about the matter. In the first place, the king himself acknowledged responsibility. During the trial of Pérez he wrote to the judges: "He knows full well the proof I have that he had Escobedo killed and the reasons he told me existed for doing it." ... Second, the king connived in the escape of the assassins hired by Pérez: the secretary's holograph notes, informing the king of his plans to spirit them away from Madrid, have survived.[11]

Political murder was a technique Philip used fairly regularly. Another writer has summarized other instances.

Philip himself deliberately and openly plotted the murder of [William of] Orange, placed a price on his head, and in 1584 saw his plans carried out. He had already had two of the greatest members of the Flemish nobility, Counts Hoorne and Egmont, condemned to death in defiance of all tradition and statute, and decapitated by the sword; two years later, in 1570, Egmont's younger brother, the Baron de Montigny, who had gone to Madrid under safe conduct, was secretly tried and garotted under Philip's personal supervision (it was officially announced he had died of natural causes). Philip accepted a plan for the murder of Elizabeth, Walsingham, Sir Francis Knollys, and Robert Beale . . .[12]

We move on to the case of Don John. Here Charles Petrie is as convinced of Philip's innocence as he was with Don Carlos. In fact he uses the same words.

The Orange propagandists have hinted, and would like to have us believe, that he [Don John] was murdered by his brother's orders, for which there is not a shred of evidence . . .[13]

Presumably this is the same shred of evidence that is missing in the cases of wrongdoing by Enron officials, Walter Sickert as Jack the Ripper, and (according to Alan Nelson) Edward de Vere as Shakespeare. More to the point, eliminating Escobedo didn't really solve Philip's problems with Don John—envy of his heroic stature and fear of his ruling a rival kingdom. (John married to Mary Stuart would control England, Scotland, the Netherlands, and perhaps eventually France. Given that accumulation of power, would he not be tempted to declare himself king of Spain as well?) Don John died a few weeks after Escobedo was murdered. Although it was reported he died of natural causes, *Leicester's Commonwealth* assures us that poisons, deftly applied, can be made to imitate the symptoms of any illness.[14]

The question of Philip's possible involvement in the death of Don John is apparently a species of 'third rail' for modern biographers—none of them will touch it. Even a writer as forthright as Parker[9] is completely mum on the subject. Only doughty Stirling-Maxwell, Don John's most thorough biographer, gives any hint of foul play.

[Don John's] body was opened for the purpose of being embalmed, when the state of the intestines exhibited appearances which some of the attendants supposed, and the camp rumour asserted, to be the effects of poison. The contents of the stomach were dry; and one side of the heart was yellow and black as if burnt, and crumbled at the touch. It was whispered in the army that Doctor Ramirez had put some deadly drug into the broth given to the patient, and that the deed had been done by orders of the King.[15]

Lorenzo. I believe we have shown that if Don John was murdered, it was done at the behest of Philip. Even if Philip were innocent, there is enough circumstantial evidence of his guilt to stimulate the imagination of a creative playwright. Thus we associate Horatio with Don John[16] and Lorenzo with Philip II of Spain.

Is there a reason the Philip character was given the name 'Lorenzo'? If there is one building in Spain associated with Philip II it is the Escorial, a combination monastery and palace begun (at the king's command) in 1563 and completed in 1584. Philip paid for the entire cost of construction. The monks who staffed it were instructed to give perpetual thanks for the king's miraculous victory over French forces in the battle of Saint Quentin, 10 August 1557, the feast day of Saint Lawrence. The official name of the Escorial monastery is 'San Lorenzo el Real'.[17]

Villuppo. Brooke and Paradise[4] comment that "The character of Lorenzo reflects the contemporary conception of Machiavelli's teachings." Englishmen around 1580 undoubtedly regarded Philip of Spain as a Machiavellian villain (although Philip himself thought he was doing God's work). The play contains a second Machiavellian villain in the subplot taking place in the Portuguese court (Scenes 1.3, 3.1). He is the one who falsely accuses his fellow courtier Alexandro of murdering Balthazar, for which Alexandro is condemned to a death he barely escapes. This villain's name is Villuppo. At first I thought that 'Villuppo' was the Portuguese equivalent of 'Philip,' but a visit to a local Portuguese dictionary quickly disabused me of that notion (the translation of 'Philip' is 'Filipe'). Further work with dictionaries revealed that the adjective 'vil' (in both Spanish and Portuguese) means 'vile'; as a noun it signifies 'a vile or despicable person'. There is an Italian word 'viluppo' which means 'tangle, entanglement, confusion, mix-up' (as we noted earlier[1] there is a puzzling tendency for characters in this play to break into Italian when excited). Philip's style as king combined micromanagement and indecision in a way that provided many examples of 'entanglement, confusion, mix-up' during his reign. Thus we conclude that the author intended Philip as the prototype for both Lorenzo and Villuppo.[18] And I still think the name 'Villuppo' was intended to evoke 'Philip' in the mind of an English-speaker.

Alexandro. If Philip is the betrayer, who is the betrayed? In the context we have been discussing, the name 'Alexandro' suggests Alexander (or Alessandro) Farnese. The son of Margaret of Parma (and thus Don John's cousin), Farnese was raised in the Spanish court, together with Don Carlos and Don John. He was one of John's commanders in the battle of Lepanto, and performed brilliantly. After John's death in 1578, Philip gave Farnese command of the Spanish forces in the Netherlands, where he was remarkably successful in subduing insurgents in the southern provinces.

> Farnese undoubtedly would have pressed the war northward if Philip II had not compelled him to participate in his plan to conquer England. He was instructed to concentrate his forces on the Channel coast preparatory to invading England, but the defeat of the Invincible Armada in 1588 ended that dream. In Spain, part of the responsibility for the disaster was laid on Farnese, and his popularity underwent a serious decline. . . . Exhausted by illness, he died at Arras, France, just in time to avoid learning of his intended disgrace at the hands of Philip II.[19]

Bel-imperia is Lorenzo's sister, so perhaps in searching for her historical counterpart we should look at Philip's sisters. Maria and Juana both married appropriately and kept low historical profiles. Philip's half-sister, Margaret of Parma, was politically prominent, but somehow doesn't fulfill expectations for the beautiful heroine of a tragedy.

> In appearance she was almost masculine. She walked like a man and her enemies made unkind remarks about the thick growth of hair on her upper lip. But they respected, for the moment, her firm handling of the political situation in Brussels.[20]

A more interesting candidate is Mary Stuart. In the play, Bel-imperia falls in love with Andrea (who dies), then with Horatio (who dies), and then forms an alliance with an older man (Hieronimo). Mary fell in love with Francis the Dauphin (who died), then with Henry Darnley (who died), and then formed an alliance with an older man (James Hepburn, Earl of Bothwell). In Scene 3.8, Bel-imperia finds herself held prisoner in a castle, exactly Mary's situation from the time she fled

Scotland in 1568. Bel-imperia is reduced to smuggling messages out to hoped-for rescuers, just as Mary was (certainly to Anthony Babington and Henry Howard, Duke of Norfolk; possibly also to Don John[21]). Mary was reputed to be beautiful ('belle'). Her resumé included queen of France, queen of Scotland, and claimant to the throne of England, which (in sum) sounds pretty imperial to me. One more clue: when Hieronimo is handing out parts for his play-within-a-play, he says of Bel-imperia "In courtly French shall all her phrases be." From the age of five until she was eighteen, Mary lived at the French court; "courtly French" was her native tongue.

Balthazar. This character's identifying characteristics are that he is a prince with a Portuguese background, and he is dominated by Lorenzo. One of Philip's biographers describes Portuguese influences on the king, then writes

> Out of this Portuguese background, which continued to influence Philip throughout his reign, the most remarkable figure to emerge was Ruy Gómez de Silva, whose mother had come to Spain as a lady of the empress Isabel [of Portugal]. Subsequently he was selected to form part of the small group of noble pages who studied with the prince. A self-effacing but strong personality, Ruy Gómez owed his success to the way in which he became the prince's shadow.[22]

Ruy Gómez was made Prince of Eboli in 1559.

Isabella is the wife of Hieronimo. I experienced a thrill of corroboration when I discovered (fairly late in the game) that Charles V's wife was Isabel of Portugal (mentioned above).

Pedringano is characterized by his duplicity and by his association with correspondence (it is his letter that convinces Hieronimo of Lorenzo's guilt). He is an accessory to the murder of Horatio and others. The following is a biographical extract for Philip's secretary, Antonio Pérez.

> The upstart secretary was hated by many of the grandees and by his rivals in the Spanish civil service. The king's favour was unstable, and to safeguard himself, Pérez intrigued with all parties: with Philip II's half-brother Don Juan of Austria and his secretary, Juan de Escobedo, against the king; with the king against Don Juan; perhaps even with the Netherlands rebels against both. When Don Juan, then governor-general of the Netherlands, sent Escobedo to Spain in 1577 to plead for his plan to invade England and liberate and marry Mary Stuart, queen of Scots, Pérez feared the exposure of his own intrigues. He

persuaded the suspicious king that Escobedo was Don Juan's evil genius and was plotting treason. The king gave his consent to the murder of Escobedo, and Pérez organized his assassination.[23]

When was the play written? A play called *Spanishe Tragedie of Don Horatio and Bellmipeia* (*sic*) was registered in London on 6 October 1592, thus providing an upper bound for the writing of the play.[4] In the introduction to *Bartholomew Fair* (1614), Ben Jonson states "He that will swear Jeronimo or Andronicus are the best plays yet, shall pass unexcepted at here as a man whose judgment shows it is constant, and hath stood these five and twenty, or thirty years." This implies the play was being performed in the period 1584-89. Baldwin has argued it cannot have been written later than the summer of 1585.[24] While this may be valid as an upper bound more stringent than that of the play's registration, Oxfordians who believe with Eva Turner Clark that *Hamlet* was written around 1584 will have trouble believing that the relatively crude *Tragedy* was penned that late.

The precipitating event in the play is the murder of Horatio. If I am correct in associating this character with the historical Don John of Austria, then it could have been written no earlier than late 1578.

Another death that occurred in 1578 was that of young Sebastian, king of Portugal, who died fighting the Berbers in Africa. His successor was Henry—sixty-eight years old, deaf, nearly blind, and dying of tuberculosis. Philip was among those with a claim to the Portuguese throne when Henry died, and he resolved to seize the opportunity. He mobilized his troops while Henry faded, and when the end came, Philip invaded Portugal. The conflict lasted from June through August 1580, and ended in victory for Spain, with Philip king of both Spain and Portugal. Since the play opens with the aftermath of an unnamed battle between Spanish and Portuguese forces, it is evident that Philip's invasion was on the author's mind. (In the play, the King of Spain exults "Spain is Portugal/ And Portugal is Spain . . . .")

If my assumptions about authorship are correct, the *Tragedy* and *Titus Andronicus* are indissolubly linked, both being Oxford's early attempts at the revenge genre (Jonson was right to associate them). When was *Titus* written? Eva Turner Clark puts it at 1576, comparing the rape and mutilation of Lavinia with 'the Spanish Fury,' the looting of Antwerp and massacre of its citizens by disgruntled Spanish troops on 4 November 1576. David Roper has studied a drawing of a scene from *Titus* apparently signed by Henry Peacham and bearing a chronogram which Roper interprets as dating the document to 1575.[25] (Several orthodox scholars read the chronogram as '1594,' but they are bound by the orthodox dating of *Titus* as 1592, conformable with the biography of Stratford Will). If Roper's interpretation of the chronogram is correct, *Titus* was written before 1576, which would seem to invalidate Clark's association of Lavinia and Antwerp. However, as Roper emphasizes, the dialog written under the drawing is substantially different from that in our current version of *Titus*. The play seems to have been revised over time. Perhaps it is a mistake on our part to think there is a unique 'date' for each play, as if Oxford tossed each one off in a month (as Stratfordians represent Shaxper as doing). Perhaps the plays were not eggs, which Oxford laid, cackled over, and then forgot about, but chicks, which he tended lovingly as they grew to robust maturity.

The idea that Shakespeare's plays were frequently and substantially revised gains support from the work of Ramón Jiménez. He has examined early history plays (such as *The Famous Victories of Henry the Fift*[26a] and *The Troublesome Raigne of John*[26b]) described as 'anonymous' by the orthodox. Citing exact parallels between scene construction and incidents portrayed between these early plays and their Shakespearean counterparts (the *Henry* trilogy and *King John*), Jiménez concludes that they all shared a common author—Oxford. In the case of *Famous Victories*, he suggests (based on the dearth of legal terminology) that this early effort was written before Oxford went to Gray's Inn, that is, while he was still a teenager. The linked plays *Famous Victories/Henry IV, V* and *Troublesome Raigne/King John* can be regarded as examples of thoroughgoing revision, carried out over a significant portion of the dramatist's lifetime.[27] And in the case of *The Spanish Tragedy*, we have specific examples of revisions made no earlier than 1597.[1,4]

Ross's edition of *The Spanish Tragedy* is useful in pointing out the author's myriad quotations from and allusions to Latin poets such as Claudian, Virgil, Curtius, Statius, and Seneca.[28] I get the impression of an eager teenager who has been burning the midnight oil and wants to show off his mastery of the literature. Perhaps the initial draft of *Tragedy* was begun at this time. Oxford's tour through Italy (then under Spanish domination) in 1575-76 would have provided him with plenty of gossip about the Spanish royal court, and Don John of Austria's reputation was still at its peak. (David Yuhas has speculated that Oxford's single-combat challenge to all comers, made in Palermo in the summer of 1575, was intended to provoke a meeting with Don John.)[29] This tour may have provided inspiration for sharpening the characterizations. Then finally, the death of Don John and the Spanish invasion of Portugal would have crystallized the drama into the version published in 1592, later revised yet again.

This paper appeared in *Shakespeare Matters* 4.4 (Summer 2005)

End Notes

1. See previous chapter, 'Who wrote *The Spanish Tragedy*?', p. 93-101.

2. Eva Turner Clark, *Hidden Allusions in Shakespeare's Plays*, Kennikat Press, 1974.

3. 'Lester' was in fact the spelling used by Leicester's nephew Sir Philip Sidney when he wrote a defense of his uncle in response to the attacks in *Leicester's Commonwealth* (1584).

4. The text used in this study is from C. F. T. Brooke and N. B. Paradise, *English Drama 1580-1642*, Heath, 1933, 98-135.

5. This colorful incident has a real-life parallel. Juana de Coello, the wife of Antonio Pérez, was imprisoned in a castle while her husband was being investigated in connection with the murder of Juan de Escobedo. She was forbidden to communicate with him, but managed to write a letter with her own blood, and have it smuggled to her husband. I regard this as further confirmation that the author of the play had Spanish court politics firmly in mind. See James Anthony Froude, *The Spanish Story of the Armada* (Scribner's, 1892), 131.

6. '*The Merchant of Venice*: 2004 and 1980.' See p. 44 in this book.

7. Henry Kamen, *Philip of Spain*, Yale University Press, 1997, 71.

8. William Stirling-Maxwell, *Don John of Austria*, Longmans, Green, 1883, vol. I, 35-7.

9. Geoffrey Parker, *Philip II*, Little, Brown, 1978, 130-2.

10. Charles Petrie, *Don John of Austria*, Norton, 1967, 50.

11. Parker, 135-6.

12. Paul Johnson, *Elizabeth I*, Holt, Rinehart & Winston, 1974, 241.

13. Petrie, 327.

14. *Leicester's Commonwealth*, D. C. Peck, ed., Ohio University Press, 1985, 82-3. See also Paul H. Altrocchi, "Poison Power: Natural Death or Murder Most Foul?" *Shakespeare Matters* 3.4 (Summer 2004), 26-30.

15. Stirling-Maxwell, vol. II, 336.

16. The alert reader, aware that Charles V died in 1558 and Don John in 1578, will object that I have identified Horatio's avenger with a historical figure who died 20 years before his son was murdered. My response is that this is precisely why the play opens with an induction scene featuring the ghost of Andrea: to show that the dead are still with us. (It is a strange fact that in the latter half of the 16th century, every year ending in '8' was unfortunate for the Habsburg family: Charles V died in 1558; Don Carlos died in 1568; Don John died in 1578, and Philip II died in 1598. What about 1588? That was the year the Invincible Armada was destroyed.)

17. Parker, 171. Saint Quentin is in France, about half way between Brussels and Paris. Kamen writes "A contemporary estimate put the number of dead in the French army at 5,200, with thousands taken prisoner. Possibly no more than 500 of Savoy's army lost their lives" (p.69). This happy circumstance anticipates the General's line in *Spanish Tragedy*: "Victory, my liege, and that with little loss" (1.2.7). About 12% of Philip's forces were English, under the command of the Earl of Pembroke. Among them were the Dudley brothers, Henry, Ambrose, and Robert. Henry was killed in the battle. Robert served with such distinction as master of ordnance that he was restored in blood by the English parliament 7 March 1558. Commanding some of the German forces was Baron von Münchhausen, who later gained a reputation as a raconteur.

18. Such functional doubling occurs in the Shakespeare plays, for example in *Twelfth Night* (Feste, Fabio) and in *As You Like It* (Touchstone, Jaques).

19. *Encyclopedia Britannica 4*, 687. Of the three 'golden lads' of the Spanish court ca. 1560 (Don Carlos, Don John, and Alexander Farnese), only Don Carlos failed to make it into the cast of *The Spanish Tragedy*. He got his revenge in 1867,

when he was cast as the eponymous hero in an opera by Giuseppe Verdi.

20. Kamen, 75.
21. Stirling-Maxwell, vol. II, 218.
22. Kamen, 27.
23. *Encyclopedia Britannica 9*, 285.
24. T. W. Baldwin, *Modern Language Notes*, June 1925; *Philological Quarterly*, 1927.
25. David Roper, "Henry Peacham's Chronogram: the Dating of Shakespeare's *Titus Andronicus*," *Great Oxford*, Richard Malim, ed., De Vere Society, Parapress, 2004, 140-50.
26. Ramón Jiménez, (a) "The Famous Victories of Henry the Fifth—Key to the Authorship Question?" *Great Oxford*, 201-7; (b) "*The Troublesome Raigne of John*: The First Shakespeare Play in Print?" talk given 9 April 2005 at the Shakespeare Authorship Studies Conference, Concordia University, Portland OR.
27. Establishment spokesperson Alan Nelson is fond of comparing Oxfordians to Creationists. This posture is amusing for its impudence, since it is Nelson who believes that Shaxper traveled from Stratford to London and in six days made himself master of a world of knowledge, including French, Italian, Greek, medicine, geography, diplomacy, court behavior, and the whole of classical literature (on the seventh day he held horses). The knowledge of Oxford as the author of the canon, on the other hand, enables one to study the evolution of a genius as he moves from the crudities of *The Spanish Tragedy* to the subtleties of *Hamlet*.
28. Thomas W. Ross, ed., *The Spanish Tragedy*, University of California Press, 1968.
29. David Yuhas, *The Shakespeare-Cervantes Code*, Columbine Paperbacks, Boulder CO, 2004, 18. I am grateful to David Yuhas for opening my eyes to the universe of Anglo-Hispanic politics beyond the Invincible Armada.

The Spanish Tragedy, Part 3

20

Oxford's *Spanish Tragedy*: More Hidden Allusions

The dramas themselves are rich and complex . . .
Many of them are three plays in one . . .
Charlton Ogburn Jr., *This Star of England*, xiii

I was settled into the supple folds of my Moroccan leather armchair, contemplating the sudden onset of turbulence in the column of smoke rising from my meerschaum. The great clock in the hallway had just struck midnight. The world seemed good. I had published my first article on *The Spanish Tragedy*,[1] which had established beyond doubt that it was Edward de Vere, Seventeenth Earl of Oxford, rather than Thomas Kyd, who had written this piece, one of the most popular plays of the 16th century. My second article[2] had just been completed: it explored the subtext of that work involving historical figures such as Emperor Charles V, Philip II of Spain, and Don John of Austria—figures active in the Continental politics of the time, mostly members of the Spanish court. I was idly musing about the last act of the *Tragedy*, in which Hieronimo stages a play for the Spanish court as part of his scheme to revenge himself on the murderers of his son, Horatio. As I mused, a feeling of *déjà vu* crept over me—somewhere, sometime, I had read another play in which the hero staged a play as part of a revenge scheme. Of course! *Hamlet*! And the character Hamlet, partly because of his interest and expertise in the theatrical arts, is regarded as perhaps the most autobiographical representation of the author, Edward de Vere, in the canon. But if Hamlet, because of his theatrical bent, is regarded as an Oxford figure, then so too *a fortiori* must Hieronimo, who does not just add "some dozen lines, or sixteen lines," but writes, produces, directs, and acts in *his* play, *Soliman and Perseda*. And if Hieronimo at some level represents Oxford, there must be a subtext involving other members of the English court. An interesting problem! No need for the cocaine needle tonight!

If Hieronimo represents Oxford, the two female figures fall quickly into place. Bel-imperia, wooed by Andrea, Horatio, and Balthazar, must be Elizabeth, herself wooed by many.[3] Isabella, Hieronimo's faithful wife, must correspond to Anne Cecil. In *Hamlet*, Ophelia (an undoubted Anne Cecil figure) dies from grief over the death of her father; in the *Tragedy*, Isabella dies from grief over the murder of her son Horatio. (This generational inversion between the two plays occurs again and again.) Subtextual identification of other characters requires more study.

Lorenzo. Two characters—Lorenzo and Balthazar—are responsible for the murder of Horatio. Lorenzo is the dominant member of this pair. It is Lorenzo who bribes Bel-imperia's servant Pedringano into naming Horatio as her current lover. It is Lorenzo who commands Pedringano to kill Balthazar's servant Serberine to cover their tracks in Horatio's murder, Lorenzo who alerts the watch so that Pedringano will be arrested, and Lorenzo who promises Pedringano a pardon, and then cruelly withholds it.

If one has read *Leicester's Commonwealth* this *modus operandi* will sound familiar—it is Leicester's. In fact, the *Commonwealth* recounts an incident so strikingly similar to Lorenzo's betrayal of Pedringano that even the orthodox community has picked up on it. It seems that a servant of Leicester's named Gates had been apprehended for a robbery, and appealed to his master for political protection.

> Gates, in the Leicester calumny,[4] is assured of Leicester's protection even after capture, and placated by the Earl with promise of a pardon. When at last no pardon is forthcoming, Gates realizes he has been deceived, and places a full account of his activities and of Leicester's complicity in the hands of an unnamed gentleman. Gates, like Pedringano, is hanged, and Leicester, like Lorenzo, escapes even censure.[5]

Like Gates, Pedringano fears the worst, and sends out a "full account of his activities," including the murder of Horatio. This letter falls into Hieronimo's hands, and sets him on the path to revenge.

If one accepts Lorenzo as a Leicester figure, it is possible to find a number of corroborating clues, each too slender in itself to be conclusive, but taken as a whole, quite convincing.

- Each is the son of a duke (Lorenzo, the Duke of Castile; Leicester, the Duke of Northumberland).

- Lorenzo claims to have captured the Portuguese prince Balthazar by stopping his horse: "This hand first took his courser by the reins" (1.2.155). Elizabeth made Leicester her Master of Horse at the very beginning of her reign, and he retained the post until his death.

- After the murder of Horatio, Lorenzo sequesters his sister Bel-imperia in the Duke's castle. When Hieronimo comes seeking her, Lorenzo says she's unavailable, but adds, with smooth bonhomie, "But, if it be aught I may inform her of, tell me, Hieronimo, and I'll let her know it. . . . Why so, Hieronimo? Use me" (3.2.59-60, 64). I find this reminiscent of Scott's quasi-fictional Leicester in *Kenilworth,* who comes bustling out of a Council meeting to greet a throng of suppliant hangers-on:

    > Poynings, good morrow, and how does your wife and fair daughter? Why come they not to court?—Adams, your suit is naught—the Queen will grant no more monopolies—but I may serve you in another matter.[6]

    Compare this with how the *Commonwealth* describes Leicester's dealings:

    > And hereof it followeth that no suit can prevail in Court, be it never so mean, except he first be made acquainted therewith, and receive not only the thanks, but also be admitted unto a great part of the gain and commodity thereof.[7]

- We have identified Bel-imperia with Elizabeth. Leicester did not literally imprison Elizabeth in a castle, but the author of *Leicester's Commonwealth* notes that by controlling the people she saw and the information she received, Leicester and his allies effectively isolated the Queen:

    > Who by their means casting indeed but nets and chains and invisible bands about that person whom most of all he pretendeth to serve, he shutteth up his Prince in a prison most sure, though sweet and senseless.[8]

Balthazar. Lorenzo and Balthazar are allies. Was there a figure in the Elizabethan court with whom Leicester might be thought to be allied? Yes—Leicester and Christopher Hatton often worked together to advance particular causes. They were both identified with the Puritan movement, Hatton presumably from conviction, Leicester from expediency (the French king and the Spanish king had each declined to support his proposed marriage to Elizabeth in return for his promise to restore England to Catholicism). Leicester and Hatton each fulsomely and repeatedly declared his love for the Queen—Hatton from conviction, Leicester probably from expediency, but who can tell? (The fact that Leicester was married three times to women other than Elizabeth makes one wonder.) Some interpersonal dynamic allowed Leicester and Hatton each to accept the other's relationship with Elizabeth, so that when an outsider (such as Oxford, Simier, Alençon or Ralegh) seemed to be gaining favor, they teamed up to oppose the intruder. The index of Hume's *Courtships of Queen Elizabeth* mentions Hatton 13 times; in only one of these instances is his name not paired with Leicester's.

The historical Hatton and the fictional Balthazar both declare their love in curiously abject, self-deprecating terms. Here is a letter from Hatton to the Queen:

> Madam, I find the greatest lack that ever poor wretch sustained. No death, no, not hell, not fear of death shall ever win me of my consent so far to wrong myself again as to be absent from you one day. I lack that I live by.
> My heart is full of woe. Would God I were with you but for one hour. I will wash away the faults of these letters with the drops from your poor Lyddes and so enclose them.
> Passion overcometh me. I can write no more. Love me: for I love you. Live for ever. Shall I utter this familiar term, farewell? Yea, ten thousand farewells. He speaketh it that most dearly loveth you. I hold you too long. Once again I crave pardon, and so bid you your poor Lidds, Farewell.
>
> > 1573, June.
> > Your bondsman everlastingly tied,
> > CH. HATTON[9]

Compare that with Balthazar's response when he finds that Bel-imperia is not responding to his advances.

> But wherefore blot I Bel-imperia's name?
> It is my fault, not she, that merits blame.

> My feature is not to content her sight,
> My words are rude and work her no delight.
> The lines I send her are but harsh and ill,
> Such as do drop from Pan and Marsyas' quill.
> My presents are not of sufficient cost,
> And being worthless, all my labour's lost.
> Yet might she love me for my valiancy:
> Ay, but that's sland'red by captivity.
> Yet might she love me to content her sire:
> Ay, but her reason masters his desire.
> Yet might she love me as her brother's friend:
> Ay, but her hopes aim at some other end.
> Yet might she love me to uprear her state:
> Ay, but perhaps she hopes some nobler mate.
> Yet might she love me as her beauty's thrall:
> Ay, but I fear she cannot love at all. [10]

The letter is in undistinguished prose, the speech in tightly structured verse, but both seem imbued with a fawning lack of self-regard. It is easy to believe that Oxford was deliberately caricaturing Hatton—he certainly did in *Twelfth Night*, where there is near-universal agreement that Malvolio represents Hatton.

Horatio. The son of Hieronimo and Isabella, Horatio participates in the capture of the Portuguese prince Balthazar, then reports to Bel-imperia on the death of her lover Andrea. They fall in love and arrange a midnight tryst, where they are ambushed by Lorenzo and Balthazar, and Horatio is murdered, in part to clear the way for Balthazar to woo Bel-imperia. His role in the play is thus quickly told, but teasing out his antecedents is more complex. I believe there are three historical figures that are alluded to in some way in the characterization of Horatio: de Vere, Wriothesley, and Oxford's infant son (plus, of course, the nominal allusion to Horatio Vere, Oxford's cousin).

> (1) *Edward de Vere.* In the period 1571-1574 Oxford was in high favor with Elizabeth. The younger Ogburn devotes an entire chapter to this affair.[11]
> We will cite one piece of evidence, a letter Gilbert Talbot (a young member of Parliament) wrote to his father in May 1573:
>> My Lord of Oxford is lately grown into great credit, for the Queen's Majesty delighteth more in his personage and his dancing and his valiantness than any other. I think Sussex doth back him all he can. If

it were not for his fickle head he would pass any of them shortly.[12]

Oxford was not murdered by Leicester and Hatton, but they consistently plotted against him for many years. Some scholars believe that Leicester suborned servants to arouse Oxford's suspicions against his wife as he was returning from his European tour, and surreptitiously provoked the quarrel with Howard, Arundel and Southwell in 1580-81. As for Hatton, Ogburn quotes a 1572 letter to him from his friend Edward Dyer advising him on how to proceed with Elizabeth:

> . . . Marry, thus much would I advise you to remember, that you use no words of disgrace or reproach towards [Oxford] to any; that he, being the less provoked, may sleep, thinking all safe, while you do awake and attend to your advantages.[13]

Apparently Hatton was not able to refrain completely from invidious references to Oxford (whose family crest featured a *Boar, rampant*), for the next year he wrote to Elizabeth, apparently thanking her for a gift.

> God bless you for ever; the branch of the sweetest bush I will wear and bear to my life's end: God witness I feign not. It is a gracious favour most dear and welcome unto me: reserve it to the Sheep, he hath no tooth to bite, where the Boar's tusk may both raze and tear.[13]

For the Horatio-Oxford identification, as in the case of Lorenzo-Leicester, there are corroborative clues in the text whose slenderness is balanced by their specificity.

- In describing the capture of Balthazar, Horatio says "But first my lance did put him from his horse." (1.2.156)
  This recalls Oxford's victories in jousting tournaments in 1571 and 1581.[14] Horatio's association with a 'lance' reminds us of the characters 'Launce' (*Two Gentlemen of Verona*) and 'Launcelot Gobbo' (*Merchant*

of Venice), as well as the pen name 'Shakespeare.'

- In Scene 1.4, Bel-imperia drops her glove, which Horatio picks up and returns. She thanks him for his pains, and Balthazar, hidden, mutters enviously "Signior Horatio stooped in happy time!" The incident has dramatic value—it prepares us for the budding romance between Horatio and Bel-imperia, and it's an early sign of Balthazar's jealousy. It also reminds us of Oxford's famous gift to Elizabeth of perfumed gloves, presented when he returned from his Continental tour in 1576.[15]

- In Scene 2.2, Horatio and Bel-imperia, newly in love, plan their midnight tryst. He asks her to pick the place, and she replies "thy father's pleasant bower. . . . The court were dangerous, that place is safe." There is a report in Morant's *History of Essex* that Elizabeth visited Edward de Vere at his estate (inherited from his father) in 'Havering utte Bower' in 1572.[16] This would have been near the beginning of their *affaire de cœur*, and the secluded location would have protected them from the danger of the court.

Identifying Horatio with Oxford means that Oxford is represented twice, since we have already characterized Hieronimo as an Oxford figure. But this doubling is more the norm than the exception: *vide* Touchstone/Jaques in *As You Like It*, Feste/Fabian in *Twelfth Night*, Valentine/Proteus in *Two Gentlemen of Verona*, and so forth.

(2) *Henry Wriothesley.* Some Oxfordians believe that Wriothesley, 3rd Earl of Southampton, was the natural son of Oxford.[17] If this is true, it makes Wriothesley a natural candidate for Horatio, the son of the Oxford figure Hieronimo. Even if it is not true, the dedications to *Venus and Adonis* and *The*

Rape of Lucrece are documentary evidence of a strong emotional bond between Oxford and Southampton, and the younger man is widely regarded as the 'Fair Youth' of the Sonnets. The accepted date for Wriothesley's birth is October 1573,[18] which would make him 10 years old in 1583, when I believe the *Tragedy* reached its final form (except for the 1597 'additions'), and 19 in 1592, when the play was first published.[19] Textual clues for this identification are sparse, the chief indication being the terms, reminiscent of the Sonnets,[17] in which Hieronimo addresses his murdered son:

> Sweet, lovely rose . . .
> Fair, worthy son . . .

(3) *Oxford's infant son.* Henry Wriothesley did not die during Oxford's lifetime, but he (Oxford) had a son who did. The parish register of the church at Castle Hedingham contains a death notice (1583 ... May 9· The Earl of Oxenford's first son).

Oxford had reconciled with his wife, Anne Cecil, about a year earlier, and she was grief-stricken at the loss. Perhaps at her husband's suggestion, she tried to assuage her grief by writing epitaphs,[20] one of which contains the lines

> Or if the mouth, time, did not glutton up all,
> Nor I, nor the world, were deprived of my son . . .

In the *Tragedy*, the grieving mother Isabella says

> Time is the author both of truth and right,
> And time will bring this treachery to light. (2.5.112-13)

Compare this with line 5.1.45 in *Measure for Measure*—spoken by *Isabella*—

> for truth is truth to the end of reckoning

and with a letter of 7 May 1603 from Oxford to Robert Cecil:[21]

> For truth is truth, though never so old, and
> time cannot make that false which once was true.

The above three candidates for association with the character Horatio contain at least a hint of textual corroboration. I would like to propose one more candidate whose historical circumstance is suggestive, although I have not been able to find any specific references in the text.

French baron Jehan de Simier arrived in London 5 January 1579. His mission was to prepare the way for his master, Hercule-François de Valois, Duc d'Alençon, who was coming to England to woo Elizabeth, an endeavor that would last for more than four years, and in the end would prove unsuccessful. Simier was an accomplished courtier, and Elizabeth delighted in his company from the very first, a development which induced paroxysms of jealous fury in Leicester and Hatton. At the end of June Simier asked Elizabeth to issue a passport for Alençon. Leicester argued passionately against it, but in the end Simier prevailed. We quote Hume:

> Shortly afterwards a desperate attempt was made by one of the Queen's guard to assassinate Simier, and it was at once concluded, doubtless correctly, that it had been done at the instance of Leicester and Hatton.[22]

Simier retaliated by informing Elizabeth of Leicester's marriage to Lettice Knollys, the widow of Walter Devereux, 1st Earl of Essex. The marriage had occurred the previous year (1578) and had been kept secret from the Queen, though an item of gossip among the courtiers. Elizabeth was furious, and banished Leicester for as long as she could stand to be separated from him.

> Soon afterwards another attempt was made upon Simier's life, this time by a shot whilst he was on the river with the Queen. He had previously lived with Castelnau at the French embassy, but now, in order to avoid the risk of his going backwards and forwards daily by water, the Queen brought him to her palace at Greenwich, and there lodged him, to the dismay and disgust of the English courtiers.

Late in 1581 Simier was again in London.

> Simier was attacked on the London 'Change by hired cut-throats, but fortunately once more escaped. He again complained to his protectress, whose rage knew no bounds. Calling Leicester to her, she called him a

murderous poltroon who was only fit for the gallows and warned him and Alençon's courtiers that if anything happened to her "ape" in England they should suffer for it.[22]

There are at least two other instances in which Leicester used murder to rid himself of a romantic rival, but I will not include the details here.[23] I believe the case of Simier is relevant to the *Tragedy* (a) because Leicester acted in concert with Hatton (at least according to Hume), and (b) because the love object involved was Elizabeth, standing in for Bel-imperia.

The *Tragedy* and *Hamlet*: the Generational Inversion. In the second paragraph of the present work we mentioned that in the *Spanish Tragedy* Isabella dies from grief over the death of her son, while in *Hamlet* there is a generational inversion: it is the daughter, Ophelia, who dies from grief over the death of her father. If we compare the fates of the five leading characters in the *Tragedy* with those of their counterparts in *Hamlet*, we see that this inversion holds in each case. *Table 1* explicitly shows these comparisons, and briefly summarizes the plot element that leads roles in the two plays to be associated. The third column lists the historical figure with whom each character in *Hamlet* is conventionally associated in the Oxfordian literature.[24] The two remarkable aspects of this comparison are (1) the consistency of the inversion—it holds for all major characters; and (2) the fact that in each case the relevant historical figure agrees in generational placement with the character in *Hamlet* rather than the corresponding character in the *Tragedy* (i.e., Gertrude was Hamlet's mother, and Elizabeth was old enough to be Oxford's mother, while the Elizabeth figure in the *Tragedy*, Bel-imperia, is of the younger generation). Is this just coincidence?

In the previous paper[2] I suggested that the plethora of quotations from Latin authors indicated that the play was initially written during Oxford's teenage years, when he had an adolescent's need to show off his learning, and that it was more or less continually revised and enriched as Oxford gained in experience, particularly as he traveled through Europe in 1575-6. Spain's annexation of Portugal in 1580 is reflected in the play. Another author has extended the reference to this conflict into 1582:

Alexandro, the Portguese Lord falsely accused in I.iii is described by the Viceroy as 'Terceira's lord' . . . It is difficult to imagine the name of the second-largest island in the Portuguese Azores as having much currency before the notable battle there of July-August 1582 . . . [25]

So Oxford's active interest in continuing to revise the *Tragedy* lasted from, say, 1567 or 1568 well into 1582, and if our speculation about the death of his infant son is correct, into May of 1583—a period of some 15 years. The grip on his imagination exerted by this material, this theme, must have been enormously strong.

The early 1580s were difficult for Oxford. In December 1580 he was vilified by three Catholic nobles whom he had accused of traitorous activities. In March 1581 he was banned from the Court and imprisoned in the Tower for impregnating Anne Vavasor. In March 1582 he was wounded in a fight with Thomas Knyvet (Anne Vavasor's uncle) and was lame for the rest of his life. A letter by his father-in-law Burghley from this period describes Oxford as "ruined and in adversity."[26]

Oxford suffered another blow in June 1583 with the death of Thomas Radcliffe, Earl of Sussex, who had been a father figure to the young Oxford, and one of his staunchest allies at court. Sussex had been a political opponent of Leicester's, and he was widely suspected to have been poisoned by Leicester. The previous year had seen the return of Lord Willoughby (Oxford's brother-in-law) from a diplomatic mission to Denmark. Is it possible that these two events, together with an emotional funk brought on by a sea of troubles, triggered a burst of creative energy that led Oxford to initiate a major revision of *The Spanish Tragedy?*—a revision that threw off the shell of inverted generational relationships and boldly displayed a one-to-one correspondence between dramatic and real—as *Hamlet*. This is of course speculation, but it is speculation about real events that happened to a real person, and to me at least it is infinitely more exciting than the airy 'could-have-beens' that infest orthodox biographies. And note that a key part of 'realizing' the Bard—making him a real person—is knowledge of works written under pen names other than 'Shakespeare.' This knowledge is unavailable to orthodox scholars—since their main argument for the plucky lad from Stratford is 'His name is on the plays!', they cannot afford to credit 'Shakespeare' with works which do not bear his name.

To write a play with two robust, coherent subtexts—combined with an overt plot that makes it a popular hit—is a staggering achievement; it requires genius of the highest order. My experience with Elizabethan dramatists has convinced me that only one of that group could have done it, and that man was Edward de Vere, the 17th Earl of Oxford.

Table 1. Generational comparison of characters in *The Spanish Tragedy* and *Hamlet* with historical figures in the Elizabethan court.

Spanish Tragedy	**Hamlet**	**Historical**
Hieronimo (old)	Hamlet (young)	Oxford (young)
[Protagonist whose family member is killed; seeks revenge]		
Isabella (old)	Ophelia (young)	Anne Cecil (young)
[Romantically linked to protagonist, kills herself from grief]		
Horatio (young)	King Hamlet (old)	Sussex (old)
[Member of protagonist's family, victim of murder]		
Bel-imperia (young)	Gertrude (old)	Eizabeth (old)
[Romantically associated with victim]		
Lorenzo (young)	Claudius (old)	Leicester (old)
[Villain, responsible for murdering family member]		

End Notes

1. 'Who Wrote *The Spanish Tragedy?*' See p. 93-101.
2. 'Hidden Allusions in Oxford's *Spanish Tragedy*,' See p. 102-15.
3. Martin A. S. Hume, *The Courtships of Queen Elizabeth* (Fisher Unwin, 1898).
4. *Leicester's Commonwealth*, D. C Peck, ed. (Ohio UP, 1985), 100-102.
5. Arthur Freeman, *Thomas Kyd: Facts and Problems* (Oxford, 1967) 58. The first researcher to note this parallel was Fredson T. Bowers in "Kyd's Pedringano: Sources and Parallels," *Harvard Studies and Notes in Philology and Literature* **13** (1931), 241-49. Another author, T. W. Baldwin [*On the Literary Genetics of Shakspere's Plays* (Illinois,

1959), 185-199] refers to a manuscript titled 'Letter of Estate' which is apparently an early version of *Leicester's Commonwealth*. He finds that the version of the betrayed-criminal story in the 'Letter of Estate' is closer to that in the *Tragedy* both in the events described and in the wording, and concludes that the *Tragedy* was the source of both versions of what he terms the Leicester "libel."

6. Sir Walter Scott, *Kenilworth* (Dodd & Mead, 1956), 195.

7. Peck, 96.

8. Peck, 93.

9. Dorothy and Charlton Ogburn, *This Star of England* (Coward-McCann, 1952), 272. Elizabeth's nickname for Hatton was 'Lyddes' (i.e. 'Eyelids') or 'Mutton' or 'Sheep.' Her nickname for Leicester was 'Eyes.'

10. *The Spanish Tragedy*, 2.1.11-28. C. F. T. Brooke and N. B. Paradise, *English Drama 1580-1642* (Heath, 1933), 106.

11. Charlton Ogburn, *The Mysterious William Shakespeare* (EPM Publications, 1984) Chapter 25, 510-36.

12. Ogburn, 511.

13. Ogburn, 503-4.

14. Ogburn, 478, 640.

15. Ogburn, 554. Examples of the use of gloves (often described as perfumed) as love-tokens: *Two Gentlemen of Verona* 2.1.1; *Much Ado* 3.4.62; *Love's Labor's Lost* 5.2.48; *Winter's Tale* 4.4.222, 4.4.250; *Troilus & Cressida* 5.2.79.

16. Ogburn, 508, 511.

17. Hank Whittemore, *The Monument* (Meadow Geese Press, 2005).

18. Ogburn, 523.

19. Freeman, 115.

20. Ogburn, 663-4.

21. Ogburn and Ogburn, 2.

22. Hume, 209-10, 278.

23. The instances referred to are the death of John Sheffield in 1568, and that of Walter Devereux, 1st Earl of Essex, in 1576.

See '*Leicester's Commonwealth*: Portrait of a Serial Killer?' (p. 133-44 in this book).

24. See, for example, Ogburn, 365-72.
25. Freeman, 53.
26. Burghley to Christopher Hatton, 12 March 1583. Quoted in Ogburn 653-4.

The Spanish Tragedy, Part 4

21

The Burbage Elegy and *The Spanish Tragedy*

As we all know, Richard Burbage was the most famous actor of his time. He originated the leading roles in many of Shakespeare's plays. When he died, he was widely mourned, and many poets wrote elegies honoring his memory. One poem in particular—*A Funeral Elegy on the Death of the famous Actor Richard Burbage who died on Saturday in Lent the 13th March 1618*[1]—has survived, although the name of its author has not. It is a long poem[2] (85 lines), but there are four lines in particular that are quoted in almost every discussion of Burbage's career:

> He's gone and with him what a world are dead
> Which he review'd, to be revived so.
> No more young Hamlet, old Hieronimo
> Kind Lear, the Grieved Moor, and more beside,
> That lived in him have now forever died.

'Hamlet' and 'Lear' are self-explanatory; the 'Grieved Moor' is of course Othello. 'Hieronimo' is the principal figure in a play called *The Spanish Tragedy*, which was enormously popular around 1580.

Orthodox scholarship attributes *The Spanish Tragedy* to Thomas Kyd; elsewhere I have argued that it is an early work by Edward de Vere, 17th Earl of Oxford.[3] If the academicians are correct, the author of the *Elegy* cites three roles by Shakespeare (i.e. Oxford) and one role by Kyd. If I am right, he cites four roles by Shakespeare/Oxford.

Now there's no reason why the poet cannot cite three Shakespearean roles and one by Kyd—he could cite one by Shakespeare, one by Marlowe, one by Webster and one by Lyly if he wanted to. But still, a 3-to-1 ratio seems peculiar. It points up the anomalous nature of attributing the *Tragedy* to Kyd in the first place. What else did he do? Academicians have given him various degrees of credit for *Soliman and Perseda*, *King*

Leir, Arden of Faversham, Edward III, and , of course, the ever-popular *Ur-Hamlet*. All of these plays (apart from the mythical *Ur-Hamlet*) have some connection to Shakespeare/Oxford.

In a recent paper[4] I pointed out a remarkable relationship between the *Tragedy* and *Hamlet*. It is that there is a one-to-one correspondence between the five main characters in *The Spanish Tragedy* and the five main characters in *Hamlet*. In addition, each character in the *Tragedy* who is of an older generation corresponds to a character in *Hamlet* who is of a younger generation, and vice versa—there is a *generational inversion*. Specifically, Hieronimo (old)—Hamlet (young), Isabella (old)—Ophelia (young), Horatio (young)—King Hamlet (old), Bel-imperia (young)—Gertrude (old), and Lorenzo (young)—Claudius (old). (See table at the end of Ref. 4.)

Thus I interpret the four lines of the poem quoted above as follows:

> (a) The anonymous author believed that all four of the roles he alluded to were by the same author. This reinforces my belief that *The Spanish Tragedy* was written by Shakespeare/Oxford.

> (b) The juxtaposition of 'young Hamlet' and 'old Hieronimo' in the same line indicates that the poet was aware that the two plays were related, and furthermore, that a *generational inversion* was one of the elements of the relationship.

I realize that these conclusions are speculative. But if speculation is outlawed, what happens to the works of Stephen Greenblatt, James Shapiro, and Stanley Wells?

End Notes

1. At the time, the new year was said to begin on 25 March (Lady Day). In modern usage, the year would be 1619.

2. The complete poem is included as Appendix 1 in a thesis by Kristýna Obermajerová entitled *Richard Burbage: The Life, Career and Acting Qualities of an Elizabethan Player*. The thesis can be accessed online by entering the title.

3. 'Who Wrote *The Spanish Tragedy*?' See p. 93-101. 'Hidden Allusions in Oxford's *Spanish Tragedy*.' See p. 102-115.

4. 'Oxford's *Spanish Tragedy*: More Hidden Allusions.' See p. 116-29.

Previously published in *The Shakespeare Oxford Newsletter* 53.1 (Winter 2017), 28.

The Leicester Papers, Part 1
22
Leicester's Commonwealth: Portrait of a Serial Killer?

Who was Leicester? Oxfordians know him chiefly as the model for Claudius in *Hamlet*. He was born Robert Dudley in 1532 or 1533 (if the latter, he was the same age as Elizabeth). His grandfather, Edmund Dudley, was beheaded by Henry VIII for 'constructive treason.' His father, John Dudley, Duke of Northumberland, was beheaded in 1553 for his attempt to make Lady Jane Grey queen rather than Mary Tudor (Lady Jane was married to his son Guildford). Robert Dudley, for his part in this conspiracy, was committed to the Tower in July 1553. He was arraigned, attainted and sentenced to death in January 1554, but was released and pardoned in October of that year. He and his brothers served with distinction in the battle of St. Quentin in Picardy in 1557, and as a reward for that service he was restored in blood.

Some sources say Dudley first met the Princess Elizabeth when he was 16, during the reign of young King Edward. He married Amy Robsart, the daughter of a provincial knight, in 1550. Elizabeth's confinement in the Tower (March-May 1554) overlapped with Dudley's, and there is a tradition that he sent her flowers during this time. At any rate, Elizabeth was strongly attracted to Dudley, and one of her first acts after her coronation was to make him her Master of Horse. The two spent much time together, and the rumor was that Dudley wanted to marry Elizabeth, thus fulfilling the family dream of putting a Dudley on the throne. An obstacle to this union was, of course, the existence of his wife Amy. She was found at the base of a stairway with her neck broken in September 1560. The Court and the diplomatic world were scandalized; on hearing the news, Mary Stuart was reported to have laughed shrilly and to have exclaimed "The Queen of England is going to marry her Horsekeeper, who has killed his wife to make room for her!" A jury declared the death an accident, but the scandal effectively prevented any marriage between Elizabeth and Dudley.

Elizabeth created Dudley Earl of Leicester on 29 September 1564, and tickled his neck during the ceremony.

What was *Leicester's Commonwealth*? It was a book purporting to be a record of a conversation between a Lawyer, a Gentleman, and a Scholar that made scandalous accusations against the Earl of Leicester. Among other things, it accused him of being responsible for the deaths (usually by poisoning) of at least eight people. It was printed in France in 1584 and distributed surreptitiously in England. Although banned by the government, it was widely read. It set the tone for the view of Leicester taken by early historians such as Camden and Naunton, but modern historians tend to give Leicester a pass, rarely if ever concluding that he killed anyone. The book itself is customarily described as "this outrageous document,"[1] "the scurrilous libel,"[2] or an "infamous tract."[3] The latter characterization is by Alison Weir, who goes on to describe it as "a virulent attack on Dudley made by an anonymous Catholic writer."

The authorship of *Leicester's Commonwealth* has been a subject for speculation since it was first published. Contemporary opinion was that it was by the Jesuit priest Father Parsons. The editor of the modern edition of the book, Dwight Peck, suggests that it "was written chiefly by Charles Arundell, probably with the assistance of all or some of the group comprising Lord Paget, Thomas Fitzherbert, William Tresham, Thomas Throgmorton, and possibly still others . . ."[4]

Knowledge is power, and our knowledge of the details of Oxford's life give us the godlike power to leap over centuries of puzzlement in a single bound. Historians have praised the skill of the author:

> It was in fact such a masterpiece of character assassination, and so brilliantly written, that many people were convinced of its veracity.[5]

> Artistically . . . it constitutes something of a minor masterpiece. Its language is often vigorous and engaging, in places . . . with . . . a delightful quality of outrageous humor. . . . it is not too much to say that the participants here take on something of the personalities expected of characters from the stage.[6]

A French edition, described by Peck as "an extremely close and accurate translation," came out in 1585. Peck considers the author of the French edition to be the same as author of the original English edition of the previous year. This author "mentions further translations into Latin and Italian shortly to appear (but which, so far as is known, never did) . . ."[7]

I'm not going to tell you who the author of the *Commonwealth* was, but if you can think of an Elizabethan courtier capable of writing masterpieces in English, who was also fluent in French, Latin and Italian, and whose characters come to life on the stage, you may be on to something.

Was Leicester a serial killer? The FBI defines a serial killer as someone who kills at least three people over an extended period of time. As we mentioned, the *Commonwealth* attributes at least eight deaths to Leicester. They are listed below.

> Amy Robsart (1560)
>
> Lord John Sheffield (1568)
>
> Cardinal Châtillon (1571)
>
> Sir Nicholas Throckmorton (1571)
>
> Walter Devereux, Earl of Essex (1576)
>
> Alice Draycot (1576)
>
> Lady Lennox (1578)
>
> Thomas Radcliffe, Earl of Sussex (1583)

Some people would add **Edward VI** (1547) and **John de Vere, 16th Earl of Oxford** (1562) to this list, but they are not mentioned in the *Commonwealth*.

In some ways, the most interesting case on this list is the first one, Amy Robsart, Dudley's first wife, who was found dead with a broken neck at the base of a stairway. I will not discuss it in detail, but will refer you to Alison Weir, who devotes 20 pages to it.[8] Weir's thesis, which both Sarah Smith and I find persuasive, is that Amy's death was arranged by William Cecil as a preëmptive strike to prevent Dudley from marrying Elizabeth. The manner of death is significant here—the broken neck immediately suggests foul play, whereas if she had been poisoned, a death from natural causes could have been claimed. As it was, a jury returned a verdict of 'death by mischance,' clearing Dudley, and we too will give him a pass.

Our program now will be to examine the three cases about which the most is known and see if we can reasonably determine Leicester to be guilty. If we do so in all three cases, we can conclude, using the FBI criterion, that he was in fact a serial killer.

Case 1: Lord John Sheffield. In 1562 John Sheffield, 2nd Baron of Butterwick, married the beautiful Douglass Howard (her father was William, Lord Howard of Effingham). In 1565 she met Dudley (now Leicester) during a visit to Belvoir Castle. A contemporary account relates that Leicester, "being much taken with her perfection, paid court to her and used all the art (of which he was master enough) to debauch her." A modern historian writes

> By the time the visit to Belvoir had ended, Douglass was much in Leicester's thrall and fearful her husband would discover her infidelity. To reassure her, Leicester allegedly wrote that he was aware of what an obstacle the unsuspecting husband was "to the full fruit of their contentment" and told the unhappy woman "that he had endeavored by one expedient already, which had failed . . ." to dispose of Sheffield. But, he said, he would try once more, and "doubted not would hit more sure."[9]

According to some accounts, Douglass dropped this letter and it was found by Sheffield's sister, who warned him about the conspiracy. He immediately set out for London to apply to Parliament for a divorce. He died 10 December 1568, at the age of 30. In May 1573 Leicester married Douglass in a secret ceremony at Esher, which he later repudiated as having no legal force. Three months later, Douglass gave birth to a son who was given the name 'Robert Dudley.' By July 1575 Leicester had grown tired of Douglass, and was actively courting Lettice Knollys, who was then married to the Earl of Essex, Walter Devereux.

Alison Weir recounts the events described above, and then writes

> No other evidence corroborates this tale, and as Leicester was invariably accused by his enemies of poisoning those about him, even such a friend as Throckmorton, little credence can be given to it.[10]

I'm having a little difficulty understanding her logic here. Perhaps it would help if I restated it as a formal PROPOSITION.

PROPOSITION: Because Leicester was **invariably** accused by his **enemies** of poisoning those about him, he is **innocent** of the death of Sheffield.

Since the opposite of **enemies** is **friends** and the opposite of **innocent** is **guilty**, we are immediately able to deduce

> COROLLARY 1: If Leicester were invariably accused by his **friends** of poisoning those about him, he would be **guilty** of the death of Sheffield.

But this is an absurdity: friends don't accuse friends of poisonings. Any person who does so is automatically an enemy. Let's try again.

> COROLLARY 2: If Leicester were **never** accused by his enemies of poisoning those about him, he would be **guilty** of the death of Sheffield.

This result seems counterintuitive, to say the least, seeming to require an unusual degree of incompetence (or politeness) on the part of Leicester's enemies. Weir presumably believes that if Leicester's enemies claim that he poisons 75% of the time, then he is 25% likely to have murdered Sheffield, and if they claim he poisons 25% of the time, his guilt in the Sheffield case is 75% assured. If you're ever on trial for murder, try to pack the jury with as many modern historians as you can get.

Case 2: Sir Nicholas Throckmorton. *Leicester's Commonwealth* gives what sounds like an eyewitness account of Throckmorton's death:

> . . . wherefore understanding that these two knights [Cecil and Throgmorton] were secretly made friends, and that Sir Nicholas was like to detect his doings (as he imagined), which might turn to some prejudice of his purposes (having conceived also a secret grudge and grief against him, for that he had written to her Majesty at his being ambassador in France that he had heard reported at Duke Memorance's table that the Queen of England had a meaning to marry her horsekeeper; he invited the said Sir Nicholas to a supper at his house in London and at supper time departed to the Court, being called for (as he said) upon the sudden by her Majesty, and so perforce would needs have Sir Nicholas to sit and occupy his Lordship's place, and therein to be served as he was; and soon after by a surfeit there taken he died of a strange and incurable vomit. But the day before his death, he declared to a dear friend of his all the circumstance and cause of his disease, which he affirmed plainly to be of poison given him in

a salad at supper, inveighing most earnestly against the Earl's cruelty and bloody disposition, affirming him to be the wickedest, most perilous and perfidious man under heaven. But what availed this, when he had now received the bait? [11]

There is a book entitled *Assassination at St. Helena Revisited* that gives a detailed account of Napoleon's death by poisoning at the hands of an agent of the French royal family. An appendix lists 32 symptoms of *chronic* and seven symptoms of *acute* arsenic intoxication. "Violent vomiting" is one of the latter. [12]

The *Dictionary of National Biography* gives the following account of Throckmorton's death:

> ... He died in London on 12 February 1571. Shortly before, he had dined or supped with the Earl of Leicester at Leicester House. According to the doubtful authority of Leicester's 'Commonwealth,' his death was due to poison administered by Leicester in a salad on that occasion ... Leicester, it is said, had never forgiven Throckmorton for his vehement opposition to the earl's proposed marriage to the queen. No reliance need be placed on this report. Throckmorton had continuously corresponded on friendly terms with Leicester for many years before his death, and they acted together as patrons of Puritan ministers ... Cecil wrote to Sir Thomas Smith of their markedly amicable relations on 16 October 1565, and described Throckmorton as 'carefull and devote to his Lordship.' [13]

It may be that Throckmorton was "carefull and devote" to Leicester, but I don't think that rules out the possibility that Leicester killed him. I remember in high school I read a story—I forget the name—about an Italian nobleman who had a grudge against a fellow citizen. For years he feigned friendship with the man, waiting for his chance, until finally he lured him into a vast array of underground catacombs on the pretext of sampling an especially rare cask of Amontillado sherry. Then he did something really awful to the man. I forget what it was. Who knows what evil lurks in the hearts of men? Not the DNB biographer.

Case 3: Walter Devereux, Earl of Essex. Appendix D of Dwight Peck's edition of *Leicester's Commonwealth* gives a succinct account of the death of Essex.

> Walter Devereux, first Earl of Essex, went into Ulster with a military force in 1573. His wife Lettice Knollys was involved with Leicester, at first as early as 1565 and then again in her husband's absence, as (probably) during the Kenilworth festivities

of 1575; she married him in 1578. Whether Essex sought revenge upon Leicester for "begetting his wife with child in his absence" may be doubted, but they were hostile toward one another, and this may have been part of the reason; on 5 December 1575, Antonio de Guaras wrote from London, during Essex's return, that "as the thing is publicly talked about in the streets there is no objection to my writing openly about the great enmity which exists between the Earl of Leicester and the Earl of Essex, in consequence, it is said, of the fact that whilst Essex was in Ireland his wife had two children by Leicester." Essex's Irish failures brought him home in 1575, but he was soon forced to go back, largely, according to Camden, because of Leicester's influence in Council . . . In late summer 1576 he was in Dublin, preparing to come home again; there he became ill and, after three week's languishing, died on 22 September. [14]

The "three week's languishing" requires that Leicester have an agent in Essex's household, in a position to administer moderate doses of arsenic over that period of time. Essex's 'yeoman of the cellar' was Roland Crompton. After Essex's death, Crompton was given a position in Leicester's household.

The *Dictionary of National Biography* sums up the matter as follows:

A report that Essex had been poisoned caused Sir Henry Sidney to order an investigation immediately after the earl's death. The rumour proved groundless; the post-mortem examination showed no trace of poison. [15]

Weir agrees:

After Essex died on 22 September, Sir Henry Sidney, the Lord Deputy of Ireland, ordered an immediate post-mortem, but, as he reported in detail to the Council, there was no evidence of foul play, nor did the doctors who attended Essex believe that he died of anything other than natural causes. [16]

Both Weir and the DNB neglect to mention that Sir Henry Sidney was in fact Leicester's brother-in-law, having married Mary Dudley on 29 March 1551. Peck is honest enough to inform the reader of that relationship, but it doesn't shake his confidence in Leicester's innocence.

Henry Sidney, despite his obvious connection with Leicester's interests, was apparently a man of very great honesty, and in the absence of harder evidence than we now have, his report should be believed. [17]

It is touching to see such wonderful faith in the essential goodness of mankind; these three historians are gleaming candles of innocence in a cynical world.

If we are to exonerate Leicester as the above historians have done, we must be convinced of two things: (1) that the medical science of the time was capable of detecting poison if it were there, and (2) that Henry Sidney reported the result truthfully. The interaction of these two conditions gives rise to three possibilities:

> (i) The post-mortem was accurate and Sidney was honest. In this case we have to join our benevolent historians in exonerating Leicester.
>
> (ii) The post-mortem was inaccurate, failing to detect poison that was actually present, and Sidney reported this result truthfully. This would count against Leicester.
>
> (iii) The post-mortem was accurate and detected poison, but Sidney reported this result untruthfully. This would also imply Leicester's guilt.

If the post-mortems of 1576 were 50% accurate and the chances of Sidney ratting on his brother-in-law are 50-50, then each of these possibilities is equally probable, but since two of them point to Leicester's guilt and only the first exonerates him, we have a 2-to-1 indication of his culpability. But can we do better in estimating the odds?

Medical science in the Elizabethan era. In 2004 we are used to precise medical analyses. When the DNB says "the post-mortem examination showed no trace of poison," the image that leaps to mind is a white-coated technician with spectacles and a clip-board reporting 'We ran the Krogheimer test for arsenic; it showed less than 5 parts per billion, normal for someone living in Dublin. Antimony and mercury levels were below the detectable limit. And we did the Fitzeau procedure for alkaloids, which also came out negative.' This is the sort of thing that could lead to the unbounded confidence in the post-mortem that our historians display. The reality was quite different.

John Hall was the son-in-law of Will Shaksper (the Stratford guy, not the playwright). He was a physician, and a highly-regarded one. When he died, the inscription in the burial register read "*Johannes Hall, medicus peritissimus*"—most skillful doctor. We can assume he was on the cutting edge of the medical practice of his time. (I emphasize he was not personally involved in any of the post-mortems discussed here.) Charlton Ogburn has given us an example of his technique:

> A seventy-year-old whom Dr. Hall treated was "oppressed with Melancholy, and a Feaver with extraordinary heat." The doctor applied "Radishes sliced besprinkled with Vinegar and Salt" to the soles of the patient's feet to draw back the "Vapours," which caused "starting and fear." [18]

One can only speculate about the Elizabethan procedure for determining if a corpse had been poisoned. Perhaps cucumber slices were placed between the toes of the deceased, and if they turned blue the test was positive.

The poisoning of Napoleon is instructive. Because of the political sensitivity of the case, the post-mortem was carried out by several doctors, each of whom concluded that he had died of natural causes. Yet when the body was exhumed twenty years later, it was in a state of perfect preservation. It was so loaded with arsenic the poor germs never had a chance to initiate the processes of decay. The authors cite a similar case:

> In all, d'Aubray's illness lasted eight months. The Marquise de Brinvilliers [his wife], whose crime was discovered, admitted she had poisoned him 28 to 30 times. . . Yet at the post-mortem examination, the doctors had judged that Monsieur d'Aubray had died a natural death. [19]

The post-mortems of Napoleon and d'Aubray were carried out over two centuries after that of Essex—yet after two centuries of medical advances, not only were both wrong, both were stunningly wrong. I can only conclude that post-mortems in 1576 were meaningless. And there is a human factor at work here—in politically sensitive cases such as these, where the possible suspect is a powerful nobleman known for his vindictive nature, it would be an audacious physician indeed who would return a finding of death by poison.

Sidney's honesty. Let's review the case against Leicester. In 1576 he had been having carnal relations with Essex's wife for perhaps 11 years. Essex knew about it and vowed revenge. By pulling strings, Leicester had got Essex shipped back to Ireland, but Leicester knew he would eventually come back to London. So Leicester had two strong motives for getting rid of Essex: (1) continued access to Lettice, and (2) self-preservation. That

Leicester had formed a relationship with Essex's 'yeoman of the bottles' is implied by the fact that Crompton joined his staff shortly after Essex died. Two other people (Robin Hunnis and Alice Draycot) who were dining with Essex were also afflicted, Draycot to the point of death. I would say the circumstantial case against Leicester is quite strong. Peck, however rejects it because of his faith in Henry Sidney's "very great honesty."

How far was Sidney willing to go to advance his brother-in-law's interests? An earlier incident may suggest an answer. In late 1560, Robert Dudley had still not despaired of persuading Elizabeth to marry him, in spite of the scandalous death of his wife Amy Robsart. He believed that if he could persuade Philip of Spain to support the union then Elizabeth would agree. Rather than approaching the Spanish ambassador himself, he sent his brother-in-law. The ambassador reported the interview as follows:

> [Sidney] began by beating about the bush very widely, but at last came to his brother-in-law's affairs and said that as the matter was now public property, and I knew how much inclined the Queen was to the marriage, he wondered that I had not suggested to Your Majesty this opportunity for gaining over Lord Robert by extending a hand to him now, and he would thereafter serve and obey Your Majesty like one of your own vassals. [20]

For a British subject to promise to serve and obey the Spanish king 'like one of his own vassals' sounds to me very much like treason, yet honest Henry Sidney was willing to make that proposal to advance his brother-in-law's interests. If by some miracle the commission looking into Essex's death had decided that he had been poisoned, would Sidney have reported that to the Council? You be the judge.

Epilogue: the death of Leicester. I must confess it was not without a rush of grim satisfaction that I read the following account of Leicester's death.

> Leicester withdrew from London at the end of August. While on the way to Kenilworth he stopped at his house at Cornbury, Oxfordshire, and there he died of 'a continual fever, as 'twas said,' on 4 Sept.1588, aged about fifty-six. Ben Jonson tells the story that he had given his wife 'a bottle of liquor which he willed her to use in any faintness, which she, not knowing it was poison, gave him, and so he died' . . . Bliss, in his notes to the 'Athenæ Oxon.' . . . first printed a contemporary narrative to the effect that the countess had fallen in love with Christopher Blount . . .

gentleman of the horse to Leicester; that Leicester had taken Blount to Holland with the intention of killing him, in which he failed; that the countess, suspecting her husband's plot, gave him a poisonous cordial after a heavy meal while she was alone with him at Cornbury. Blount married the countess after Leicester's death, and the narrator of the story gives as his authority William Haynes, Leicester's page and gentleman of the bedchamber, who saw the fatal cup handed to his master. But the story seems improbable in face of the post-mortem examination, which was stated to show no trace of poison. [21]

Ah, yes—the trusty post-mortem examination, which has done so much to sanitize the modern reputation of Elizabeth's favorite, now exonerates his widow, who, driven to distraction by her grief, seeks to alleviate it by immediately marrying her late husband's Master of Horse. As a keen observer of human nature once remarked, "'Tis sport to see the engineer hoist on his own petard."

NOTE: *This paper was originally given as a talk at the Shakespeare Fellowship Oxford Day Banquet, 30 April 2004, in Cambridge, Massachusetts. The audience was empanelled to act as a jury. Leicester was unanimously voted guilty on all three counts (Sheffield, Throckmorton, Essex). He thus fulfills the FBI's definition of a serial killer.*

BIBLIOGRAPHY

Dictionary of National Biography, ed. Leslie Stephen and Sidney Lee, Oxford University Press, 1917

Leicester's Commonwealth, Dwight C. Peck, ed., Ohio University Press, Athens OH, 1985

Luke, Mary M., *Gloriana: the Years of Elizabeth I*, Coward, McCann & Geoghegan, New York, 1973

Ogburn, Charlton, *The Mysterious William Shakespeare*, EPM Publications, McLean VA, 1984

Richardson, Mrs. Aubrey, *The Lover of Queen Elizabeth*, Werner Laurie, London, 1907

Ross, Josephine, *Suitors to the Queen*, Coward, McCann & Geoghegan, New York, 1975

Weider, Ben, and Sten Forshufved, *Assassination at St. Helena Revisited,* Wiley, New York, 1995

Weir, Alison, *The Life of Elizabeth I,* Ballantine, New York, 1998

References

1. Richardson, p. 317
2. DNB VI, 118
3. Weir, 95,
4. Peck, 31
5. Weir, 353. In using the word 'veracity,' Weir unconsciously got it right.
6. Peck, 41-2
7. Peck, 11
8. Weir, 93-112
9. Luke, 391-2
10. Weir, 291
11. Peck, 85
12. Weider, 507
13. DNB XIX, 813
14. Peck, 267
15. DNB V, 896
16. Weir, 304
17. Peck, 268
18. Ogburn, 317
19. Weider, 227
20. Ross, 97
21. DNB VI, 119

This paper appeared in *Shakespeare Matters* 3.4 (Summer 2004)

The Leicester Papers, Part 2

23

The Earl of Leicester in the Plays of Shakespeare

Robert Dudley, Earl of Leicester, was one of the most powerful politicians in the Elizabethan court. His power stemmed largely from his relationship with the Queen, who was head-over-heels in love with him; their stormy but passionate relationship lasted from his appointment as Elizabeth's Master of Horse (shortly after her accession in 1558) to his death in 1588, a period of thirty years. He had a dark complexion, which led to the nickname, used mostly by his enemies, of 'Gypsy.' Elizabeth's nickname for him was 'Eyes.' He was known for his love of ornate clothing.

Leicester had a reputation as a poisoner. *Leicester's Commonwealth*, a book that was published surreptitiously in 1584 (and subsequently banned by the Queen) accused him of being implicated in eight known murders, and implied he was probably responsible for many more not yet known. In the mid-1560s Leicester became involved with a court beauty who was the wife of Lord John Sheffield. In December 1568 Sheffield died suddenly at the age of 30. Leicester married his widow, who bore him a son, named Robert Dudley. Around 1575 Leicester became involved with Lettice Knollys, the wife of Walter Devereux, Earl of Essex. Essex died in 1576 at the age of 35, probably poisoned by Leicester. Leicester repudiated his marriage to Sheffield's widow and married Lettice. As the author of *Leicester's Commonwealth* put it,

> For first his Lordship hath a special fortune, that when he desireth any woman's favor, then what person so ever standeth in his way hath the luck to die quickly for the finishing of his desire. [1]

Edward Albee has observed that the source material for a playwright is the people he knows, rather than the people he doesn't know. There is no doubt that Oxford knew Leicester. Thus we are justified in examining the plays written by Oxford under the pen name 'Shakespeare' for characters resembling

Leicester. The clues are (1) an illicit relationship with a queen, (2) a swarthy complexion, (3) intent to murder, especially by poison, and (4) a love of ornate clothing, often implied by a reference to tailors. With this in mind, let's look at a sample of the plays in which the Leicestrian allusions seem particularly clear.

HAMLET. Scholars have long noted parallels between the *dramatis personæ* in *Hamlet* and real-life figures in the Elizabethan court, the most obvious example being the councilor Polonius, a caricature of William Cecil, Lord Burghley.[2] The process of identification accelerated after the publication in 1920 of J. Thomas Looney's *Shakespeare Identified*, which revealed Edward de Vere, 17th Earl of Oxford, as the true author of the Shakespeare plays and the model for the central figure in *Hamlet*. Eva Turner Clark, writing in 1931, suggested originals for 12 of the characters in the play,[3] including Leicester as the model for the usurping poisoner, Claudius. Below we list the overt parallels between Leicester and Claudius.

(1) Each was the consort of the queen of the realm.

(2) Each achieved that position on the basis of sexual attraction.

(3) Each wielded political power on the basis of his relationship with the queen.

(4) Each used poison to gain personal advantage.

Did Leicester kill Oxford's father? A literal interpretation of the parallels between events in *Hamlet* and those in the Elizabethan court would require that Leicester be responsible for poisoning Oxford's father. The traditional gloss (offered by Clark, for example) is that Leicester was suspected of poisoning Thomas Radcliffe, Earl of Sussex. *Leicester's Commonwealth* states

> The late Earl of Sussex wanted not a scruple for many years before his death of some dram that made him incurable . . . [Leicester's] treacheries towards the noble late Earl of Sussex in their many breaches is notorious to all England.[4]

Shakespeare Confidential

Sussex was a father figure to Oxford, overseeing the younger man's introduction to military action in 1570, and encouraging his first dramatic productions. However, the more literal interpretation may in fact be true. A later researcher, Gwynneth Bowen,[5] searched the records and found that through a complex arrangement Leicester had obtained control of almost all the Oxford lands on the death of the 16th Earl, de Vere's father. Oxford was thus substantially disinherited by Leicester, just as Hamlet was by Claudius. And once the indenture giving Leicester control of the Oxford lands on the death of the 16th Earl was signed, Leicester had a strong motive for accomplishing that death. In fact, the 16th Earl was dead two months after the signing. In the play *Hamlet*, the prince stages 'The Murder of Gonzago' to see by Claudius's reaction whether he is guilty of the murder of Hamlet's father. It's on the line "He poisons him in the garden for his estate" that Claudius rises and flees the room. Could Oxford have staged *Hamlet* to see if Leicester was guilty of the murder of the 16th Earl? Was *Hamlet* Oxford's Mousetrap?

We have indicated that Leicester is to be identified with Claudius, but identity in the Shakespeare plays is like identity in a dream—shifting, fluid and mutable. Take Laertes. When Polonius is giving instructions to Reynaldo (2.1), Laertes is clearly Burghley's eldest son, Thomas Cecil, who sowed his wild oats as a student in Paris, seducing wenches and stealing from his tutor. At this point, one is puzzled by the name: classically, Laertes is the father of Ulysses, not the son of Nestor. The puzzle is cleared up at the end of Act 4, when Laertes plots with Claudius to avenge his father's death by wounding Hamlet with a poisoned sword. The notion of poisoning would immediately make the well-informed Elizabethan think of Leicester, and suddenly realize that **LAERTES** is a perfect anagram for **A LESTER**.[6] Laertes' line "I bought an unction of a mountebank" would confirm the identification—the word 'mountebank' is Italian, and immediately suggests Dr. Julio Borgarucci, an Italian physician who was a prominent member of Leicester's entourage and reputedly his mentor in the toxic arts. *Leicester's Commonwealth* mentions his use of "the Italian ointment procured not many years past by his surgeon or mountebank of that country,"[7] clinching the reference to Borgarucci.

We have mentioned that one of Leicester's nicknames was 'Gypsy'—Sussex's dying words were "Beware the Gypsy. He will betray you. You do not know the beast as well as I do." [8] During the Dumb Show (3.2), Ophelia asks Hamlet "What means this, my lord?" Hamlet responds with a strange phrase

> Marry, 'tis miching mallecho—it means mischief.

Partridge (and others) identify 'mallecho' as a form of the Welsh gypsy word 'maleko,' meaning 'beware'.[9] Hamlet's line is spoken as the Pantomime Queen yields to the usurping poisoner. I submit that the reference to Leicester is as unmistakable as it is subtle: a Gypsy word meaning 'beware' can be read as 'Beware the Gypsy.'

There's another occasion in the play where a line takes a strange turn. Hamlet, newly returned to Denmark (4.7), writes to Claudius and says "Tomorrow shall I beg leave to see your kingly eyes . . ." Why "eyes"? Wouldn't it be more natural to say something like ' . . . I beg leave to appear in your royal presence'? Then we recall that 'Eyes' was Elizabeth's pet name for her 'sweet Robin.' Richardson gives us a letter from Leicester to Elizabeth in which the favorite makes fulsome use of this intimacy:[10]

> I most humbly thank my most gracious lady for her great comfort showed toward her absent Õ Õ, by the testimony of her own sweet hand, which never yieldeth less joy than greatest contentation both to body and mind...Your Majesty's most faithful and most bounden ,
>   R. LEYCESTER

KING LEAR. In May 1573 Gilbert Talbot wrote a letter to his father, the Earl of Shrewsbury, containing the following information:

> My Lord of Leicester is very much with Her Majesty, and she shows the same great good affection to him that she was wont. Of late, he has endeavoured to please her more than heretofore. There are two sisters now in the court that are very far in love with him, as they have been long: my lady Sheffield and Frances Howard. They (of like striving who shall love him better) are at great wars together and the Queen thinketh not well of them, and not the better of him.[11]

My lady Sheffield' is Douglass Howard, a court beauty who married John Sheffield in 1562. Reading Talbot's letter, one immediately thinks of Regan and Goneril's rivalry for Edmund in *King Lear:*

Goneril (to Edmund):

> This kiss, if it durst speak
> Would stretch thy spirits up into the air ...
> To thee a woman's services are due ... (4.1)

Regan (to Goneril's servant): ...

> Edmund and I have talk'd
> And more convenient is he for my hand
> Than for your lady's ... (4.5)

Goneril: I had rather lose the battle than that sister
Should loosen him and me. (4.7)

In the play, Goneril poisons Regan, then kills herself when Edmund is slain by Edgar. In real life, Douglass Sheffield took Leicester for her lover, then conspired with him to poison her husband, a task they had accomplished by the end of 1568. In 1573, Leicester yielded to Douglass's demands and staged a secret wedding ceremony. In 1574 she bore him a son, who was named Robert Dudley. The following year, Leicester pursued an affair with another court beauty, Lettice Knollys, who (as we noted above) was married to the Earl of Essex. This obstacle was overcome by the death of Essex in 1576, and Leicester and Lettice were joined in holy wedlock in 1578, the groom having declared that his secret marriage to Douglass Sheffield was of no legal force. After marrying Lettice, Leicester was careful to refer to Robert Dudley as "my base son" to avoid giving the impression that he (Leicester) was a bigamist. This gives point to the opening scene of *Lear*—

Kent: Is this not your son, my lord?

Gloucester: His breeding, sir, hath been at my charge.
I have so often blushed to acknowledge him, that now I am brazed to it. . . .
Though this knave came something saucily into the world before he was sent for,
yet was his mother fair, there was good sport at his making, and the whoreson must be acknowledged.

—as well as to Edmund's brilliant soliloquy on bastardy (1.2). Note again how fluid the identities are: Edmund starts out as Robert Dudley *fils*, but before long is identified with his father, the unscrupulous politician beloved of two sisters.

TITUS ANDRONICUS. We have already noted parallels between Leicester and Claudius in *Hamlet*. There's a reference to Leicester's dark complexion that we haven't mentioned yet. It occurs during Hamlet's confrontation with Gertrude in her bedroom; he shows her portraits of the elder Hamlet and Claudius, and says

> Could you on this fair mountain leave to feed,
> And batten on this moor? . . . (3.4)

Etymologically, a Moor is someone from Morocco and a Gypsy is someone from Egypt, but to an audience in misty, rain-swept England, that's a distinction without a difference. In *Titus Andronicus* the chief villain is Aaron the Moor. He is involved in a passionate, illicit affair with Tamora, newly made queen, which eventually results in the birth of an illegitimate son. He is introduced to the audience in a soliloquy at the beginning of Scene 2.1. Its explicitness took my breath away:

> Then, Aaron, arm thy heart and fit thy thoughts,
> To mount aloft with thy imperial mistress,
> And mount her pitch, whom thou in triumph long
> Hast prisoner held, fettered in amorous chains . . .
> Away with slavish weeds and servile thoughts!
> I will be bright, and shine in pearl and gold,
> To wait upon this new-made emperess.
> To wait, said I? To wanton with this queen . . .

In case anyone should think this is simply a generic, nonspecific relationship between a dark-complected subject and a queen, the author has helpfully included the specific detail of Leicester's well-known love of ornate clothing ("I will be bright, and shine in pearl and gold"). Note too the intensely sensual imagery (" mount her pitch . . . fettered in amorous chains . . . wanton with this queen"). No wonder it was politically important to attribute authorship of the plays to a bumpkin from Stratford who couldn't possibly know what went on at the court of the Virgin Queen.

1,2 HENRY VI. One of the joys of being an Oxfordian is that we learn so much from other Oxfordians. The 2003 conference of the Shakespeare Fellowship was held in Carmel, California. One of the events of the conference was a performance of *2 Henry VI* by the Pacific Repertory Theatre. The performance was preceded by a talk given by Barbara Burris, in which she pointed out that the illicit relationship between Queen Margaret and the Earl of Suffolk in the play mirrored the illicit relationship between Queen Elizabeth and the Earl of Leicester in real life.

Once this parallel is pointed out, textual confirmation practically jumps off the page. In *1 Henry VI* Suffolk is in France and encounters Margaret, daughter of the impoverished king of Naples. He immediately falls in love with her, but remembers there is an obstacle to their union (5.3.81):

> Suffolk (aside): Fond man, remember that thou hast a wife,
> Then how can Margaret be thy paramour?

This, of course, was precisely Leicester's situation in 1560, before his wife, Amy Robsart, was found with a broken neck at the bottom of a stairway. Suffolk solves his problem by persuading King Henry to marry Margaret. He then exclaims (5.4.107):

> Margaret shall now be Queen, and rule the King;
> But I will rule both her, the King, and realm.

These are the last words in the play. *Leicester's Commonwealth* lays out in great detail just how completely Leicester ruled England on the strength of his intimate relationship with the queen.

In *2 Henry VI* a group of nobles, including Margaret (now queen) and Suffolk, discuss murdering Gloucester, the Lord Protector. Suffolk volunteers for the job (3.1.72):

> But say the word, and I will be his priest.

A footnote in the Riverside edition glosses the phrase "be his priest" as *perform the last offices for him*; for me the phrase evokes the disturbing image of a communion performed with a poisoned host. Historically, the *Dictionary of National Biography* has the following comment:

> On 28 Feb. [1447] Gloucester was dead, probably by a natural death, for Suffolk, though freely accused of the murder, was never formally charged with it . . .[12]

We have previously shown with what unwarranted optimism the *DNB* approaches questions of guilt and innocence.[13]

You may object that it is a far stretch to associate a figure in a history play with an Elizabethan courtier when the play dealt with events which occurred more than a hundred years before. However, the association between Suffolk and Leicester also occurred to someone writing in 1584. This author was describing the dangers run by monarchs in showing too much favor to an unscrupulous courtier. He wrote

> In the third [example] ([Henry VI] being a simple and holy man), albeit no great exorbitant affection was seen toward any [by Henry],yet his wife Queen Margaret's too much favor and credit (by him not controlled) towards the Marquess of Suffolk that was after made Duke, by whose insti[gation] and wicked counsel she made away first the noble Duke of Gloucester and afterward committed other things in great prejudice of the realm and suffered the said most impious and sinful Duke [of Suffolk] to range and make havoc of all sort of subjects at his pleasure (much after the fashion of the Earl of Leicester now, though not yet in so high and extreme a degree).

The above passage is from *Leicester's Commonwealth*.[14] A growing number of Oxfordian scholars believe it was written by Oxford himself. Thus we have confirmation of the Suffolk-Leicester connection straight from the horse's mouth, so to speak.

RICHARD III and 3 HENRY VI.: Nina Green manages the online discussion group *Phaeton*. In 1998 she posted a discussion[15] of the extensive parallels between Richard III and Leicester, summarized below.

1. Richard's ruthless ambition to be king parallels Leicester's.
2. Richard's marriage with Anne Neville, whose husband he had killed, parallels Leicester's marriage to Lettice Knollys.
3. Richard's appointment as Protector. When Elizabeth was suffering from smallpox and believed she was dying, she named Leicester as Lord Protector. Fortunately she recovered.
4. Richard's entrapment of his brother, the Duke of Clarence, is mirrored by Leicester's entrapment of his cousin, the Duke of Norfolk.
5. Richard orders Catesby to spread rumors that "Anne, my wife, is very grievous sick" prior to having her murdered (4.2). Similarly, Leicester spread rumors about Amy Robsart's illness before she was killed.
6. Both Richard and Leicester made public displays of piety for political gain.

In addition, Green points out that both were responsible for multiple murders, and both were virtually friendless at the time of their deaths. She concludes that "surely the foregoing are sufficient to demonstrate that Shakespeare made deliberate use of the reign of Richard III to portray the danger which Leicester's ambitions posed to the state."

The character of Richard Plantagenet, later Duke of Gloucester and eventually Richard III, does not appear in *1 Henry VI*. He appears in *2 Henry VI*, but only sporadically, spouting the same type of defiant boilerplate as most of the other characters. Then halfway through *3 Henry VI* he suddenly comes to life with a stunning speech, 72 lines long, in which his ambition for the crown is nakedly revealed. It ends with the lines

> I can add colors to the chameleon,
> Change shapes with Proteus for advantages,
> And set the murderous Machevil to school.
> Can I do this, and cannot get the crown?
> Tut, were it farther off, I'll pluck it down.

But Richard started this speech with the conviction that there were too many obstacles between him and the crown:

> Well, say there is no kingdom then for Richard;
> What other pleasure can the world afford?
> I'll make my heaven in a lady's lap,
> And deck my body in gay ornaments,
> And witch sweet ladies with my words and look.
> O miserable thought! And more unlikely
> Than to accomplish twenty golden crowns!
> . . .
> And am I then a man to be belov'd?
> O monstrous fault, to harbor such a thought!

Since Leicester was notorious for his conquests, this sounds to me like Richard is saying that he is *not* Leicester, or more accurately, that the author is making a distinction, adding characteristics that are not Leicester-like. What are these characteristics? They are enumerated in this same speech.

> Why, love foreswore me in my mother's womb;
> And for I should not deal in her soft laws,
> She did corrupt frail nature with some bribe,
> To shrink mine arm up like a wither'd shrub,
> To make an envious mountain on my back,
> Where sits deformity to mock my body . . .

Richard is a hunchback. Is there a figure in the Elizabethan court who was a hunchback? Yes, Robert Cecil. Cecil is distinct from Leicester in not being a ladies' man, but do Cecil and Leicester share any characteristics? They were both unscrupulous manipulators, political Machiavels. I suggest that the protagonist of *Richard III* is a composite of Robert Cecil and Leicester.

When was *Richard III* written? Eva Turner Clark says that it dates from 1581 and that it was inspired by Oxford's imprisonment in the Tower for impregnating Anne Vavasor. In 1581 Robert Cecil was 18 years old, probably too young to be the protagonist in a major tragedy. Hank Whittemore[16] and Bill Boyle[17] have proposed that a political deal was made in 1601, in the wake of the Essex Rebellion, whereby Southampton's life was spared in return for Oxford's pledge of anonymity with regard to the literary works we associate with the name 'Shakespeare.' If this was in fact the case, it seems natural to me that Oxford would have spent the remaining years of his life revising his plays to give them a sharper edge, introducing themes and speeches that would have been too critical, too scandalous to include when the plays were actually being performed at court. Who in Elizabeth's waning days had the power to negotiate and enforce such a deal? The obvious answer is Robert Cecil, now 38 years old and at the height of his powers. I suggest that after the deal of 1601, Oxford took his revenge on Cecil by revising *3 Henry VI* and *Richard III* so as to sharpen allusions to Robert Cecil, thus enhancing the satirical bite that makes these plays so fascinating even today.

End Notes

1. Dwight C. Peck, ed., *Leicester's Commonwealth*, Ohio University Press, 1985, 81.

2. George Russell French, *Shakespeareana Genealogica*, Macmillan, London, 1869.

3. Eva Turner Clark, *Hidden Allusions in Shakespeare's Plays*, 3rd Edition ed. Ruth Loyd Miller, Minos Publishing Co., Jennings LA, 1974.

4. Peck, 85, 92. 'Wanted not a scruple' is equivalent to 'required no medication,' implying perfect health.

5. Gwynneth Bowen, *Shakespeare Authorship Review* **24**, Spring 1971, 9-10.
6. 'Lester' was the spelling used by Leicester's nephew Sir Philip Sidney in his unpublished rejoinder to *Leicester's Commonwealth* (see Mrs. Aubrey Richardson, *The Lover of Queen Elizabeth*, Werner Laurie, London, 1907: 309-312).
7. Peck, 89.
8. Charlton Ogburn, *The Mysterious William Shakespeare*, EPM Publications, McLean VA, 1984, 666.
9. Eric Partridge, *Dictionary of Slang and Unconventional English*, Macmillan, New York, 1967, 518. The *Oxford English Dictionary* says that 'miching' is probably the same as 'mitching,' for which it offers the synonym 'skulking.'
10. Mrs. Aubrey Richardson, *The Lover of Queen Elizabeth*, Werner Laurie, London, 1907, 131.
11. Alison Weir, *The Life of Elizabeth I*, Ballantine, New York, 1998, 209-1.
12. *Dictionary of National Biography*, ed. Leslie Stephen and Sidney Lee, Oxford University Press, 1917, IX 511.
13. '*Leicester's Commonwealth*: Portrait of a Serial Killer?' See p. 133-44.
14. Peck, 188.
15. Nina Green, *Phaeton*, 5 December 1998.
16. Hank Whittemore, "1601: 'authorize thy trespass with compare,' " *Shakespeare Matters* 3.4 (Summer 2004), 1+.
17. Bill Boyle, "With the *Sonnets* now solved ..." *Shakespeare Matters* 3.4 (Summer 2004), 1, 11-21.

Presented at the First Dutch Shakespeare Authorship Conference Utrecht, the Netherlands, 9 July 2004

The Leicester Papers, Part 3
24
All's Well That Ends Well: Who Is Parolles?

If *Hamlet* is the most autobiographical of Oxford's plays, surely *All's Well That Ends Well* is a close second. It concerns Bertram, a young nobleman who has recently lost his father, and is being pressured by his country's ruler to marry a young woman who, though beautiful and intelligent, comes from common stock. Dismayed by this insult to his aristocratic origins, he flees the court to seek military adventures in an ongoing war on the Continent. Historically, Edward de Vere, 17th Earl of Oxford, married Anne Cecil, daughter of William Cecil (a commoner who had recently been promoted to baron by Elizabeth) in December 1571. Shortly after that, he and a companion traveled without permission to Belgium, where Protestant insurgents were fighting the occupying Spanish.

With this, it is easy to identify Bertram with Oxford and Helena with Anne, and the aged councilor Lafew seems to be a benign portrait of Cecil. But there is another character who is important to the play, whose historical antecedents (if any) are harder to winkle out—Parolles, a braggart, coward and liar who has attached himself to Bertram. I will review what previous scholars have said about this character.

- **Eva Turner Clark** practically invented the game of identifying Shakespeare's characters with historical figures, but in this case she is uncharacteristically silent, saying only "The identity of Parolles . . . is of interest but has not been fixed."[1]

- **Claire McEachern** is Professor of English at UCLA, and is thus a member of the Stratfordian establishment. Guild rules prevent her from associating a character in the plays with any actual person, living or dead, so she invokes an abstraction: ". . . in Parolles, Shakespeare animates the convention of the braggart soldier, or *miles gloriosus*: scarves, flags, drums and bombast, but beneath all the noise, a cowardly heart." [2]

- **The Elder Ogburns** write "Parolles is intended to stand for the talkative side of Oxford himself..." [3] This is no doubt true, but what Shakespeare play does *not* have a character who is in love with words? (Don Armado, Mercutio, Berowne, Jaques, Autolycus—the list goes on.)

- **Charlton Ogburn** finally gives us a flesh-and-blood figure to associate with Parolles; he nominates an adventurer named *Rowland Yorke*, a sometime servant and traveling companion of Oxford's.

> Arrested on a charge of felony in 1580, Yorke was unmasked in 1584 in a plot to betray Ghent to the Duke of Parma . . . Having with the help of friends managed to get back to England, he ingratiated himself with Philip Sidney and wangled from Sidney's uncle, the Earl of Leicester, command of Zutphen Sconce (a strategically located fortification), which, to pay back a grudge against the Earl, he surrendered to the Spanish. . . . We know him, I should guess, for his contribution to Parolles in *All's Well*, a braggart captain and follower of Bertram's whose baneful influence on the young Count is exorcised only when he is shown up as a coward and traitor.[4]

In reading and rereading the play I became aware of a number of characteristics exhibited by Parolles that suggested another fleshly figure: *Robert Dudley*, Earl of Leicester (mentioned above as 'Sidney's uncle'). Leicester was never traveling companion to Oxford, but some general characteristics lead me to believe that Oxford had Leicester in mind when he created Parolles. These characteristics are discussed below.

Ornate Clothing. Lafew says of Parolles " . . . there can be no kernel in this light nut; the soul of this man is in his clothes" (2.5.42-4).In a later speech (4.5.1-7), Lafew is more specific:

> . . . your son was misled with a snipt-taffeta fellow there, whose villainous saffron would have made all the unbak'd and doughy youth of a nation in his color. Your daughter-in-law had been alive

> at this hour, and your son here at home, more advanc'd by the King than by that red-tail'd humble-bee I speak of.

A note in the *Riverside Shakespeare* describes 'snipt-taffeta' as "wearing a garment of taffeta slashed to show a rich lining of contrasting color". That description, together with 'saffron' and 'red-tail'd', conjures up an image very much like the contemporary portrait of Leicester shown on the opposite page.

Bellicosity. Parolles urges Bertram to flee the French court and seek military adventure in Italy:

> To th' wars! . . . To th' wars, my boy, to th' wars! . . . To other regions! France is a stable, we that dwell in't jades. Therefore to the war! (2.3.275-85)

One historian writes "Leicester's was one of the most insistent voices in favour of intervention [in support of the Dutch rebels] . . . Walsingham would support Leicester whenever he promoted a more aggressively Protestant and militant policy in the privy council debates than that to which Elizabeth inclined." [5]

Tension with Senior Court Official. Lafew, who is the King's chief counsellor, meets Parolles in Scenes 2.3 and 2.5. In both cases verbal fireworks occur. In one example, Parolles protests "My lord, you do me most insupportable vexation," and Lafew replies, "I would it were hell-pains for thy sake, and my poor doing eternal . . ." (2.3.184-263).

Historically, Elizabeth's chief counsellor was William Cecil, Lord Burghley. He and Robert Dudley, Earl of Leicester, were long-time antagonists, and their enmity is discussed in every account of the politics of the period. Here is one brief example:

> To Cecil, Dudley had from the start of the reign been the key trouble-maker at court and he would remain a potential danger until Elizabeth was safely married to someone else. [6]

Cowardice. The extreme cowardice of Parolles is comically revealed in Scene 4.3. He has been captured, bound and blindfolded by men he believes to be enemy foreigners; actually, they are under the command of two French officers who want to show Bertram the true nature of his supposed friend. Under interrogation, he not only reveals a plethora of military information, but roundly insults Bertram, who is looking on.

To testify as to Leicester's nature, we turn to the author of *Leicester's Commonwealth*, who some scholars (including myself) believe to be the author of *All's Well*—Edward de Vere. If this is true, his testimony must be accorded special weight.

> A third cause of this manner of the lady [Amy Robsart]'s death may be the disposition of my Lord [of Leicester]'s nature, which is bold and violent where it feareth no resistance (as all cowardly natures are by kind), and where any difficulty or danger appeareth, there more ready to attempt all by art, subtilty, treason, and treachery. . . .But in the men whom he poisoned, for that they were such valiant knights, the most part of them, as he durst as soon have eaten his scabbard as draw his sword in public against, he was enforced (as all wretched, ireful, and dastardly creatures are) to supplant them by fraud and by other men's hands. [7]

Figure 8 - Robert Dudley, Earl of Leicester[9]

Specific Clue 1. Early in the play (1.1.35) it is mentioned that the ailment from which the King is suffering is a fistula in the leg. Oddly enough, starting around 1569, Queen Elizabeth also suffered from a fistula in the leg. In the play (2.3.104-66) much is made of the monarch's implacable insistence that Bertram marry the commoner Helena. The senior Ogburns write "This is surely a strong indication that Oxford was ordered to marry Anne ....."[3] Court audiences watching the play could appreciate the striking parallel, and would be pointed in the right direction by the coincidence of a fistula in both the King and Elizabeth.

Specific Clue 2. In one of their explosive encounters, Lafew says to Parolles, "So, my good window of Lettice, fare thee well. Thy casement I need not open, for I look through thee" (2.3.213-4). 'Lettice' was an Elizabethan spelling for 'lattice', so Lafew is apparently saying 'You are a latticed window, and I see through you'. In the First Folio, 'Lettice' is capitalized, suggesting the name of Lettice Knollys, a court beauty who married Walter Devereux in 1561, and was rumored to have carried on a "wild flirtation" with Leicester in the fall of 1565 (Devereux died in 1576, and Lettice married Leicester in 1578).[8] Court members would have been well aware of the Leicester-Lettice affair, so Lafew's line would have been like pinning a label, 'This is Leicester!', on Parolles.

So reading between the lines of *All's Well*, we can come up with a coherent picture of Oxford around 1572. He is feeling miffed about being ordered (by Elizabeth) to marry Anne Cecil, but is rather ashamed of himself—hence his unsparing treatment of Bertram. There is as yet no reason to question Anne's chastity, so Helena (unlike Desdemona, Imogen, Hermione or Hero) is not accused of adultery. Oxford's portrayal of Lafew as an insightful councillor shows he is on good terms with Lord Burghley. But what delight he takes in skewering Leicester as a braggart, liar and coward! And he has deniability—if reproached by a Leicester ally, he can simply say 'I wasn't referring to Leicester at all—Parolles is merely the classic stock figure, a *miles gloriosus*'.

Figure 9 - Lettice Knollys

End Notes

1. Eva Turner Clark, *Hidden Allusions in Shakespeare's Plays* (Kennikat Press, 1974), 124.

2. Claire McEachern, ed., *All's Well That Ends Well* (Penguin, 2001), xxxvi. The traditional *miles gloriosus* received a literal incorporation in the Broadway musical *A Funny Thing Happened on the Way to the Forum* (1962).

3. Dorothy and Charlton Ogburn, *This Star of England* (Coward-McCann, 1952), 168. In their excellent chapter on *All's Well* (160-73), the Ogburns point out that Oxford made two unauthorized trips to Belgium—one in 1571 just before he married Anne Cecil, and one in 1574.

4. Charlton Ogburn [Jr.], *The Mysterious William Shakespeare* (EPM Publications, 1984), 564. For more on Yorke, see Mark Anderson's *'Shakespeare' By Another Name* (Gotham, 2005), xv, 60, 112-16, 120, 136.

5. Sarah Gristwood, *Elizabeth and Leicester* (Viking, 2007), 266.

6. Neville Williams, *All the Queen's Men* (Macmillan, 1972), 96.

7. D. C. Peck, ed., *Leicester's Commonwealth* (Ohio UP, 1985), 92.

8. See 'Robert, Earl of Essex—Who's Your Daddy?', p. 162-68.

9. If only we could have printed this in color!—the very image of a "snipt-taffeta fellow … that red-tailed humble bee." Readers with the internet are invited to search 'Robert Dudley images.' The portrait can also be found on p. 48 of *All the Queen's Men*, by Neville Williams (Macmillan, 1972).

The Leicester Papers, Part 4

25

Robert, Earl of Essex—Who's Your Daddy?

Things are seldom what they seem,
Skim milk masquerades as cream;
High-lows pass as patent-leathers,
Jackdaws strut in peacock feathers
—W. S. Gilbert

In 1559 Robert Dudley, later created Earl of Leicester, was the handsome, dashing courtier who was just appointed the Queen's Master of Horse.[1]

In 1587 Robert Devereux, 2nd Earl of Essex, was the handsome, dashing courtier who was just appointed the Queen's Master of Horse.[2]

There are many other curious parallels between the lives of these two men:

- Both acquired power in the Elizabethan court by means of a personal relationship with the Queen.

- In May 1590, Elizabeth granted Essex the 'farm of sweet wines,' a lucrative import monopoly. The previous beneficiary of this grant was Leicester.[3]

- Both Leicester and Essex availed themselves freely of the sexual resources available to them. The 1584 pamphlet *Leicester's Commonwealth* says of Dudley: "Neither holdeth he any rule in his lust besides only the motion and suggestion of his own sensuality ... What he best liketh, that he taketh as lawful for the time ... There are not (by report) two noblewomen about her Majesty ... whom he hath not solicited by potent ways: neither contented with this place of honor, he hath descended to seek pasture among the waiting gentlewomen of her Majesty's Great Chamber ..."[4] Essex is described as indulging in "a bold pattern of promiscuity" at the Court, conducting affairs with four of the Maids of Honor at the same time, while his wife, Frances

Walsingham (daughter of the spymaster and widow of the sainted Sir Philip Sidney), was pregnant.[5]

- Both Leicester and Essex were improvident, spending freely to maintain their positions and accumulating enormous debts. When Leicester died he owed the Queen £25,000, plus a similar amount to private creditors; in his will he noted "I have always lived above any living I had (for which I am heartily sorry)".[6] As for Essex, a biographer describes his preparations for the military campaign in the Netherlands: "Ignoring his existing debts, he ran up bills for the best part of £1,000 in the course of recruiting and equipping a train of some 700 gentlemen and 1,585 common soldiers to follow him into battle. In vain did his grandfather, Sir Francis Knollys, reproach him for his extravagance: 'wasteful prodigality hath devoured and will consume all noble men that be willful in expenses,' he warned in a long letter that pointed out that even if Essex sold the lands that he was free to sell, he would still be hopelessly in debt."[7]

- Both men were put in charge of overseas military campaigns that ended disastrously. In September 1585, Elizabeth named Leicester commander of an expeditionary force to be sent to the Netherlands to help the Dutch in their struggle to overthrow the tyranny of Spain. He landed at Vlissingen on 10 December, and the Dutch received him ecstatically. He and his officers traveled from city to city, feasting "with abundant pomp" and receiving the accolades of the city officials. One author comments "Leicester was committed not so much to leading an armed force as to conducting a royal progress—in which, naturally, he was reveling."[8] In March 1599 Elizabeth appointed Essex commander of a force to sail to Ireland and put down the rebels led by Tyrone. Rather than engage the rebels, Essex and his party traveled from city to city, being fêted by the local English. A courtier reported Elizabeth's reaction: "The Queen is nothing satisfied with the Earl of Essex's manner of proceeding, nor likes anything that is done; but says she allows him £1000 a day to go on progress."[9]

- Both men were said to be tall and handsome. A description of Leicester: "He had dark brown hair with a reddish tint (the tint was more pronounced in his beard and moustache), fine brown eyes, and a long prominent nose, with a bridge to it, rather like the Queen's own: she seems to like such noses, for Essex's was similar."[10] A description of Essex: "He was tall, long-faced, with a broad forehead from which he brushed back his fierce red hair. His nose was aristocratic, with a high bridge, almost Roman, his fingers slender but manly. When his stubble permitted he ventured to sprout a fine ginger beard and moustache."[11]

Figure 10 - The leftmost portrait is of Robert Devereux, 2nd Earl of Essex. One of the men labeled A (center) or B (right) is his biological father. Which one? You decide! Identifications are in note 21 of the End Notes.

Essex's mother. Lettice Knollys was born in 1540. In 1561 she married Walter Devereux, then Viscount Hereford, later created 1st Earl of Essex. Robert Lacey describes her as follows:

> She was a beautiful woman in the dark sullen fashion that can infuriate men with desire—and women with jealousy. She flaunted her beauty shamelessly, first to capture Walter Devereux, but soon after her marriage to capture other lovers. Lettice Devereux and Leicester had met while Walter, Lettice's husband, was still alive, and through the autumn of 1565 they had carried on a wild flirtation of which Walter was most probably unaware but which infuriated Elizabeth to the point of a blazing quarrel between the Queen and her favourite. [12]

In July 1573 Walter Devereux embarked for Ireland at the head of an expedition to put down rebellion there. In July 1575 Leicester staged an enormous extravaganza at his country seat of Kenilworth, a last-ditch attempt to persuade Elizabeth to marry him. Unbeknownst to the Queen, Lettice was staying with him at the time. Devereux returned to England in

Shakespeare Confidential

November 1575. In December, Antonio de Guaras, a Spanish agent, reported the following:

> As the thing is publicly talked of in the streets, there is no objection to my writing openly about the great enmity that exists between the Earl of Leicester and the Earl of Essex in consequence, it is said, of the fact that, while Essex was in Ireland, his wife had two children by Leicester. Great discord is expected. [13]

Due in large part to political pressure exerted by Leicester, Devereux was sent back to Ireland in July 1576. He died two months later under suspicious circumstances.[14] In 1578 Leicester married Lettice, thus becoming stepfather to Robert Devereux, 2nd Earl of Essex.

Leicester's. generosity. When a male lion takes over a pride containing a lioness with cubs, he kills the cubs and impregnates the lioness, ensuring the primacy of his own genetic material. Similar behavior occurs among humans: the abuse or murder of a child by a stepfather or live-in boyfriend is, sadly, an all-too-frequent occurrence. Thus it is heartwarming to note the benevolence with which Leicester, a man of many flaws, treated his stepson, Essex.

- It was Leicester who introduced Essex to the Court in 1584.

- When Leicester was planning his expedition to the Netherlands in August 1585, he appointed Essex his 'general of horse,' a great honor for a 19-year-old.

- Leicester rewarded Essex for his participation in a skirmish at Zutphen in September 1586 by making him a 'knight banneret.'

- On 11 April 1588 Essex was awarded an honorary Master of Arts at Oxford, the university of which Leicester was chancellor.[15]

- Leicester made Essex a major beneficiary of his will, but the property would devolve to him only after the death of his mother.[16] Since Essex was executed in 1601 and Lettice didn't die until 1634, the bequest did not improve Essex's financial position.

Essex was fortunate in having what seems to be the kindest stepfather in all England. The man could not be expected to do more for his own flesh and blood.

When was Essex born? The birth date of Robert Devereux is strangely elusive. All historians are agreed that he was born in November, but some of them say it was the 10th, others the 19th. There is an even greater divergence of opinion with regard to the year: some say 1565, others say 1566, and a third group (including most modern historians) opts for 1567. It is known that he entered Trinity College, Cambridge, in May 1577, which makes the later date seem unlikely.[17] The *DNB* gives the date as 19 November 1566. If this is indeed the correct date, and if the "wild flirtation" between Lettice and Leicester in the fall of 1565 lasted (however surreptitiously) into February, it is physically possible that Leicester was in fact Essex's biological father. Perhaps the 1st Earl suspected this. One writer notes that Essex (Walter Devereux) had been deeply suspicious over his wife's flirtation with the Favourite ten years before (in 1565), and particularly over the later arrival of a son, Robert, who could have been Leicester's and for whom, perhaps in consequence, he held, according to Sir Henry Wotton, "a very cold conceit," giving his affection to his second son, Walter.[18]

Was Leicester capable of getting children? Most assuredly so. The rumor that Lettice bore him a daughter while Walter Devereux was in Ireland has enough corroborative detail to be convincing.[13] In August 1574, Lady Douglass Sheffield, under the impression that she was married to Leicester, bore him a son, who was suggestively named 'Robert Dudley.' Leicester openly acknowledged him as his heir until he tired of Lady Douglass and married Lettice; after that he was careful to refer to the younger Robert as "my base son," to avoid giving the impression that he (Leicester) was a bigamist. Around 1579 Lettice bore Leicester a son, again named 'Robert' and given the title 'Lord Denbigh.' Leicester immediately began making plans to marry his heir to the infant Arabella Stuart, who had a claim to eventual succession to the throne. He was crushed when his 'royal imp' died at the age of five.

Essex and Sidney. Every biography of Essex tells of his touching friendship with Sir Philip Sidney, the Flower of English Knighthood. Both went with Leicester to fight the Spanish in the

Low Countries, and both took part in the skirmish at Zutphen in 1586. Sidney was wounded in the leg. Gangrene set in, and he died two weeks later, bequeathing to Essex "my best sword," and charging him to take care of his wife, Frances. Essex fulfilled this obligation by marrying her, while continuing his wicked ways with the Maids of Honor. If Leicester was Essex's father, Essex and Sidney were more than best pals, they were *first cousins*, since Sidney's mother was Mary Dudley, Leicester's sister. To me, this possible blood relationship makes the deathbed scene even more poignant.

Is there a gene for overreaching? Leicester's grandfather, Edmund Dudley, was commissioned by Henry VII to raise money for the crown. Edmund did this so ruthlessly that he overreached, becoming so unpopular that when Henry VIII succeeded to the throne he had to behead Edmund to prevent rebellion. Leicester's father, John Dudley, cunningly married his oldest son, Guildford, to Lady Jane Grey, whose ancestry made her a candidate for the crown. When Edward VI died in 1553, John proclaimed his daughter-in-law to be queen. But he had overreached; Mary Tudor had the support of the people, and John, Guildford and Lady Jane Grey were executed for high treason. Leicester's failed expedition in the Netherlands would show him to be an overreacher even if crimes such as bigamy and serial murder[14] did not, but somehow he was cunning enough, or charming enough, or deep enough in the Queen's favor to avoid paying the supreme penalty. Was Essex an overreacher? His biographer says so specifically and repeatedly,[19] in the last instance when discussing the 'Essex rebellion' of 1601. If Robert Devereux was Robert Dudley's natural son, he represents the fourth generation of that family to be executed for treason.[20]

End Notes

1. *Dictionary of National Biography* (Oxford, 1917), VI, 112. Dudley was named Master of Horse 11 January 1559.
2. Robert Lacey, *Robert, Earl of Essex* (Atheneum, 1971), 43. Lacey writes that Elizabeth made Essex Master of Horse on 18 June 1587; the *DNB* (V, 876) gives the date as 23 December 1587.
3. *DNB* V, 877.

4. *Leicester's Commonwealth*, Dwight C. Peck, ed. (Ohio University Press, 1985), 88.

5. Arthur Gould Lee, *The Son of Leicester* (Gollancz, 1964), 93.

6. Lacey, 49.

7. Lacey, 35.

8. Paul Johnson, *Elizabeth I* (Holt, Rinehart & Winston, 1974), 267.

9. Johnson, 397.

10. Johnson, 119.

11. Lacey, 24.

12. Lacey, 15-16. This author is not a rumor-monger, but rather a rumor-squelcher. Thus when he describes the 1565 encounter between Lettice and Leicester as "a wild flirtation," one suspects that it involved considerably more than expressive glances and whispered compliments.

13. Alison Weir, *The Life of Elizabeth I* (Ballantine, 1998), 303. Since Walter Devereux didn't leave for Ireland until 1573, neither of the two children to which de Guaras refers could have been his. *Leicester's Commonwealth* (p. 82) mentions one child, a daughter, born to Lettice while Walter was in Ireland, and says the child was raised by Lady Chandos, the wife of William Knollys, who was Lettice's older brother and a friend of Leicester's.

14. '*Leicester's Commonwealth*: Portrait of a Serial Killer?' See p. 133-44.

15. *DNB* V, 876.

16. Lacey, 50.

17. Lacey Baldwin Smith, *Treason in Tudor England* (Princeton, 1986), 193.

18. Lee, 28.

19. Lacey, 35, 311.

20. Edmund Dudley, John Dudley, Guildford Dudley, Robert Devereux.

21. Portrait A is of Walter Devereux, Essex's putative father. Portrait B is of Robert Dudley, Earl of Leicester. All three drawings are from *The Official Baronage of England* by James E. Doyle (Longmans, Green, 1886).

Previously published in *Shakespeare Matters* 4.3 (Spring 2005)

26
Two Gentlemen of Verona: Questions Answered

Berners W. Jackson was a professor of English at McMaster University in Hamilton, Ontario. He edited the 1964 and 1980 editions of *Two Gentlemen of Verona* in the Pelican series of Shakespeare's plays. In his introduction he poses a number of intriguing questions about the play, given below in italics. My responses follow.

(1) *How does one go by ship from Verona to Milan?*

Major cities in 16th-century Italy were connected by an intricate system of rivers and canals that made travel by boat or barge easier and more efficient than travel by land. Chapter 2 of *The Shakespeare Guide to Italy* by Richard Roe (2011) is devoted to a description of this system. Verona is located on the Adige river, and Roe, citing a map from 1713, specifies a water route from Verona to Milan involving the Adige, Tartaro, Po, and Adda rivers and associated canals. In 1573 (two years before Oxford visited Italy) the last leg of the journey was shortened by the widening of the Martesana Canal. Roe comments "A commodious passenger vessel, or cargo ship, could now travel from the Po, up the Adda, and then, on the improved Martesana Canal, enter the Naviglio Interno, and thus reach the heart of Milan."

(2) *Why do the characters, when they are in Milan, sometimes speak as if they were in Verona or Padua?*

Please be more specific.

(3) *Why are there two Eglamours, and what does happen to the second one?*

The *dramatis personæ* of the Pelican edition lists only one Eglamour, "agent for Silvia in her escape". The last we hear of him is described by the Third Outlaw:

> Being nimble-footed, he hath outrun us,
> But Moyses and Valerius follow him.
> ... We'll follow him that's fled.
> The thicket is beset; he cannot scape. (5.4.7-11)

Thus his fate is ambiguous, but ambiguity in Shakespeare should not be surprising. A 'Sir Eglamour' is mentioned in Scene 1.2 as one of Julia's suitors, but I see no reason to differentiate him from the character in Act 5.

(4) *Why does Proteus speak as if he had only seen Silvia's picture, when he has, in fact, seen her?*

According to the note for line 2.5.207 in this edition (p. 37), "He has seen only her outward appearance".

(5) *Why does Proteus use Speed, Valentine's servant, to deliver his letter to Julia?*

The two servants, Speed and Launce, provide most of the comic relief in the play, Speed being the witty corrupter of words and Launce being the dolt. The Author wanted to finish Scene 1.1 with fast-paced verbal invention, so he chose Speed to deliver the letter. Since Proteus and Valentine are essentially two aspects of the same person, it doesn't really matter whose servant delivers the letter.

(6) *[a] Why does Valentine lie to the outlaws about the reason for his banishment, and [b] why does Shakespeare have the third outlaw banished from Verona (Valentine's city) for what was essentially Valentine's crime,*

plotting to steal away a lady closely related to the ruler?

[a] Valentine has been banished by the Duke of Milan for plotting to elope with Silvia, the Duke's daughter. The interview with the Outlaws goes as follows:

>   1st Outlaw.   What, were you banished thence?
>   Valentine.   I was.
>   2nd Outlaw.   For what offence?
>   Valentine.   For that which now torments me to rehearse:
>   I killed a man, whose death I now repent,
>   But yet I slew him manfully in a fight,
>   Without false vantage or base treachery. (4.1.23-9)

But a reading of *Taming of the Shrew* suggests that, at least for young men in Shakespeare's early plays, claiming to have killed a man is simply the default explanation for an anomalous situation. Here is Lucentio explaining to his servant Biondello why he (Lucentio) has changed clothes with his other servant, Tranio.

>   Lucentio.   Your fellow Tranio here, to save my life,
>   Puts my apparel and my count'nance on,
>   And I for my escape have put on his;
>   For in a quarrel since I came ashore
>   I killed a man, and fear I was descried. (*Shrew* 1.1.228-32)

(Of course the real reason for the exchange of clothes is to allow a disguised Lucentio to woo Bianca.)

It would be presumptuous to think that this repeated reference to a killing is an indication of a violent episode in the Author's youth. Yet the fact is that when he was 17, Edward de Vere was involved in a fracas with Thomas Bricknell, an undercook, which ended with the wounding and eventual death of Bricknell.[1]

[b] The Author wants the Outlaws to be menacing, but (since they are pardoned and welcomed back into

society at the end) not *too* menacing. What better crime to attribute to one of the band than one we have just seen our sympathetic hero commit?

(7) What is the mystery of the "wrong letter" that Julia almost delivers inadvertently to Silvia at 4.4.120?

I asked this question of Paige Clark, who portrayed Julia in the Boston-based Actors' Shakespeare Project production of *Two Gentlemen* in January 2013. Her answer was that in her mind the "wrong letter" is the one she originally got from Proteus and tore up (1.2.96); she has pasted it back together and keeps it with her at all times.

(8) What is the point of having Silvia accede to Proteus's request for her picture?

Fetching the portrait is the device the Author uses to set up a meeting between Silvia and the disguised Julia. This meeting has at least two important functions:

(a) It allows Silvia to express contempt for Proteus and sympathy for the spurned Julia, thus helping to flesh out a character that is on the whole rather thinly written.

(b) It gives Julia the chance for speeches that are dramatically effective because the audience knows more than Silvia does—namely that the 'page' is Julia herself.

While the above points are valid in the context of the playwright's craft, I believe a response can also be made in the context of 'Silvia' as a real person. It is this: Silvia is hedging her bets. Valentine is banished, and Thurio is an odious buffoon. Who's left? Proteus is handsome and virile; he has behaved badly, but apparently for the best of reasons—he's madly in love with her. As W. S. Gilbert has noted, "A reformed rake is a useful implement of husbandry."[2] So at some level she thinks "Let's give him the picture and see what happens."

(9) *Was there an Emperor at Milan as well as a Duke, or are they two titles for the same role?*

Richard Roe has researched this question; his findings are given in Chapter 3 of *The Shakespeare Guide to Italy*. On 10 March 1533, Charles V, the Holy Roman Emperor, entered Milan to receive the fealty of Francesco, Duke of Milan. The city had made elaborate preparations for the ceremony, including an 'imperial arch of triumph' designed by Giulio Romano, the artist mentioned in *The Winter's Tale*. Roe notes that "The Milanese made the great tournament and tiltyard ready," which reminds one of Panthino's line (1.3.29-30)

> 'Twere good, I think, your lordship sent him thither.
> There shall he practice tilts and tournaments . . .

Emperor Charles V returned to Spain shortly after the ceremony.

ADDITIONAL COMMENT

It is curious that neither Berners Jackson (who posed the above questions) nor any other orthodox scholar has gone to Italy to try to dig out the answers. But in retrospect, the reason is apparent: they believe that Will Shaxper of Stratford was the Author—there is no indication he ever left England, so what is to be learned in Italy? Besides, it is useful to display a list of apparent geographical gaffes to prove that the Author never left England, hence he must be the Stratford lad.[3]

References

1. Charlton Ogburn, *The Mysterious William Shakespeare* (Dodd Mead, 1984), p. 454.
2. Jane W. Stedman, *Gilbert Before Sullivan* (U. Chicago Press, 1967), p. 205.
3. See 'Six Reasons Why Stratfordian 'Scholarship' is So Bad,' p. 58-9.

27
Plays on 'Oxford'

Oxfordian scholars have long noted the occurrence in the Shakespeare plays of 'Ver' *words* (veritable, vertue), *both in English and in French* (ver = worm, Ver = spring). *The question was raised,*[1] *are there also veiled allusions to the name* Oxford?

It can be argued that 'Arthur Brooke', juvenile author of the long poem *Romeus and Juliet*, is the young Oxford's *nom de plume* (a ford is a place where a brook can be crossed). In *Merry Wives of Windsor* one of the main characters is Master Ford, who is obsessed with suspicions about his wife's fidelity. When meeting with Falstaff he assumes the name 'Brook'. In the final scene, Falstaff ruefully says "I do begin to perceive that I am made an ass," and FORD replies "Ay, and an OX too" (5.5.120).

A more subtle play on the name 'Oxford' is the frequent appearance in the plays of the name 'Falconbridge'—it occurs in *The Merchant of Venice, Love's Labor's Lost, Henry V, 1 Henry VI, 3 Henry VI*, and most prominently in *King John*, where the real hero of the play is Philip (the Bastard) Falconbridge, who can be strongly identified with the author. De Vere habitually signed his name 'Oxenford', a version related to 'Falconbridge' in that they both consist of an animal[2] (two syllables) followed by a means of crossing a river (one syllable). You are going to object that this relationship is so farfetched as never to occur in real life, but in 1881 the second-greatest English playwright did exactly the same thing. William Gilbert, in writing the comic opera *Patience*, wanted to satirize the 'fleshly poet' Algernon Swinburne, so he named the corresponding character 'Reginald Bunthorne', the two last names each consisting of an animal followed by a feature of the landscape. The 'Falconbridge' in *Merchant of Venice* is one of Portia's failed suitors, and a comedic self-portrait of the artist (1.2.66-76).

And finally there's the clown Lavatch in *All's Well That Ends Well*. 'Lavatch' is an anglicization of *la Vache*, French for 'the Cow', a creature which is closely related to the Ox. Lavatch is a witty Clown, similar to Feste in *Twelfth Night*, and thus of a type generally associated with Oxford himself. The unflattering name shows Oxford in a self-deprecating mood, consistent with his characterization of Bertram, another authorial figure.

End Notes

1. Phaeton, 23-4 Dec 2011.
2. An account of a mock tournament in Italy in which Oxford participated noted that "He carries for device a falcon . . . " (see Julia Cooley Altrocchi, 'Edward de Vere and the Commedia dell'Arte', *Shakespeare Authorship Review*, Autumn 1959).

28
Gilbert and the Bard

William S. Gilbert was the most popular playwright of the 19th century. His comic operas, with music by Arthur Sullivan, include *H.M.S. Pinafore, The Pirates of Penzance,* and *The Mikado.* These works are in constant production today, almost 150 years after they were written.

Gilbert knew his Shakespeare. He was fascinated by Hamlet, writing a spoof of the play (*Rosencrantz and Guildenstern*) that served for several charity performances.[1] His long comic opera, *The Mountebanks* (1892) has a subplot in which two carnival performers, Bartolo and Nita, are transformed into clockwork figures of Hamlet and Ophelia.[2] Gilbertians have long known about the quote from *Hamlet* in *Ruddigore* ("Alas, poor ghost!")[3] and the allusion to *Macbeth* in *Princess Ida* (Melissa's "*are men* stuck in her throat" echoes Macbeth's "*Amen* stuck in my throat").[4]

For some years I have participated in a group that meets semimonthly to read the plays of Shakespeare out loud. Occasionally in these readings we would encounter a scene or situation that reminded me strongly of a similar situation in one of Gilbert's works without being as specifically allusive as the examples given above. Four of these scenes are discussed below.

I. The Band of Brothers.

I'm thinking of a theatre piece based on two brothers—one good, the other bad. The good brother has a faithful old servant named Adam; he (the brother) is in love with a beautiful girl whose name evokes the loveliest of flowers, and is so smitten that he can scarcely speak in her presence. The bad brother commits terrible deeds, but later undergoes a sudden reformation which allows the good brother to marry his rosaceous sweetheart.

The Gilbertian will immediately identify this plot as that of

Ruddigore (1887), while the Shakespeare scholar will be sure it is *As You Like It* (ca. 1580).

They are both right. In Gilbert's libretto, Ruthven Murgatroyd loves Rose Maybud while his brother Despard performs villainies, and in Shakespeare's play the trio is Orlando and Oliver du Boys plus Rosalind. Gilbert probably gave Ruthven's aged servant the same name as Orlando's to show that he was aware of the situational similarities.

II. Cross-dressing.

In Shakespeare's early play *Two Gentlemen of Verona*, Silvia is the queen bee of the country. The beautiful daughter of the ruling duke, she is being wooed by Valentine (the good guy) and Proteus (not so good). In entering the race for Silvia, Proteus has abandoned Julia, his former sweetheart. Though heartbroken, Julia does not give up—she dons masculine attire, and thus disguised, adopts the pseudonym 'Sebastian', and gets herself hired as Proteus's page. He sends her to Silvia's boudoir to pick up a painting she has promised him. Silvia is aware that Julia has been dumped by Proteus and is sympathetic, even though she has never met Julia. She asks 'Sebastian' "How tall was she?" (referring to Julia), and 'Sebastian' replies

> About my stature; for at Pentecost,
> When all our pageants of delight were played,
> Our youth got me to play the woman's part,
> And I was trimmed in Madam Julia's gown,
> Which served me as fit, by all men's judgments,
> As if the garment had been made for me,
>   (4.4.157-62)

In Gilbert and Sullivan's *Princess Ida* (1884) a similar situation occurs, but with genders reversed. Prince Hilarion and his companions have entered the grounds of the Princess's feminist university, where male trespassers will be put to death. As the courtiers jokingly try on (female) academic robes they are interrupted by the Princess, and (aware of the death penalty) are forced to adopt female personæ. Ida, who was betrothed to Hilarion in childhood, asks if he has grown up to be good-looking, and the disguised Hilarion replies

> Pretty well,
> I've heard it said that if I dressed myself
> In Prince Hilarion's clothes (supposing this

> Consisted with my maiden modesty),
> I might be taken for Hilarion's self. [5]

Is this parallel unique to Gilbert's adaptation, or does it also occur in Gilbert's source, Tennyson's 1847 poem, *The Princess*? Here is how Tennyson deals with the incident (the voice is Hilarion's):

> But while he jested thus,
> A thought flash'd thro' me which I clothed in act,
> Remembering how we three presented Maid,
> Or Nymph, or Goddess at high tide of feast,
> In masque or pageant at my father's court.
> We sent mine host to purchase female gear;
> He brought it, and himself, a sight to shake
> The midriff of despair with laughter, holp
> To lace us up, till each, in maiden plumes
> We rustled: him we gave a costly bribe
> To guerdon silence, mounted our good steeds,
> And boldly ventured on to the liberties.[6]

Thus Tennyson's description of the cross-dressing lacks the sly self-referencing of both Shakespeare's and Gilbert's accounts, and Gilbert may have had *Two Gentlemen* in mind when he wrote *Princess Ida*.

III. First Encounters

Iachimo and Imogen. In *Cymbeline*, a young man named Posthumus has got himself engaged to the king's only daughter, the beautiful Imogen. For this effrontery he is banished to Italy, where he meets Iachimo, a smooth-talking cad who goads him into betting that Iachimo cannot seduce Imogen. The would-be seducer travels to England, meets Imogen, and is stunned by her beauty (Scene 1.6).

> Iach. All of her that is out of door most rich!
> If she be furnished with a mind so rare
> She is alone th' Arabian bird, and I
> Have lost the wager. . . .
>
> Imo. You are as welcome, worthy sir, as I
> Have words to bid you . . .
>
> Iach. Thanks, fairest lady.
> [aside] What, are men mad?
> Hath nature given them eyes . . . ?
>
> Imo. What, dear sir,
> Thus raps you? Are you well?

Dick Dauntless and Rose Maybud. We have encountered Rose Maybud before (see 'Band of Brothers', above); she is the most beautiful girl in the quaint little village of Reddering. Ruthven Murgatroyd (the 'good brother') is in love with her, but is too shy to declare his feelings, so he calls upon Dick Dauntless, a swaggering mariner, to woo her by proxy (*Ruddigore*, Act I).

Dick.	[aside] By the Port Admiral, but she's a tight little craft! Come, come, she's not for you, Dick, and yet—she's fit to marry Lord Nelson! By the flag of Old England, I can't look at her unmoved.
Rose.	Sir, you are agitated
Dick.	Aye, aye, my lass, well said! I am agitated, true enough!—took flat aback, my girl, but 'tis naught—'twill pass.
Rose.	Can I do aught to relieve thine anguish, for it seemeth to me that thou art in sore trouble? This apple—?

I find these scenes amusingly parallel, but perhaps the parallelism simply stems from the similarity of the situations.

IV. Outlaws with Worthy Qualities

Recall that in *Two Gentlemen of Verona*, Valentine has been wooing Silvia. They plan to elope, but Proteus tips off the Duke (her father), who then banishes Valentine from Milan. Valentine sets out alone to return to Verona, but in the midst of a wilderness he is set upon by a band of Outlaws, and just as Ruth and the Pirate King do with Frederic in *Pirates of Penzance* (1880), they insist he join the group. Valentine accepts their offer, at least partially influenced by their stated intention to kill him if he refuses.

However, we soon find that the Outlaws' apparent fierceness is tempered by high ethical standards.

Valentine.	I take your offer, and will live with you, Provided that you do no outrages On silly women or poor passengers.
3rd Outlaw.	No, we detest such vile base practices . . (4.1.68-71)

And when Silvia encounters the Outlaws, she gets this comforting reassurance:

1st Outlaw.	Come, I must bring you to our captain's cave.

> Fear not; he bears an honorable mind,
> And will not use a woman lawlessly.
> (4.4.12-14)

We have encountered a comparably conscientious group of *banditti* before, in Gilbert's *Pirates*. An apprentice explains how their high moral standards limit the financial viability of their enterprise.

> Frederic. Well, then, it is my duty, as a pirate, to tell you that you are too tender-hearted. For instance, you make a point of never attacking a weaker party than yourselves, and when you attack a stronger party you invariably get thrashed.

Gilbert's pirates, like Shakespeare's outlaws, do not use women lawlessly—when they abduct Major-General Stanley's daughters, they do not embark on careers of unlicensed pleasure, but rather seek out a Doctor of Divinity to regularize any personal relationships that might ensue.

Two Gentlemen is a comedy, so when the final scene rolls around, the Duke recognizes what a fine, manly fellow Valentine is, and allows him to marry Silvia. Proteus is reconciled with Julia. And the Outlaws? Compare Valentine's apologia

> These banished men, that I have kept withal,
> Are men endued with worthy qualities.
> Forgive them what they have committed here,
> And let them be recalled from their exile.
> They are reformed, civil, full of good,
> And fit for great employment, worthy lord. (5.4.153-8)

with that of piratical spokeswoman Ruth:

> One moment! Let me tell you who they are.
> They are no members of the common throng,
> They are all noblemen who have gone wrong!

to which the Major General replies

> No Englishman unmoved that statement hears.
> Because, with all our faults, we love our House of Peers!

Thus *Two Gentlemen* and *Pirates* share the themes of (1) the protagonist forced to join an outlaw band, which (2) turns out to have high ethical standards, perhaps (3) because it is composed of men of worthy quality (i.e., noblemen) who have become estranged from the wider community. I find it hard to believe that Gilbert did not have *Two Gentlemen* in mind as he wrote the ending of *Pirates*.

End Notes

1. George Rowell, *Plays by W. S. Gilbert* (Cambridge UP, 1982), 172-8. A detailed examination of the play was given by Ralph MacPhail Jr. at the *Gilbert Sesquicentennial Conference*, MIT, 1986.
2. This subplot has been adapted into a free-standing one-hour musical entertainment entitled *Put a Penny in the Slot*. It was performed by the Boston-based Royal Victorian Opera Company in 1992-93.
3. *Hamlet* 1.5.4. *Ruddigore*, Act II (*Modern Library* 441)
4. *Princess Ida*, Act II (*Modern Library* 321). *Macbeth* 2.2.28-9.
5. *Princess Ida*, Act II (*Modern Library* 322-3)
6. G. Robert Stange, ed., *The Poetical Works of Tennyson* (Houghton Mifflin, 1974) 121-2.

Previously published in GASBAG *(the newsletter of the Univ. Michigan Gilbert & Sullivan Society) XLVI No. 2 Spring 2016).*

29
Billy Budd and *The Monument*

Billy Budd, Foretopman, is Herman Melville's last literary work. He was working on it almost to the day of his death, 27 September 1891. His wife put the manuscript into a tin breadbox, where it remained for over thirty years. Eventually the manuscript was passed on to a scholar by Melville's granddaughter, and *Billy Budd* was included in a uniform edition of Melville's works in 1924.[1] It has since come to be regarded as a classic—a poignant and layered parable of the human condition.

Billy Budd. The story concerns a sailor of radiant beauty (he is frequently referred to as "the Handsome Sailor"). The time is 1797, and England is at war with Napoleonic France. The British navy must be manned, and Billy is impressed—forcibly transferred from a merchant ship to a man-o'-war, the *Indomitable*. There he incurs the enmity of Claggart, the Master-at-Arms, whose responsibility it is to detect and suppress any mutinous inclinations among the seamen. Claggart sets Billy up by having one of his subordinates propose a *sub-rosa* meeting to Billy. The young sailor indignantly refuses to participate, but does not report the incident to the authorities. This sin of omission allows Claggart (reporting to the captain of the ship) to represent Billy as the leader of a mutinous plot. The captain, stunned by an accusation so at odds with what he has seen of Billy's behavior, calls for an immediate face-to-face confrontation. Billy has one flaw: when under stress, he has difficulty speaking. When Claggart repeats the accusation to Billy's face, he struggles to respond, then reflexively strikes Claggart, who is killed by the blow. The captain, agonizingly aware of Billy's essential innocence, is nevertheless forced to order Billy's immediate trial and execution.

The Monument is Hank Whittemore's groundbreaking analysis of Shakespeare's Sonnets.[2] Whittemore sees the Sonnets as divided into three groups. Sonnets 1-26 are addressed to the 'Fair Youth,' with the first seventeen urging him to marry and get an heir. In common with most scholars, Whittemore identifies the 'Fair Youth' as Henry Wriothesley, the 3rd Earl of Southampton. Whittemore takes the further step of postulating that Southampton is the natural son of Edward de Vere, 17th Earl of Oxford, by Queen Elizabeth. As the son of the queen, Southampton is the natural heir to the throne. The last group (Sonnets 127-154) is mostly addressed to the Dark Lady, the queen who defaulted on promises made to Oxford, the author of the Sonnets. The central group of 100 sonnets constitutes a set of chronologically arranged messages to Southampton during the time he was imprisoned and under sentence of death for his participation in the Essex Rebellion, which took place 8 February 1601.

Lytton Strachey has written a convincing account of the Essex rebellion.[3] He tells it as a power struggle between handsome, dashing Robert Devereux, 2nd Earl of Essex, and the queen's chief advisor Robert Cecil, son of the late Lord Burghley. A leader must be chosen to command English forces putting down the rebellion in Ireland. Wise heads discourage Essex from volunteering for the post, pointing out how difficult it is for foreign troops to suppress insurgents in their native land, but Cecil manipulates council discussions in such a way that Essex finally blurts out that he is the right man for the job. He goes to Ireland at the head of 17,500 troops, naming his best friend, the Earl of Southampton, as his Captain of Horse. The campaign in Ireland is a disaster, and Essex, fearing that Cecil is turning the queen against him, rushes back to England to give the queen an explanation of his military difficulties and assure her of his love. He is accompanied by Southampton and a group of loyal soldiers. The queen is displeased by his precipitate return, in defiance of her express command. Tensions grow between them, until finally a note from Cecil requiring Essex's presence at a council meeting leads Essex to believe he will be arrested. He takes to the streets with a band of his followers (including Southampton), intending to take control of the Court and remove Cecil from access to the queen. The uprising is ill-planned, and soon defeated. Essex and four of his followers are tried and executed. Strangely, the sentence of his chief follower,

Southampton, is commuted to life imprisonment. No official explanation for this commutation has ever been given.

The story of *Billy Budd* runs strongly parallel to that of the Essex Rebellion. In both cases a handsome protagonist, more or less naïve, is manipulated by a wily plotter into a position which leads him to an emotional act of violence, a deed for which the power structure decrees that he must be executed. The question we will now consider is this: was Herman Melville aware of this parallelism, was it something that he consciously used in constructing his last literary work, or is it simply a coincidence? If Melville was consciously using material from the Elizabethan period, we would expect to find indications of it in the details of the work. Let us look more closely at some of the characters in *Billy Budd*.

The Captain of the *Indomitable*. In a stunning display of candor, Melville gave his captain the name 'Edward Vere,' the name of the author of the Sonnets, the Shakespeare plays, and (some believe) the biological father of Southampton. It's as if C. S. Lewis gave his self-sacrificing lion in the *Narnia* series the name 'Jesus Christ.' It's as if you came across a 'Where's Waldo' drawing where Waldo is standing on a pedestal in the foreground holding a banner saying 'Here I Am!' (In Melville's defense, the name 'Edward de Vere' was not as well known in 1891 as it is today.)

But perhaps we're being too hasty, jumping to a conclusion. Perhaps Melville simply chose the name at random. What are the characteristics of the captain?

> In the navy he was popularly known by the appellation "Starry Vere." [659] [4]

For many of us, the term "starry" recalls the mullet on the shield in the Vere family crest (Fig. 11). This seems to support our original hypothesis, that Melville was deliberately referring to Edward de Vere.

"But wait," cries the Orthodox Scholar, "Melville tells us where he got the name. It's from the poem 'Appleton House,' written around 1652 by Andrew Marvell. It even provides the appellation 'starry'!"

> This 'tis to have been from the first
> In a domestic heaven nursed,
> Under the discipline severe
> Of FAIRFAX and the starry VERE [5]

Shakespeare Confidential

The phrase "discipline severe" in the quoted portion of the poem leads one to assume that it deals with naval exploits. It is actually a panegyric to the beauties of the woods surrounding the Yorkshire country home of Thomas Fairfax (1612-1671), and to the charms of his daughter Mary, who Marvell tutored.[6] The *Dictionary of National Biography* gives Fairfax a fairly detailed treatment, including his matriculation at St. John's College, Cambridge, and his service in the Low Countries under Edward de Vere's cousin, Sir Horace Vere.[7] He got along so well with Sir Horace that he married his daughter Anne (she is the "Vere" mentioned in the poem).

Melville gives his captain's full name as "Edward Fairfax Vere." The *DNB* lists an 'Edward Fairfax' (d. 1635) as a translator and poet whose works were especially valued by James I and Charles I.[8] There is some mystery about his origins: his name is missing from some genealogies. In one he is listed as a son of Sir Thomas Fairfax (1560-1640, grandfather to the Thomas Fairfax mentioned above, with a dotted line connecting him to a brother, Sir Charles. One historian describes him as a natural son of Sir Thomas.

Coat-of-Arms of the de Veres

Figure 11 - Coat of Arms of the Earls of Oxford

Aside from family connections, the name 'Fairfax' itself can be construed as significant. In Elizabethan times, 'Vere' was pronounced to rhyme with 'Fair'. Some Oxfordians assert that de Vere used 'fair' as a code word for 'Vere.' 'Fax' can be viewed as a Latin noun. The dictionary [9] gives three definitions: (1) a torch (2) a firebrand, instigator (3) light, flame, shooting star. I leave it to the reader to decide whether any of these terms can be applied to Edward de Vere.

Melville says explicitly that his Vere is "allied to the higher nobility" [657], and gives his philosophy in some detail [660-1]:

> He had a marked leaning toward everything intellectual. He loved books, never going to sea without a newly replenished library, compact but of the best. . . . His settled convictions were as a dyke against those invading waters of novel opinion, social, political, and otherwise, which carried away as in a torrent no few minds in those days . . . While other members of that aristocracy to which by birth he belonged were incensed at the innovators

mainly because their theories were inimical to the privileged classes, Captain Vere disinterestedly opposed them because they seemed to him not alone incapable of embodiment in lasting institutions, but at war with the peace of the world and the true welfare of mankind.

One need only read Ulysses' *degree* speech in *Troilus and Cressida* (scene 1.3) or Menenius's *tale of the belly* in *Coriolanus* (1.1) to see how closely the above convictions agree with those held by the author of the Shakespeare canon.[10] Toward the end of the novel Melville recounts Captain Vere's death in a battle with the French, and makes this final observation [736]:

The spirit that spite its philosophic austerity may yet have indulged in the most secret of all passions, ambition, never attained to the fullness of fame.

This was certainly true of Edward de Vere at the time Melville was writing. Perhaps the situation is changing.

Shakespearean Allusions. For the alert reader, *Billy Budd* is filled with names and phrases reminiscent of Shakespearean or Elizabethan characters, inserted almost subliminally. This starts early in the story: the lieutenant who abducts Billy from his merchant ship [640] is named Ratcliffe, reminding us of Thomas Ratcliffe, 3rd Earl of Sussex, under whom de Vere served in putting down the Northern Rebellion of 1569-70. Sussex, a father figure to de Vere, died in 1583, probably poisoned by his political enemy, the Earl of Leicester. Ogburn has suggested he was the model for the murdered king in *Hamlet*.[11] Another reminder of the murdered king: "[Claggart's unobserved] glance would follow the young sea-Hyperion [Billy] with a settled . . . expression" [688] . Hamlet twice refers to his father as the sun god Hyperion: first in a soliloquy (1.2) and then in his confrontation with Gertrude (3.4). Admiral Nelson is mentioned several times and is usually referred to as "Sir Horatio," again reminding us of *Hamlet*. A sailor who befriends Billy is described as "an old Dansker, long anglicized in the service . . ." What is Hamlet if not an anglicized Dane? In fact, the term could be applied to the entire Vere family: Ogburn says "the de Veres must in origin have been Vikings— Danes to the Anglo-Saxon English . . . "[12] The old Dansker is described as "an *Agamemnon* man" [668], reminding us of the Greek general in *Troilus and Cressida*. Elsewhere we are told

"Sir Horatio, being with the fleet off the Spanish coast, was directed by the Admiral in command to shift his pennant from the *Captain* to the *Theseus* . . ." [657] (the Duke of Athens in *Midsummer Night's Dream* is named Theseus). The world of *Billy Budd* is one in which half the warships are named after characters in Shakespeare! And it goes on. Another passage [670] refers to a conversation between the Dansker and Billy: ". . . the old sea-Chiron, thinking that perhaps for the nonce he had sufficiently instructed his Achilles . . ." The overt reference is to Chiron, the wise centaur of Greek legend, but Chiron is also one of Tamora's mischievous sons in *Titus Andronicus*. And of course Achilles is another character in *Troilus and Cressida*. At one point we are told " . . . something exceptional in the moral quality of Captain Vere made him . . . a veritable touch-stone . . . " [698]; with this statement we have not only a reference to the 'allowed fool' in *As You Like It*, but one which links the Oxford figure in that play directly with Captain Vere (with a 'veritable' thrown in for free). On three separate occasions, Melville refers to Billy's 'welkin eye' (i.e. one that is sky-blue) [640, 670, 678]. The phrase is from *The Winter's Tale* (1.2.136). The jealous king Leontes applies it to his young son, who subsequently dies from grief at the supposed death of his mother. A poignant moment in *Billy Budd* involves Captain Vere's reaction when he discovers that Billy's blow has killed Claggart [702].

> Slowly he uncovered his face; and the effect was as if the moon emerging from the eclipse should reappear with quite another aspect than that which had gone into hiding.

The reader familiar with the Sonnets will immediately think of Sonnet 107, which alludes to the death of Elizabeth:

> The mortal moon hath her eclipse endured . . .

Billy Budd as Henry Wriothesley. The quote from *Billy Budd* given immediately above [702] continues directly as follows:

> The **father** in him, manifested toward Billy thus far in the scene, was replaced by the military disciplinarian. (emphasis added)

Melville mentions Captain Vere's fatherly relationship to Billy on two other occasions. Just after Claggart has accused Billy to his face, Captain Vere perceives his difficulty in speaking and says "There is no hurry, my boy. Take your time, take your time." [701]. The author describes these words as "fatherly in tone." Later, Melville says of the captain "He was old enough to have been Billy's father." [720]. Lewis Carroll enunciated the rule "What I tell you three times is true."[13] Melville has told us three times that Captain Vere represents Billy's father.

When we turn to *The Monument*, we find that Billy's name is as explicit as Captain Vere's. Whittemore's study of the Sonnets has led him to propose that because of their political implications they are written in a special language involving coded references to the protagonists in the drama of Southampton's arrest, imprisonment, death sentence, and finally, commutation of that sentence. Whittemore asserts that in this context, the word 'bud' always refers to Southampton as "the budding flower of the Tudor Rose Dynasty" {61}.[2] Below we give examples of the use of 'bud' in the Sonnets (the number of the sonnet is followed by the page {in curly brackets} on which Whittemore discusses the symbolism).

> Within thine own bud buriest thy content --- Sonnet 1 {61}

> Rough winds do shake the darling buds of May --- Sonnet 18 {134}

> And loathsome canker lives in sweetest bud --- Sonnet 35 {246}

> When summer's breath their masked buds discloses --- Sonnet 54 {336}

> And buds of marjoram had stol'n thy hair --- Sonnet 99 {533}

If Whittemore's view of the Sonnets is correct, the name 'Budd' points to Southampton as unambiguously as the name 'Vere' points to Oxford.

It could be argued that Whittemore's association of the word 'bud' with Southampton, though consistent and tightly argued, is mere speculation. However, there is a contemporary source that makes that association directly and unambiguously. Some time after 1590, Thomas Nashe dedicated a work[14] to Southampton and addressed him in the following words:

> Pardon, sweete flower of matchless Poetrie
> And fairest bud that red rose ever bore . . .

Some Oxfordians believe that 'Thomas Nashe' was one of Oxford's pen names.

Early in the novel, as Lieutenant Ratcliffe is impressing Billy, he converses amicably with Captain Graveling,[15] commander of the merchant ship on which Billy has been serving. Graveling, reluctant to lose Billy, laments "Lieutenant, you are going to take my best man from me, the jewel of 'em" [642]. On first reading this, I thought that 'jewel' was a strange term for a mariner to use describing one of his crew. However, *The Monument* explains that 'jewel' has a special significance. In Sonnet 27, the first commemorating Southampton's imprisonment, he is described as "a jewel (hung in ghastly night)" {208}. Whittemore's commentary mentions a similar use of 'jewel' in Sonnet 96. He also quotes two examples from the plays in which 'jewel' is equated with 'son': "As for my sons, say I account of them as jewels" (*Titus Andronicus*, 3.1); "Had our prince, Jewel of children, seen this hour (*The Winter's Tale*, 5.1). A related word is 'ornament,' also used to refer directly to Southampton (Sonnets 1, 21 {60,162}). Throughout the novel, Billy is referred to as "the Handsome Sailor," the nautical equivalent of "the Fair Youth."

After Claggart's death, Captain Vere convened a drumhead court, over which he presided until the verdict was reached. After the verdict, the captain had a private conversation with Billy in which he told him of the sentence. Melville notes " . . . the condemned one suffered less than he who mainly had effected the condemnation . . ." [720]. As the ranking peer in England, Edward de Vere participated in the Chamber proceedings that resulted in a death sentence for Southampton {202-268}. Sonnets 40-44 express Oxford's anguish at seeing his son tried and convicted {277-300}.

Billy Budd as the Works of 'Shakespeare.' The identification of Billy Budd as Henry Wriothesley, as discussed above, cannot be the whole story, since Billy was executed and Wriothesley was not. Why was he not? In Whittemore's interpretation, de Vere struck a bargain with Robert Cecil whereby Wriothesley's life would be spared if he relinquished all claim to the throne. This condition required that literary traces of his royal parentage be obscured, leading to the further requirement that de Vere's name be permanently disassociated from his works. This sundering of the works from their author, their father, is the metaphoric execution that takes place on the deck of the *Indomitable*, and is the reason that Vere/de Vere "never attained to the fullness of fame" [736]. There are hints of Billy's status as a creation early in the story. As Billy is being mustered into the service, an officer asks him his place of birth [648].

> "Don't you know where you were born?—who was your father?"
>
> "God knows, Sir."
>
> Yes, Billy was a foundling, a presumable bye-blow, and, evidently, no ignoble one. Noble descent was as evident in him as in a blood horse.

The Old Dansker calls him "Baby Budd," the name by which he is eventually known throughout the ship, and one that suggests something that has been created [669]. At the moment of execution, Billy cries out "God bless Captain Vere!" a cry that is echoed by the assembled crew [729]. Oxford has been blessed by his literary works—they are the reason hundreds (or thousands) of people are interested in him today, and this interest from a knowledgeable public echoes the response of the crew.

We have discussed the significance of Billy's last name. His first name is a nickname for 'William.' A possible reason for the choice of this name in connection with the works of 'Shakespeare' is left as an exercise for the reader.

The Old Dansker. This character is Billy's confidant, the one he turns to when puzzled by events aboard the ship. Melville writes that his relationship to Billy is "patriarchal," as indeed the nickname ('Baby Budd') he bestows on the Handsome Sailor would imply. I suggest that the Dansker is a second father figure, bearing that relationship to Billy in his persona representing the Shakespeare canon. The Dansker is known to the crew as "Board-her-in-the-smoke," due to a scar and blue-peppered complexion from wounds he received in a sea-battle [668]. I lay awake several nights trying to puzzle out the meaning of "Board-her-in-the-smoke" in a Shakespearean context. It finally occurred to me that a 'board' is a pasteboard rectangle used for the cover of a book. As a verb in this context, 'board' means "to bind (a book) in boards,"[16] thus (by extension) 'to publish.' 'Smoke' can be read as 'that which obscures or deceives,' as in the phrase 'smoke and mirrors.' Thus the Dansker's nickname is equivalent to 'publish deceptively,' which is a thumbnail description of what happened with the First Folio (with its allusions to 'Stratford' and 'Swan of Avon'), and strengthens the hypothesized connection between Billy and the Shakespeare canon.

Billy Budd as Essex. While I believe that the strongest associations are with Southampton and the Works, there are three circumstances that point directly to Essex, and I would be remiss if I did not mention them. (1) During the trial, Essex maintained that his reasons for the uprising were patriotic, to prevent England being sold to Spain, and that he had heard the queen's secretary, Robert Cecil, state that the Spanish Infanta's claim to the succession was as good as anybody's. Cecil had been hiding behind the arras (like father, like son), and he suddenly revealed himself, making an impassioned speech to the assembly in which he roundly condemned Essex. This face-to-face confrontation parallels that between Claggart and Billy in the novel. (2) Historically, Essex is executed. Billy Budd is executed, Southampton is not. (3) The moment before the axe fell, Essex "asked God to bestow His blessing upon Elizabeth . . . " {295}, thus prefiguring Billy's "God bless Captain Vere!"

Claggart as Robert Cecil. It is clear that functionally Claggart represents Robert Cecil, the wily plotter who set up Essex and Southampton and then brought the full force of the law down on them. To what extent has Melville alluded to Cecil's personal characteristics? He introduces Claggart as follows [662]:

> Claggart was a man of about five-and-thirty, somewhat spare and tall, yet of no ill figure on the whole. His hand was too small and shapely to have been accustomed to hard toil. . . . His brow was of the sort phrenologically associated with more than average intellect; silken jet curls partly clustering over it, making a foil to the pallor below, a pallor tinged with a faint shade of amber . . . This complexion, singularly contrasting with the red or deeply bronzed visages of the sailors, and in part the result of his official seclusion from the sunlight, though it was not exactly displeasing, nevertheless seemed to hint of something defective or abnormal in the constitution and blood.

Cecil's most prominent physical characteristic was his humpback. Melville has chosen not to refer to it ("no ill figure"), perhaps reluctant to make his villain too operatic. However he hints obliquely to "something defective or abnormal . . ." Ogburn, on observing a portrait of Robert Cecil at Hatfield House, noted its pallor.[17] Cecil was born on 1 June 1563, and thus was 37 at the time of the Essex Rebellion, close enough to "about five-and-thirty." Discussing Claggart's career, Melville continues [666]:

> The superior capacity he immediately evinced, his constitutional sobriety, ingratiating deference to his superiors, together with **a peculiar ferreting genius** manifested on a singular occasion, all this capped by a certain austere patriotism, abruptly advanced him to the position of master-at-arms. (emphasis added)

This sounds like Cecil to me. It apparently would to Lytton Strachey as well, since he wrote of "the gentle genius of Cecil." A biographer of the Cecil family says of Robert Cecil that he was "noted for a sort of grave, gentle sweetness." He goes on to say "His complex nature, glinting forth through his mask of apparent gentleness, baffled people and made them feel uneasy; all the more because events showed it to be combined with such a formidable capacity quietly to eliminate his opponents"[18] In his biography of Oxford, Mark Anderson, referring to the period around 1593, writes

> Robert Cecil had begun to augment his father's extensive espionage networks with his own cabal of agents and assassins.[19]

Melville comments on the consequences of Claggart's position as master-at-arms [666]:

> His place put various converging wires of underground influence under the Chief's control, capable when astutely worked through his understrappers of operating to the mysterious discomfort, if nothing worse, of any of the sea-commonality.

Melville emphasizes Claggart's unpopularity with the crew by pretending to minimize it [665].

> But the less credence was to be given the gun-deck talk touching Claggart, seeing that no man holding his office in a man-of-war can ever hope to be popular with the crew. Besides, in derogatory comments upon anyone against whom they have a grudge, or for any reason or no reason mislike, sailors are much like landsmen; they are apt to exaggerate or romance it.

Cecil was markedly unpopular. Ogburn says that "execrations of Robert Cecil, who was blamed for [Essex's] fall, were scrawled on walls, even those of Whitehall."[20] Anderson discusses Cecil's unpopularity in Shakespearean terms.

> In 1597, the play *Richard III* had first appeared in print. The analogy between Shake-speare's humpbacked usurper and the power-hungry Robert Cecil was hardly obscure and not hard to

apprehend. Common libelers, for instance, were fond of comparisons between Cecil and Richard III. ("Richard [III] or Robin [Cecil], which was worse?/ A crook't back great in state is England's curse . . .") [19]

And finally, we have another nickname puzzle. Claggart's first name is John [662], but the Old Dansker consistently refers to him as "Jemmy Legs" [670-1]; 'Jemmy' is a nickname for 'James,' not for 'John.'[21] Our identification of Claggart with Robert Cecil provides a clue. Cecil almost single-handedly engineered the deal that transported James VI from Scotland to the British throne; in that sense he was the 'legs' of James I.

Our old friend, the Orthodox Scholar, objects to the above analysis. "Nonsense!" he snorts, "That is the most pestiferous pile of speculative garbage I have ever read. The author can't make up his mind whether Edward de Vere is the Captain or the Old Dansker. He can't make up his mind whether Billy Budd represents Southampton, Essex, or an inanimate pile of books." Exactly. Melville is not in the business of simply retelling a historical tale with the names changed. What he has done (I believe) is he has taken a number of threads from a historical occurrence and woven them into his own story of moral ambiguity and the human condition.[22]

In the physical sciences, a theory is esteemed to the extent that its reach exceeds its grasp—that is, to the extent that it sheds light on phenomena other than those it was intended to explain. The prime example is the quantum theory, which was devised by Max Planck around 1900 to account for the distribution of wavelengths in light emitted by a perfect absorber (a 'black body'). In 1905 Einstein used the theory to explain aspects of the photoelectric effect. Then Niels Bohr adapted it to explain the structure of the hydrogen atom. Eventually it was developed to the extent that it explained all of microscopic electrodynamics, and potentially all of chemistry. The theory that Hank Whittemore propounds in *The Monument* was crafted to explain Shakespeare's Sonnets. I believe it illuminates at least one level of Herman Melville's *Billy Budd* as well.

End Notes

1. Andrew Delbanco, *Melville* (Knopf, 2005), p. 290. Chapter 12 (288-322) has a valuable treatment of *Billy Budd*.
2. Hank Whittemore, *The Monument* (Meadow Geese Press, Marshfield Hills, Massachusetts, 2005). Numbers in curly brackets {xy} refer to pages in this book.
3. Lytton Strachey, *Elizabeth and Essex* (Harcourt Brace, New York, 1928) 189-275.
4. Page numbers [in square brackets] refer to *Billy Budd* in *The Portable Melville*, ed. Jan Leyda (Viking, 1952), 637-739.
5. *Poetical Works of Andrew Marvell*, ed. J. R. Lowell (Little, Brown; Boston, 1857), 7-33.
6. *Encyclopedia Britannica* **7**, 895.
7. *Dictionary of National Biography* (Oxford, 1917) VI, 1005-13.
8. *DNB* VI, 995-6.
9. *Cassell's Latin Dictionary* (Macmillan, 1968)
10. See also Charlton Ogburn, *The Mysterious William Shakespeare* (EPM Publications, 1984) 241, 249-50.
11. Ogburn, 666-7, 696-7.
12. Ogburn, 417.
13. Lewis Carroll, *The Hunting of the Snark* (Kaufmann, 1981) 21.
14. Thomas Nashe, *Choice of Valentines* (quoted in "A Royal Shame" by Paul Altrocchi, *Shakespeare Matters* 4.4, Summer 2005, pp. 1,12-17).
15. Captain Graveling's name may be the first hint in the novel that there is an Elizabethan subtext: the decisive battle in the defeat of the Spanish Armada is the *Battle of Gravelines*, 8 August 1588. Gravelines is a French coastal village near Calais. See David Howarth, *The Voyage of the Armada* (Viking, 1981) 175-92.
16. *Oxford English Dictionary*, 2nd Edition (Clarendon, 1989) II, 339.
17. Ogburn, 199.
18. David Cecil, *The Cecils of Hatfield House* (Houghton Mifflin, 1973) 91, 118. The author is a direct descendant of Robert Cecil.

19. Mark Anderson, *Shakespeare by Another Name* (Penguin, 2005) 273, 305.
20. Ogburn, 753-4.
21. The *OED* (VII, 212) defines *Jemmy* as "A pet-form and familiar equivalent of the name JAMES ."
22. I am grateful to the late Elliott Stone for alerting me to the presence of Captain Edward Vere in *Billy Budd*.

>(Presented at the *Third Dutch Shakespeare Authorship Conference*, Utrecht, the Netherlands, 2 June 2006)

30
Defending John le Carré

In 2010, James Shapiro published a book punningly titled Contested Will. *It was presented as a psychological study of those who questioned the authorship of the man from Stratford, but was actually an attempt to destroy the Oxfordian movement, and as such was cunningly conceived* ('Let's not talk about why the Stratford guy never wrote any letters—let's talk about why Walt Whitman, Sigmund Freud, and Orson Welles were crazy'). *Below is an imagined defense of the Frenchiness of John le Carré using arguments similar to those used by Shapiro.*

I saw the film *Tinker, Tailor, Soldier, Spy* the other day. It's taken from a novel of the same name by John le Carré, who has written a number of well-regarded novels dealing with espionage in the Cold War.

There is a fringe group of loonytics who maintain that these novels were in fact written by David Cornwell, an Englishman. Their motivation is obvious: they are anti-Gallic snobs who just can't believe that these acclaimed novels were written by someone with a Gallic surname—'It HAD to be an Englishman', they huff.

In addition, these deluded creatures claim that the detailed knowledge of spycraft revealed in these works is a result of Cornwell's years of work in the British secret service. This is a preposterous claim, a rank and demeaning denigration of the awesome power of the human imagination.

I understand that Professor James Shapiro is currently at work on a book exposing these 'Cornwellians' for the charlatans they really are. The working title of the book is *Occupied John*.

Posted on the Phaeton ListServ, 4 January 2012

31

Listening to *The Winter's Tale*

Prologue: the Text. On the off chance that there are readers who are not familiar with ***The Winter's Tale***, I will give a brief summary of the events therein.

Leontes (King of Sicilia) has been entertaining his childhood friend Polixenes (King of Bohemia) for nine months; finally Polixenes determines it is time for him to go home. Leontes pleads with him to stay longer, but Polixenes refuses, saying that it is urgent that he return. Finally, Leontes tells his pregnant wife Hermione to urge his friend to stay. Hermione does so and is successful—Polixenes promises to stay another week. Leontes immediately becomes jealous of the fact that his friend yielded to Hermione's persuasion rather than to his. This jealousy quickly takes over his mind, and he becomes obsessed with the idea that he has been cuckolded, and that the child Hermione is carrying is Polixenes' and not his own. He turns to Camillo, one of his principal advisors (and cupbearer to his guest), suggesting that Camillo "bespice a cup, to give mine enemy a lasting wink"—that is, poison Polixenes. Camillo pretends to agree, but then warns Polixenes. They both immediately flee the court and set sail for Bohemia.

The flight of Polixenes and Camillo further convinces Leontes that his suspicions were justified, and that those two plus Hermione were all involved in a plot to kill him. He publicly accuses her of adultery and treason, and has her imprisoned. While confined she gives birth to a baby girl.

Enter Paulina, perhaps the most forceful woman in the entire Shakespeare canon. She is the wife of Antigonus, another of Leontes' chief counselors. She visits the prison, swaddles the new-born babe, and presents it to Leontes, hoping that the sight of the child will soften Leontes' heart. The king's suspicions are unabated; he pronounces the child a bastard and orders it to be burnt alive, then softens slightly and commands Antigonus to take it to "some remote and desert place quite out of our dominions" and there abandon it.

The climax of the first part of the play is Leontes' trial of Hermione. She defends herself eloquently, but the king remains obdurate. Just then, officials that Leontes has sent to the Oracle of Apollo return. The Oracle's judgment: "Hermione is chaste, Polixenes blameless, Camillo a true subject, Leontes a jealous tyrant, his innocent babe truly begotten, and the King shall live without an heir, if that which is lost be not found." Leontes, unmoved, says there is no truth in the Oracle, and the report is a falsehood. A servant enters with the news that Leontes' young son Mamillius, overcome with the trauma of his mother's disgrace, has died. The death of his beloved son shocks Leontes out of his jealous rage: "Apollo's angry, and the heavens themselves do strike at my injustice!" The news affects Hermione as well—she falls to the ground, and Paulina pronounces her dead.

In the final episode of the act (3.3), the scene shifts to the seacoast of Bohemia.[1] As a storm gathers strength, Antigonus fulfills his lord's dread command and leaves the infant in an exposed location, together with some jewels and a hint about her identity. Antigonus himself is then exposed to the world's most famous stage direction: "Exit, pursued by a bear."

Act 4 starts with an actor representing 'Time' announcing the passage of 16 years. The abandoned infant—Perdita—has been raised by a kindly shepherd, and now, as the most beautiful maiden of the countryside, is presiding as queen of the spring festival. She is being wooed by Florizel, the son of Polixenes and heir to the kingdom of Bohemia. Polixenes has noticed his son's frequent absence from the court. He discusses the situation with Camillo, who, since they fled Leontes' court together, has been Polixenes' most trusted advisor. Now they decide to follow Florizel in disguise to find out how he has been spending his time. Thus they wind up at the shepherds' spring festival. Florizel is celebrating his betrothal to Perdita, and admits to the disguised Polixenes that he intends to marry her without telling his father. Polixenes, enraged, threatens to disinherit Florizel and to kill both Perdita and her foster father, and then leaves in a huff. Florizel wants to marry Perdita and flee the kingdom; Camillo, who has been longing to return to Sicilia, proposes that they flee to Sicilia and visit Leontes, purporting to bear greetings from a reconciled Polixenes. When

Florizel and Perdita leave, Camillo informs Polixenes of the plan.

The next scene (5.1) takes place in the Sicilian court. Courtiers are discussing the need for the king to remarry and beget an heir, but Paulina extracts from the penitent Leontes a promise never to marry, unless it be to a woman chosen by Paulina. Then Florizel enters with Perdita, and spins a yarn about his father having sent him to greet Leontes, and his "wife" Perdita being the daughter of the king of Libya. A noble of the Sicilian court enters with the news that Polixenes has just arrived, accompanied by Camillo, the shepherd, and his son. Their meeting with Leontes results in the disclosure that Perdita is his long-lost daughter, which brings great joy to the king. Perdita sorrows to hear of her mother's death, but is intrigued by the news that Paulina has a marvelous statue of Hermione, executed by "that rare Italian master, Julio Romano." In the final scene, the royal party visits Paulina's home to gaze upon the statue. Leontes is transfixed, and moves to kiss the statue, but Paulina prevents him, saying the paint is not yet dry. She then proclaims "I'll make the statue move," and cries "Music! awake her! strike!" Hermione, now living, descends from her platform and embraces Leontes. There is general rejoicing.

The Orthodox view. Mainstream scholars classify *The Winter's Tale* as one of Shakespeare's 'late comedies' or 'romances,' all supposedly written near the end of his career (other examples are *Pericles, Cymbeline,* and *The Tempest*).[2] *The Riverside Shakespeare* estimates that these four plays were all written between 1607 and 1611.[3] (A. L. Rowse, with the air of someone who has been looking over the dramatist's shoulder as he writes, asserts that "[the play] seems to have been written at Stratford in one onrush in the winter of 1610-11").[4] Oxfordian scholar Eva Turner Clark, writing in 1930, dates these plays as considerably earlier—from the late 1570s through the early 1580s.[5] Clark's dating puts *Pericles* (1577) and *Cymbeline* (1578) in Oxford's early period (right after *Timon of Athens* and *Titus Andronicus*), and *The Tempest* (1583) and *The Winter's Tale* (1586) in the middle of his mature period (the former just after *Othello*, the latter between *2 Henry IV* and *Henry V*). Thus the Stratfordian and Oxfordian datings of these plays are hugely discrepant —the average difference is almost 30 years! Occasionally an orthodox scholar will almost stumble across the truth: writing of the 'romances,' Northrop Frye notes " . . . there's a strong tendency to go back to some of the conventions of the earlier plays, the kind that were produced in the 1580s."[6]

In preparing for this paper I read a few pieces by orthodox critics, and found myself in a strange world, one in which the plays have no subtext. One frequently used approach is to analyze the characters as if they were real people, often with extravagant admiration:

> The characterization of Perdita is the glory of the fourth act. Her charming modesty and diffidence about her role as the humble sweetheart of a disguised prince make her hold back as mistress of the feast and her father's hostess, until she is gently reproached by the shepherd. . . . Though she is, unknown to herself, a princess, yet she is a child of nature.[7]

Another approach is to discuss the form of the drama in abstract terms:

> In *The Winter's Tale*, however, Shakspeare has not opened up the whole region of the marvelous; he has described the wonderful, not so much in its outer form as in its ideal nature and character. In fact, it exists here only in the incomprehensibility of outward contingency and the mysterious connection of the latter with the actions and fortunes of the dramatic characters. . . . [Shakespeare] could hardly have intended merely to dramatize a traditional tale; the play is not called "**A** Winter's Tale," but "**The** Winter's Tale." The poet's intention here was again, as it were, to hold the mirror up to nature, to show the body of the time its pressure.[8]

I haven't the faintest idea what all that means.

Subtext Layer 1: Sir Walter Ralegh. John Russell French seems to have been the first person to publish material relating Shakespeare's characters to historical figures. His essay, 'Notes on Hamlet,' appeared in 1869.[9] He correctly associated Polonius with Lord Burghley, but being a Stratfordian, he got everyone else wrong—in particular, he associated the Oxford figure 'Hamlet' with Sir Philip Sidney (we now know that Sidney was the prototype for Boyet in *Love's Labor's Lost*, Slender in *Merry Wives of Windsor*, and (most hilariously) Andrew Aguecheek in *Twelfth Night*).

Eva Turner Clark was the first Oxfordian to pursue this line of investigation. Published 10 years after the Looney epiphany,[10] her book *Hidden Allusions in Shakespeare's Plays* displays a breadth of scholarship and an intensity of focus that surely qualifies the author as a modern Paulina.[11] Clark (inspired by Hamlet's statement that "The players are the abstract and brief chronicles of the time") studied the plays in search of 'topicalities'—allusions to contemporary events. This approach, given Clark's deep and detailed knowledge of historical characters and happenings, has yielded abundant fruit. Her book is invaluable in understanding the plays, and pragmatically, in dating them.

Clark's take on *The Winter's Tale* is influenced by a very specific 'topicality' that occurs early in the play. King Leontes is speaking to his son, Mamillius, a boy of perhaps seven or eight.

Leontes. Mamillius, art thou my boy?

Mamillius. Ay, my good lord.

Leontes. I' fecks!
Why, that's my bawcock.
What! hast smutch'd thy nose?
They say it is a copy out of mine.
Come, captain,
We must be neat; not neat, but cleanly, captain

(1.2.119-23)

A Pomeranian observer at the Elizabethan court, Herr Lupold von Wedel of Kremzow, has left a description of a similar occurrence:

> As long as the dancing lasted she (the Queen) summoned young and old and spoke continuously. All of them knelt before her. She chatted and jested most amiably with them, and pointing with her finger at the face of one Master or Captain Rall (Ralegh), told him that there was smut on it. She also offered to wipe it off with her handkerchief, but he anticipating her removed it himself. They say that she now loves him beyond all others, and this one may easily credit, for but a year ago he could scarcely keep one servant, whereas now owing to her bounty he can afford to keep five hundred.[12]

I find the specificity of this allusion to the 'smutch'd nose' quite convincing, especially since the king playfully addresses his son as "captain' (Ralegh was Elizabeth's Captain of the Guard). Ralegh and Elizabeth were said to have had similarly shaped 'Roman' noses; hence Leontes' line " . . . thy nose? They say it is a copy out of mine."

Clark goes on to find other plausible references to Ralegh. The historian Naunton (author of *Fragmenta Regalia*) wrote that "Ralegh had gotten the Queen's ear in a trice, and she began to be taken with his elocution, and loved to hear his reasons to her demands; and the truth is, she took him for a kind of oracle, which nettled them all"[12] (the visit to the Oracle of Delphos is a significant part of the third act). Clark adds that "Doricles, the name assumed by Florizel, is probably made up of 'de' and 'oraculum,' meaning 'of oracles,' again a reference to Ralegh."[12] The Shepherd, assumed to be Perdita's father, says of Florizel

He says he loves my daughter:

I think so too; for never gaz'd the moon
Upon the water as he'll stand, and read,
As 'twere, my daughter's eyes . . . (4.4.171-4)

Clark points out that the moon, personified as Cynthia, frequently refers to Elizabeth, and that 'water' was the queen's nickname for Ralegh.[12] ('Water' may have been the customary Elizabethan pronunciation of 'Walter': Ralegh's wife, who spelled phonetically, invariably rendered his name as "Sur Wattar.")[13] The passage is thus a reflection of Elizabeth's infatuation with Ralegh.

In another striking observation, Clark points out that the archaic word 'fardel,' meaning 'bundle' or 'burden,' is used six times in *The Winter's Tale*—it is used only one other time in the entire canon, when Hamlet asks "Who would fardels bear?" Ralegh was born in the Devon village of Fardell; his father was known as Walter Ralegh of Fardell.[12]

As noted above, establishment scholars are oblivious to the possibility of a subtext in Shakespeare's plays. Thus they innocently believe that 'Sicilia' is simply a fancy name for Sicily, and that 'Bohemia' refers to the actual historical kingdom. This viewpoint is so ingrained that they merrily sneer at the author for alluding to the 'seacoast' of Bohemia (see, however, Note 1). Clark, with her deeper knowledge of the time and greater awareness of the subtlety of the author, points out that members of the Leicester faction, fiercely opposed to the policies of William Cecil, Lord Burghley, mockingly referred to England as *Regnum Cecilianum*—Cecil's kingdom.[14] The phrase is virtually homophonic with the Latin term for the 'Kingdom of Sicily': *Regnum Sicilianum*. Thus Oxford is guardedly suggesting that the events in his play have some relevance to historical events in the Elizabethan court—that is, that 'Sicilia' can be read as 'England.' Clark sees Perdita as the personification of Ralegh's infant colony in Virginia (a settlement named after Elizabeth's public persona).[14] Thus 'Bohemia' can be read as 'the American colonies,' a wild landscape teeming with dangerous animals (like bears). This identification is in accord with the humility of the Bohemian courtier Archidamus when (in the opening speech of the play) he apologizes to Camillo for the "great difference betwixt our Bohemia and your Sicilia." All these considerations (among others) lead Clark to declare " . . . *The Winter's Tale* concerns itself . . . with the rise to fame of Sir Walter Ralegh and his schemes for exploring and colonizing the New World."[14]

When I began studying *The Winter's Tale* I started with Clark's essay, and found this conclusion surprising. Over the years I had read about Oxford's strained relations with his first wife (Anne Cecil), his father-in-law (Burghley), his brother-in-law (Robert Cecil), and the arch-villain of the Elizabethan court (Leicester), and I expected to find these relationships reflected in the plays (as indeed they are). But Ralegh? Why would Oxford base a play on Ralegh?

After doing more reading, I found that Ralegh loomed larger in Oxford's life than I had realized. Ralegh was born no later than 1554, and was thus just a bit younger than Oxford. There are strong parallels between the careers of the two men. Both were courtiers who enjoyed a season of high favor with the queen, and then were cast into the Tower for a sexual transgression.[15] Both were poets, both had military aspirations, both sailed against the Invincible Armada in 1588. Both sought to be named Warden of the Stannaries in Cornwall, both sought to be named Governor of Jersey. There are strong distinctions as well: Ralegh was successful in his quest for the Stannaries and Jersey; Oxford was not. Ralegh had a distinguished military career, commanding troops in Ireland (1580-81) and participating in the glorious raid on Cadiz (1596); Oxford did not. Oxford had one big advantage—rank. His lineage was the most ancient in England, dating back to the Norman Conquest, while Ralegh was the son of a country squire. Thus it was that Oxford felt humiliated when it was Ralegh's letter to the queen (written at Burghley's request) that restored the earl to the queen's favor in 1583. Ralegh wrote to Burghley describing his efforts on Oxford's behalf, adding

> And the more to witness how desirous I am of your Lordship's favour and good opinion, I am content, for your sake to lay the serpent before the fire as much as in me lieth; that, having recovered [his] strength, myself may be most in danger of his poison and sting.[16]

Ralegh is referring to the folk tale about the man who finds a frozen snake, and taking pity on it, brings it to his house and warms it, whereupon the recovered serpent bites him. This identification of de Vere with a serpent curiously foreshadows the scene with the Clown bearing the viper-laden basket in *Antony and Cleopatra* (5.2.241-79).

Cleopatra. Hast thou the pretty worm of Nilus there, That kills and pains not?

Clown. Truly, I have him; but I would not be the party that should desire you to touch him, for his biting is immortal; those that do die of it do seldom or never recover.

Richard Whalen has pointed out that 'worm,' an archaic term for 'serpent,' when translated into French is 'ver' (pronounced 'Vere').[17]

Oxford's attitude towards Ralegh can be illustrated by a remark he made after the trial of Essex in 1601, a trial in which Ralegh played a prominent role as witness for the prosecution. Elizabeth and some courtiers were in the Privy Chamber; the queen was playing the virginals. A messenger entered with the news of Essex's execution. Oxford observed bitterly "When Jacks start up, heads go down."[18] But Oxford was not Ralegh's enemy. When Ralegh was executed in 1618, the fatal bite had been administered 15 years earlier by Robert Cecil, whose machinations had resulted in Ralegh's trial and conviction on charges of treason.[19]

Subtext Layer 2: the Play as Autobiography. Even with my newly-won knowledge of the relations between Oxford and Ralegh, I felt that my understanding of the play was incomplete. Things just didn't add up. For example, in the scene between Leontes and Mamillius quoted above, in which Leontes comments on his son's 'smutch'd nose,' Ralegh is to be identified with Mamillius, whereas the references to 'fardels' occur in a scene with the thief Autolycus. Mamillius and

Shakespeare Confidential

Autolycus are not the most important figures in the play. It was then I determined to listen to *The Winter's Tale* with my own ears. When I did so, one of the early scenes caught my attention immediately. Leontes has been trying to persuade his childhood friend Polixenes to extend his stay. Polixenes pleads urgent business at home. Leontes tells Hermione to try her hand at persuading Polixenes.

Hermione	You'll stay?
Polixenes	No, madam.
Hermione	Nay, but you will?
Polixenes	I may not, verily
Hermione.	Verily? You put me off with limber vows, but I, Though you would seek t' unsphere the stars with oaths, Should yet say "Sir, no going." Verily, You shall not go; a lady's 'verily' is As potent as a lord's. Will you go yet? Force me to keep you as a prisoner, Not like a guest: so you shall pay your fees When you depart, and save your thanks. How say you? My prisoner? or my guest? By your dread 'verily,' One of them you shall be. (1.2.44-56)

This unrelenting drumbeat of 'verily's reminds us that the author is a Vere, and hints that the events of the play are of direct relevance to his personal situation.[20] (The effect is heightened if one looks at this scene in the First Folio, where 'verily is spelled **Verely** .)[21] And once we see this, the penny drops and the light comes on. Of course! Hermione is one of the chaste women wrongly accused of infidelity that inhabit so many of the plays: Imogen in *Cymbeline*, Hero in *Much Ado*, Mariana in *Measure for Measure*, Diana in *All's Well that Ends Well* and most famously, Desdemona in *Othello*. Hermione is Anne Cecil, Oxford's first wife, whose painted statue graces the Cecil tomb in Westminster Abbey. Once we recognize this, a number of other relationships fall into place. We see the jealous Leontes as Oxford himself, and Polixenes, associated with the wilderness of 'Bohemia,' is identified as Ralegh, the man

Oxford had so many reasons to be jealous of. Perdita reminds us of Oxford's first daughter Elizabeth, who at one time was betrothed to Henry Wriothesley, 3rd Earl of Southampton, the Fair Youth of the Sonnets—and thus the prototype of Florizel. And we can associate Mamillius, the son who dies of grief, with Anne and Oxford's infant son who died shortly after birth in May 1583.

Figure 12 - Mildred Cooke

The chief advisor of the sovereign of England at this time was William Cecil, Lord Burghley. Leontes, king of Sicilia, has two principal advisors—Camillo and Antigonus. Camillo, in rejecting the king's suggestion that he poison Polixenes, acquires tints of Elizabeth's secretary William Davison and Mary Stuart's keeper Amyas Paulet, who similarly resisted hints from Elizabeth that Mary could be disposed of without the necessity of a public execution.[22] We shall later find reasons for associating Antigonus with Burghley.

In telling the story of *The Winter's Tale* we mentioned the scene (2.3) in which Paulina shows the infant girl to Leontes, hoping to effect a reconciliation. A similar incident happened to Oxford. While he was estranged from Anne, the Lady Katherine Bertie, Duchess of Suffolk, contrived to present the infant Elizabeth Vere to him.[23] Thus it has become customary to regard Lady Suffolk as the original of Paulina. We have suggested that Paulina's husband, Antigonus, in his capacity as counselor to the throne, acquires a measure of identification with Burghley. As it happens, Burghley was married to a woman as strong-willed as Paulina—namely, Mildred Cooke. In the play, Leontes has a number of lines in which he suggests that Antigonus is hen-pecked.

> Leontes Away with that audacious lady! Antigonus,
> I charg'd thee that she should not come about me:
> I knew she would.

Shakespeare Confidential

Antigonus	I told her so, my lord, On your displeasure's peril and on mine, She should not visit you.
Leontes	What? canst not rule her?
Paulina	He shall not rule me.
Antigonus	La you now, you hear! When she will take the rein I let her run.
Leontes	Thou dotard, thou art woman-tyred; unroosted By thy Dame Partlet here.

(2.3.42-76)

Cecil family historian David Cecil has provided us with a description of Burghley's wife:

> Mildred Cooke was the daughter of Sir Anthony Cooke, Governor to the young Prince Edward . . . [She was] famous as one of the most learned girls in England. One can believe it from her portrait. With her lofty brow, compressed lips and pale, stern eyes, she looks like the most formidable kind of lady academic. Many found her alarming; which is hardly to be wondered at, seeing that, in addition to talking Greek as easily as English, she was a well-informed and combative arguer for the Protestant cause.[24]

"Combative arguer" is Paulina in a nutshell. Since Mildred Cooke was Oxford's mother-in-law, I find it easy to imagine that he had no difficulty using her character appropriately as he wrote *The Winter's Tale*. And the Duchess of Suffolk, the woman who presented Oxford with his infant child, was his sister's mother-in-law.

Subtext Layer 3: Mary of Scotland. While studying *The Winter's Tale* I was simultaneously reading a life of Mary Queen of Scots by John Guy,[25] a biographer who is notably more sympathetic to Mary's cause than others I have read. Guy describes in great detail Mary's conflicts with the factious Scottish nobles. In March 1566 a group of them, led by her husband Darnley, burst into her private chamber; they murdered David Rizzio, her secretary, and took Mary captive. She persuaded Darnley to help her escape, and with the aid of James Hepburn, Earl of Bothwell, they did so, riding furiously to Bothwell's stronghold of Dunbar. Three months later Mary, now restored to power, gave birth to the boy who became James VI of Scotland and eventually James I of England. In February of the next year (1567) Darnley was himself murdered.

Bothwell was accused of the crime and was brought to trial in April, but by this time Edinburgh was filled with his armed supporters, and he was acquitted. A month later he and Mary were married.

Bothwell was now so powerful that other nobles felt threatened, and a group calling themselves 'the Confederate Lords' banded together to oppose him.[26] Both sides raised armies, which confronted each other at Carberry Hill in June but did not come to blows. A settlement was reached in which Bothwell's life was spared and Mary was taken into custody by the rebels and confined to a castle on the island of Lochleven.

The Confederate Lords now proceeded to try Mary in the court of public opinion. A systematic campaign was mounted, accusing Mary of being complicit in Darnley's murder and consumed by lawless passion for Bothwell. Guy summarizes the story spread by the Lords:

> [Mary] was not a proper queen. She had disqualified herself because she was guilty of "moral turpitude." . . . Mary's "furious love" for Bothwell had "proved" that she was unable to control her passions. Carnal lust had led her first to commit adultery with a married man and then to conspire with him to murder her husband so that she could be free to marry her lover.[27]

These are precisely the accusations Leontes makes against Hermione.

Leontes
I have said
She's an adultress; I have said with whom:
More—she's a traitor, and Camillo is
A federary with her, and one that knows
What she should shame to know herself,
that she's a bed-swerver . . .(2.1.87-93)

Officer [at trial].
"Hermione, queen to the worthy Leontes, King of Sicilia, thou art here accused and arraigned of high treason, in committing adultery with Polixenes, King of Bohemia, and conspiring with Camillo to take away the life of our sovereign lord the King, thy royal husband . . . "   (3.2.12-17)

In this context the blameless Hermione represents Mary Stuart (Guy finds Mary innocent of any complicity in Darnley's murder)[28] while the accusatory Leontes stands in for the Confederate Lords.

The climax of *The Winter's Tale* is the scene (5.3) in which

Paulina displays to the sorrowful Leontes a statue of Hermione, supposedly executed by "that rare Italian master, Julio Romano." The statue is so lifelike that Leontes is moved to kiss it, but Paulina forestalls him, saying she will "make the statue move." She exclaims "Music! awake her! strike" and the statue comes to life—indeed, it is Hermione, who joyfully greets her daughter.

Within the framework of the play, there are two possibilities here: either there was a statue made by Julio Romano which magically came to life, or Hermione did not die when the death of her son was announced, but was kept in seclusion by Paulina for 16 years until Perdita's arrival in court. I believe the text supports the latter scenario: Hermione's supposed death is announced by Paulina and is not corroborated by any other character. The scene in which the statue comes to life is adroitly stage-managed by Paulina.

In May 1568 Mary Stuart managed an escape from Lochleven and raised an army to help her regain power. Her forces were defeated in battle at Langside, and she fled to England, expecting that her cousin Elizabeth would support her efforts to regain her throne. Instead she was placed under house arrest. For 15 years she was guarded by George Talbot, Earl of Shrewsbury. Much of this time she spent in the company of Talbot's formidable wife, Bess of Hardwick, gossiping and embroidering, much as one imagines that Hermione and Paulina would have spent the queen's 16 years of sequestration. Bess of Hardwick, twenty years older than Mary and described as "a woman of masculine understanding and conduct"[29] thus becomes another candidate for identification with the forthright Paulina.

In 1586, either as a result of her conspiratorial nature, or enmeshed in a 'sting' operation contrived by Walsingham (depending upon your viewpoint), Mary was shown to have been involved in the Babington plot. In October of that year she was brought to trial, an event that markedly resembles Hermione's trial (3.2). Both defendants show great composure and dignity.

Mary.   Search your consciences. Look to your honor!
        May God reward you and yours for your judgment against me.[30]

Hermione.	... but thus, if powers divine
	Behold our human actions (as they do),
	I doubt not then but innocence shall make
	False accusation blush . . . (3.2.28-32)
	For behold me,
	A fellow of the royal bed . . . a great king's daughter,
	The mother to a hopeful prince, here standing
	To prate and talk for life and honor
	(3.2.37-41)

The latter quote strikingly and precisely describes Mary's position—former queen of France, wife of Francis II of France, daughter of Scotland's James V, and mother of the future James I of England. It is almost as if the playwright had been present at the trial. Actually, he was—Lord Oxford was one of the peers who sat in judgment at Mary's trial, duty-bound to render the predetermined verdict of 'guilty.'

For about a week after I had perceived the parallels between Hermione's trial and Mary Stuart's, I preened myself on having made an original contribution to the study of *The Winter's Tale*. However, I felt uneasy. *This Star of England*, the massive tome written by the elder Ogburns, contains so many insights—might they have preceded me in this one? I don't own the book, so I ordered a copy through interlibrary loan. When it finally arrived, I feverishly tore it open and found this description:

> The play is replete with casual allusions to public persons and events—notably to Raleigh and his affairs, including the colonizing of Virginia. But the central core is the terrible ordeal of Hermione, and her integrity and nobility of spirit in the face of inimical authority. Foredoomed, she stands before Leontes and his court and defends herself with a poise and dignity truly regal.
>
> Hermione's trial is that of Mary Stuart, which had just taken place, in October 1586, while Leontes represents English authority (Leo) in the person of the English peers and lawyers who participated in the legalistic formality, their unanimous verdict a foregone conclusion.[31]

Alas! my dreams of scholarly glory have crumbled into dust. (Perhaps not. The *Cymbeline* papers, p. 219-38, seem to be an original contribution.)

One wonders how Elizabeth reacted to the play. Was she amused by the references to Ralegh? Did she think 'Oh, there Edward goes again, castigating himself for the way he treated poor little Anne Cecil'? Was she outraged at the sympathetic treatment accorded her would-be supplanter Mary Stuart? Or did she think 'Yes, Edward got it right—queens are always chaste and pure. Or at least should be regarded as such.'

Subtext Layer 4: Perdita as the Works. Clark and the elder Ogburns have both suggested that on one level, the lost princess Perdita represents Oxford's plays and poems, commonly attributed to 'Shakespeare.' Adopting this viewpoint is rather like shaking up a kaleidoscope—the elements cohere again into a pattern, but it's a different pattern. If Perdita is the Works, her mother Hermione becomes Oxford, and the accusations of Leontes remind us of the slanders directed against Oxford by Henry Howard and Charles Arundel in December 1580.[32] Bucolic Bohemia, with its sheep-shearing festival and queen of the May, becomes Stratford-on-Avon. And the father and son—Shepherd and Clown—who take charge of Perdita and are thereby engentled— become John and William Shaxper.

A possible indication that Perdita represents the Works occurs as the babe is being abandoned on the Bohemian coast.

<pre>
Antigonus   Poor wretch,
                  That for thy mother's fault art thus expos'd
                  To loss, and what may follow!
                                              (3.3.49-51)
</pre>

That is, the indiscretions or lack of judgment of the author—Oxford—have led to the possibility that the Works will be suppressed—lost to future generations. Note that Antigonus—the Burghley figure—seems to believe that the 'mother' is indeed at fault. It seems likely that historically much of the pressure to suppress or censor Oxford's writings came from Burghley. Another parallel is that the Shepherd and Clown, representing the Shaxpers *père et fils*, gain financially by their association with Perdita ("This is fairy gold, boy . . . keep it close"). And note the quantum jump in social status achieved by the rustics:

<pre>
Clown.   Try whether I am not now a gentleman
                  born.
</pre>

Autolycus	I know you are now, sir, a gentleman born.
Clown.	Ay, and have been so any time these four hours.

(5.2.134-6)

Of special significance is the 'fardel'—bundle or pack—containing objects left with the abandoned infant Perdita which provide clues to her true identity. As the Third Gentleman says:

> They found with it the mantle of Queen Hermione's;
> her jewel about the neck of it; the letters of Antigonus
> .(5.2.32-4)

Similarly, Oxford has left clues in the Works pointing to the identity of the author. Earlier we mentioned the drumbeat of repeated 'verily's in the play's second scene; in Scene 5.2 the Second Gentleman utters a similarly resonant line:

> This news, which is called true, is so like an old tale,
> that the verity of it is in strong suspicion.

The bundle contains the letters of Antigonus—and Burghley's collected letters have proved invaluable in providing a picture of Oxford's private life, a context essential for understanding the plays and Oxford's authorship thereof.

Subtext Layer 5: Autolycus. Thus far I have given short shrift to a character who is the most multifaceted figure in the play—Autolycus, the professional thief whose musical entrance opens Scene 4.3. As a character, Autolycus has some curious characteristics. In terms of the plot, he is entirely peripheral—so much so that I was able to summarize the plot of the play at the beginning of this paper without once mentioning him. Yet he dominates the second half of the play. The author allows him to address the audience directly, a rare privilege, but one which is shared with other figures who boast of their cunning and lack of scruples, such as Falstaff, Edmund, Aaron the Moor, and Richard the Third.

The dictionary defines *mercurial* as "eloquent, clever, shrewd, thievish . . . quick, changeable." Autolycus is all of these. In classical literature, Autolycus was a mythical thief, the son of Mercury, the god of thieves—thus the Autolycus in the play is literally *mercurial*. Describing the mythical character, one author writes "Autolycus was able to escape with anything he got his hands on and, if need be, to make it change its color or form." [33] Again we find the emphasis on *changeability*, again appropriate for this character, for is there a more protean figure in the canon than Autolycus? Consider the range of personæ he adopts: (1) he enters in Scene 4.3 and addresses the audience, presumably in his 'true' persona. (2) Clown enters, and Autolycus immediately throws himself on the ground, pretending to be the victim of a mugging. He claims the mugging was perpetrated by— (3) a fictional or off-stage 'Autolycus,' described as "a servant of the Prince" who was "whipt out of the court" (4.3.87-90). (4) In Scene 4.4 Autolycus shows up at the sheep-shearing festival as a pedlar selling ballads and "trumpery," disguised by a false beard. (5) Later in that scene he appears as a random passer-by, a "poor fellow" who is forced by Camillo to change clothes with Prince Florizel to facilitate the latter's elopement. (6) Still later, Autolycus encounters Shepherd and Clown, and doffing the false beard, appears to them as an arrogant courtier who, in return for gold, will arrange for them an audience with the king. (7) Then after the rustic pair have gained status by proving that Perdita is Leontes' daughter, Autolycus attaches himself to them as their humble follower. (I will refer to these avatars as 'Autolycus 1, Autolycus 2 . . . etc.)

This is a dizzying set of transformations—seven personæ in three scenes!— and the subtext of the character seems to be equally changeable. The elder Ogburns take Autolycus to be "whimsically, the bohemian side of Oxford," [34] and there is evidence for this in the text, particularly in references to the character's career as a courtier. In his initial soliloquy (presumably speaking as the 'real' Autolycus) he says

[Aut. 1]   I have serv'd Prince Florizel, and in my time wore
three-pile, but now I am out of service.
(4.3.13-14)

In his persona as a mugging victim, Autolycus gives us a name-clue—

[Aut. 2]   O that ever I was born!

Clown   I' th' name of me—

—which can be read as 'I was born E. Vere,' followed by 'Using *my* name!' (we have previously seen that Clown represents Will Shaxper of Stratford). Aut. 2 then goes on to describe his assailant (Aut. 3) to Clown:

[Aut. 2] I knew him once a servant of the Prince. I cannot tell, good sir, for which of his virtues it was, but he was certainly whipt out of the court. (4.3.89-90)

The word 'virtue' comes from the Latin *vir*, meaning 'man,' thus 'virtue' has the root meaning of 'manly quality.' It was for the 'manly quality' of impregnating Anne Vavasor that Oxford was 'whipt out of the court' and imprisoned in the Tower when the child was born in 1581.[35] Note too that 'virtues' is a 'ver'-word, spelled **'Vertues'** in the First Folio. But then as the dialog proceeds, the descriptions of Aut. 3 take an ambiguous turn.

[Aut. 2]. . I know this man well; he hath been since an ape-bearer, then a process-server (a bailiff), then he compass'd a motion of the Prodigal Son, and married a tinker's wife within a mile where my land and living lies; and having flown over many knavish professions, he settled only in rogue. Some call him Autolycus.

Clown Out upon him! . . . He haunts wakes, fairs, and bear-baitings.

[Aut. 2] Very true, sir; he, sir, he. That's the rogue that put me into this apparel. (4.3.94-104)

So we have references to various phases of rural show-business—trained monkeys, puppet shows, bear-baitings. Is this a sardonic look at Oxford's theatrical activities, or is it pure invention? Or is it a summary of Stratford Will's career before he became a wealthy grain merchant? If Aut. 1, the disgraced courtier, stands for Oxford, perhaps his shadow-figure, the rural entertainer and thief Aut. 3, represents Stratford Will. Is it not a pretty conceit?—the playwright de Vere, adopting the pen name 'William Shake-speare,' finds that he has a shadow-figure, William Shaxper, who steals credit for his matchless plays. The alert reader will object: 'Wait a minute—we already have a Shaxper figure—the Clown, son of the Shepherd!' Ah, but that's on another level of subtext. Besides, the play is a dream, not a phone book.

Shakespeare Confidential

Autolycus next enters, singing, as a pedlar, disguised with a false beard and selling all kinds of goods (Aut. 4; 4.4.218). The villagers are particularly interested in the sheet-music he sells ("The ballad is very pitiful, and as true"). He exits at the end of another song, then reenters 272 lines later to soliloquize, displaying the same cunning persona as in his initial address to the audience. "I have sold all my trumpery," he exults, and recites a list of his profitable transactions, reminding one of Diana Price's account of Stratford Will's conjectured commercial activities, which include brokering pirated plays and selling second-hand costumes.[36] His soliloquy is interrupted by the entrance of Camillo and Prince Florizel, followed by the forced exchange of clothes with Florizel.

The word 'trumpery' is used twice in Shakespeare's plays—once in *The Tempest* and once in *The Winter's Tale*. In both cases the word is associated with a rascally commoner donning the clothes of a nobleman (in *The Tempest*, it is the drunken steward Stephano, seeking to depose Prospero as lord of the island). A similar event takes place in the Induction of *Taming of the Shrew*, where the drunken tinker is dressed in the Lord's finery as a jest. Charlton Ogburn, writing about *The Tempest* and *Shrew*, has pointed out how suggestive the exchange of clothing is, identifying Stephano and Sly as Shaxper-figures, commoners taking the place of a noble.[37] So Autolycus—thief and disgraced courtier—represents Stratford Will (the putative author) as well as Edward de Vere (the real author).

Closing Quotes.

"There is no subtext in Shakespeare."
Stratfordian John Basil, *Will Power* (Applause, 2006) 26.

"In Shakespeare, topical allusion is rare . . . "
Stratfordian Jonathan Bate, 'The Mirror of Life, *Harper's Magazine* (April 2007) 41.

"Who is so blind as he that will not see?"
John Ray, *English Proverbs* (1670) 64.

" . . . Now if one takes [Shakespeare's] thirty-seven plays with all the radar lines of the different viewpoints of the different characters, one comes out with a field of incredible density and complexity; and eventually one goes a step further, and one finds that what happened . . . is something quite different from any other author's work. It's not Shakespeare's view of the world, it's something which actually resembles reality. A sign of this is that *any single word, line, character or event has not only a large number of interpretations, but an unlimited number. Which is the characteristic of reality."*

Peter Brook, in Ralph Berry, *On Directing Shakespeare* (Croom Helm, 1977) 114-5.

End Notes

1. Charlton Ogburn wrote "The most famous error alleged in Shakespeare is the attribution of a seacoast to Bohemia. From Ben Jonson to Louis B. Wright, critics have ridiculed Shakespeare for that, not troubling to inform themselves that the Kingdom of Bohemia under King Premyal Ottaker (1253-1278) stretched to the Adriatic, and in 1526, upon the accession of the first Hapsburg to the throne of Bohemia, the realm of the King of Bohemia comprised the Archduchy of Austria, which bordered the Adriatic between territories of the Venetian Republic." (*The Mysterious William Shakespeare*, EPM Publications, 1984; 307.)

2. *The Riverside Shakespeare*, ed. G. Blakemore Evans (Houghton Mifflin, 1974) viii.

3. *Riverside* 1479, 1517, 1564, 1606.

4. A. L. Rowse, *The Annotated Shakespeare*, Vol. III (Orbis, 1978) 769.

5. Eva Turner Clark, *Hidden Allusions in Shakespeare's Plays*; 3rd Revised Edition, ed. Ruth Loyd Miller (Kennikat Press, 1974) 60, 79, 584, 749.

6. *Northrop Frye on Shakespeare*, ed. Robert Sandler (Yale, 1986) 155.

7. Hallett Smith in *The Riverside Shakespeare*, 1566.

8. Hermann Ulrici, *Shakspeare's Dramatic Art*, Vol. II (London, 1876) 30 *et seq*.

9. John Russell French, *Shakspeareana Genealogica* (Macmillan, 1869) 301-310.

10. J. Thomas Looney, *"Shakespeare" Identified*, Third Edition, ed. Ruth Loyd Miller (Kennikat, 1975).

11. A list of modern Oxfordian 'Paulina's would have to include Dorothy Ogburn, coauthor of another seminal text, *This Star of England*, and Ruth Loyd Miller, editor of the 1974 edition of Clark's book.

12. Clark, 750; 754-5; 763; 767.

13. John Winton, *Sir Walter Ralegh* (Coward McCann, 1975) 162. Another example of the 'water-Walter' homophony occurs in *2 Henry VI*, 4.1.31-35.
14. Clark, 631; 762, 749.
15. With someone other than the Queen.
16. Dorothy and Charlton Ogburn [Sr.], *This Star of England* (Coward McCann, 1952) 380.
17. Richard Whalen, " 'The Queen's Worm' in *Antony and Cleopatra*," *Shakespeare Oxford Newsletter* 34.2 (Summer 1998) 12-13.
18. Charlton Ogburn, *The Mysterious William Shakespeare* (EPM Publications, 1984), 755.

    Oxford was punning on 'Jack,' meaning 'a common fellow,' and 'jack,' the mechanism in the virginal that raises a plectrum when a key is depressed. There had long been rivalry between Ralegh and Essex, and Ralegh had testified for the prosecution in Essex's trial.

19. Winton, chapters 17, 22.
20. An even stronger case for the autobiographical nature of the play is made by C. Richard Desper and Gary C. Vezzoli in "A Statistical Approach to the Shakespeare Authorship Question," *The Elizabethan Review* 1.2 (Fall 1993) 36-42. Desper and Vezzoli point out that *The Winter's Tale* translated into French is 'le Conte d'Hiver,' which is homophonic with 'le Conte de Vere' ('the Vere story') and virtually homophonic with 'le Comte de Vere' ('the Earl de Vere').
21. Doug Moston, ed. *The First Folio of Shakespeare 1623* (Applause, 1995) 278. Oddly enough, the modern spelling, 'verily,' is used elsewhere in the First Folio (e.g. line 5.3.64, p. 302).
22. Clark, 752-53.
23. Dorothy and Charlton Ogburn, 138-9.
24. David Cecil, *The Cecils of Hatfield House* (Houghton Mifflin, 1973) 61-2.
25. John Guy, *Queen of Scots: the True Life of Mary Stuart* (Houghton Mifflin, 2004).
26. The ringleaders of the Confederate Lords were James Douglas, Earl of Morton, Archibald Campbell, Earl of Argyll, John Stuart, Earl of Atholl, and Lord Erskine, Earl of Mar (Guy, 319).

27. Guy, 373.

28. Guy, Chapter 19, 285-301.

29. Guy, 435.

30. Guy, 474.

31. Dorothy and Charlton Ogburn, 746-7.

32. Mark Anderson, *Shakespeare by Another Name*, (Gotham, 2005) 166-7.

33. Edward Tripp, *Crowell's Handbook of Classical Mythology* (Crowell, 1970) 128. It is instructive to take this sentence and substitute 'Oxford' for 'Autolycus' and 'incorporate in his plays' for 'escape with.' The sentence then reads "Oxford was able to incorporate in his plays anything he got his hands on and, if need be, to make it change its color or form."

34. Dorothy and Charlton Ogburn, 759.

35. Anderson, 172.

36. Diana Price, *Shakespeare's Unorthodox Biography* (Greenwood Press, 2001).

37. Ogburn, 746-7, 762-3.

Presented as the keynote address at the
Fourth Dutch Shakespeare Authorship Conference,
Utrecht, the Netherlands, 8 June 2007.

32
Cymbeline: the Hidden History Play

Shakespeare's *Cymbeline* is not a well-known play. It seems to have been stitched together from devices that were successful in other plays—e.g. *Evil Italian Stirs Jealousy* (*Othello*), *The Evil Queen* (*Macbeth, Titus Andronicus*), *Servant Refuses Order to Kill* (*Winter's Tale*), *Changeling Children* (*Winter's Tale, Midsummer Night's Dream*), *Death-Feigning Potion* (*Romeo & Juliet*), and of course, those ever-popular standbys, *Virtuous Woman Accused of Adultery* and *Woman Disguised as a Boy*, with examples too numerous to mention.

In spite of its patchwork construction, *Cymbeline* is a fast-moving play that can engage audiences. The Boston-based *Actors' Shakespeare Project* mounted a production in February 2012 that was very successful. It was performed in an empty commercial space, rather than in a proscenium theatre. The staging was reminiscent of *commedia del' arte*—there was much doubling of parts, actors not in a given scene were seated on the sidelines, and they frequently played musical instruments to augment the action.

The Ur-cast of *Cymbeline*. When I start to study a play I usually turn to Eva Turner Clark's *Hidden Allusions in Shakespeare's Plays*[1] for a preliminary look at what she calls 'topicalities'—historical figures or events that are mirrored by allegedly fictional figures or events in the play. I am using the word 'Ur-cast' to designate the historical figures thus mirrored in a given play. For example, in Kenneth Branagh's 1998 film of *Hamlet*, the main characters are Hamlet, Gertrude, Claudius, Polonius, and Ophelia, the cast of players representing these characters is Branagh, Julie Christie, Derek Jacobi, Richard Briers, and Kate Winslet, while the corresponding Ur-cast is Oxford, Elizabeth, Leicester, Burghley, and Anne Cecil.

The Queen and Cloten. One of the main characters in *Cymbeline* is the Queen, a character so iconically evil that she needs no name. In the play, she dabbles in poisons, and schemes to marry her son (from a previous marriage) to the king's daughter Imogen, which (if accomplished) would make him effective heir to the throne. Clark associates her with Catherine de' Medici, dowager queen of France, whose reputation had been tarnished by her role in the massacre of Protestants and by incidents of poisoning. She was the mother of François, Duke of Alençon, who was an active suitor for the hand of Queen Elizabeth during the period 1578-81. If his suit had been successful, he (like Cloten) would have been consort king of England. In the play, Cloten (rhymes with 'rotten') is portrayed as a vicious, self-absorbed braggart. The aptness of his identification with Alençon is illustrated by historian J. L. Motley's description[2] of the duke:

> Francis, Duke of Alençon . . . was, upon the whole, the most despicable personage who had ever entered the Netherlands.
>
> His previous career at home had been so flagrantly false that he had forfeited the esteem of every honest man in Europe. . . .
>
> The world has long known his character. History will always retain him as an example to show mankind of mischief which may be perpetrated by a prince, ferocious without courage, ambitious without talent, and bigoted without opinions.

This sounds like perfect Cloten.

Cymbeline. This character is ostensibly based on the early king of Britain Kimbelinus, described in Geoffrey of Monmouth's *Historia Regum Britanniae* (1136), but there is little overlap with this historical figure. He had two sons—Guiderius and Arviragus—but they were *not* stolen in infancy and raised in a mountain cave, as in the play.

For a guy the play is named after, Cymbeline is surprisingly passive. In the course of the action, he makes only three decisions: (1) He banishes Posthumus (this happens before the play begins and is probably the Queen's idea). (2) He decides to stop paying tribute to Rome, a decision he explicitly blames on the Queen (see 5.5.463). (3) He decides to resume paying tribute to Rome, a puzzling move, since they just fought a successful war to stop payment.

Clark describes Cymbeline as "a composite of Queen Elizabeth of England and Henry III of France," probably because they were both reigning monarchs during Alençon's courtship of Elizabeth. The Henry III attribution is confusing, since he was Catherine de' Medici's son, not her husband, but Henry is said to have relied heavily on his mother's advice, so perhaps that's the allusion. Actually, come to think of it—high in government circles, father of a marriageable daughter, tendency to bumble—Cymbeline looks a lot more like Lord Burghley than Elizabeth or Henry III. However, on further reflection, I'm inclined to associate Cymbeline with Edward IV, father of Elizabeth of York (Imogen), and of Edward and Richard, the 'Princes in the Tower' (Guiderius and Arviragus). Like Cymbeline, Edward IV married an attractive widow who was ambitious for the political advancement of her son.

Posthumus and Imogen. If you believe what other characters say about him, Posthumus Leonatus is the hero of the piece; if you judge him by his actions, not so much. Expository dialog at the start of the play reveals that he is a "poor but worthy" gentleman who has married Imogen—the king's daughter and heir to the kingdom. Cymbeline, at the insistence of the Queen, has banished Posthumus for this effrontery. The Author also suffered a banishment— although Oxford was Elizabeth's favorite in 1578, by 1581 he had accused a group of Catholic nobles of plotting against the queen, and their counter-accusations carried enough weight to get Oxford banished to the Tower. The lands Oxford had inherited from his father had largely been pried away from him, initially by Leicester, over time by Burghley, and on the occasion of his 1575-76 Grand Tour, by himself. Oxford fits the 'poor and banished' template very neatly.

In her chapter on *Cymbeline*, Clark includes the anecdote of Elizabeth's castigation of Thomas Radcliffe, 3rd Earl of Sussex, for a supposed paucity of plate displayed on the sideboard. This was during a 'progress' through the East Counties, and the group (which included two envoys from Alençon) had reached the town of Long Melford. Oxford was a particular friend of Sussex, and reacted to his friend's humiliation by refusing the Queen's request to dance before the French envoys. Clark suggests that *Cymbeline*, with its portrayal of the odious Cloten, was written partly as a protest against the unfair treatment of Sussex. She further suggests that the character Posthumus is a composite of Sussex and Oxford. Posthumus may be a composite, but I don't see Sussex in the mix—he was never poor, and he was never exiled.

I believe that Clark overestimates the importance of the Incident of the Insufficient Plate. Not only has it led her to inflate Sussex's contribution to the character of Posthumus, it has caused her to misinterpret the play's references to 'Milford Haven'. Clark refers to Imogen's questioning Pisanio about the distance to Milford Haven (3.2.64-67) and concludes that 'Milford Haven' must be code for 'Long Melford', the town SE of London where Elizabeth met with Alençon's envoys. This interpretation ignores the obsessive regularity with which the name of the Welsh harbor is mentioned throughout the play. Like the tolling of a great bell, 'Milford' or 'Milford Haven' occurs no less than 17 times[3]. Its importance is underscored when Imogen wakes from the coma induced by the Queen's potion; the first thing she says is "Yes sir, to Milford Haven, which is the way?" (4.2.291). I can only conclude that 'Milford Haven' is code for Milford Haven, the place where Henry Tudor landed his forces in 1485 in his successful campaign to overthrow Richard III.

Figure 13 - Elizabeth of York

I greatly admire Eva Turner Clark and her work, so I am happy to report that I agree with her assessment of the character of Imogen. Insofar as she is being sought in marriage by Cloten/Alençon, she is Elizabeth, and as she is the virtuous woman wrongly accused, she is Oxford's wife, Anne Cecil.

Posthumus. The library I attend has a shelf labeled 'New Books', and one afternoon I plucked out a tome entitled *Elizabeth of York*; it was a biography of the eldest child of Edward IV, written by Alison Weir. I was idly leafing through it when I saw a phrase that struck me like a thunderbolt, and each particular hair stood on end, much like the quills of the fretful porpentine. The phrase was

". . . Henry Tudor, the posthumous son of Edmund Tudor . . ."[4]

Shakespeare Confidential

I checked. It was true—Edmund Tudor died 3 November 1456, and Henry Tudor was born 86 days later, on 28 January 1457. This fact sheds a dazzling new light on the significance of the 'hero' of *Cymbeline*, and also accounts for his unusual name—Henry Tudor was literally 'posthumous'.

The identification of Posthumus with Henry Tudor has implications for our understanding of the character of Imogen. Before invading England, poor, exiled Henry Tudor had pledged that (if victorious) he would marry Elizabeth of York, daughter of the deceased Edward IV, thus uniting the houses of York and Lancaster and ending the Wars of the Roses. He won at Bosworth Field (22 August 1485), was crowned (30 October 1485) and fulfilled his promise by marrying Elizabeth (18 January 1486). Thus both Imogen and Elizabeth of York are king's daughters, heirs to the kingdom, who marry a soldier born posthumously, that soldier having won a battle on English soil.

We stated earlier that Posthumus is at least partially Oxford. Our finding that the character's posthumous birth is significant raises the question: was Oxford born posthumously? It turns out the answer depends on who you think his father was. If you think it was John de Vere, 16th Earl of Oxford, the answer is definitely 'no'. The accepted date for Oxford's birth is 2 April 1550;[5] John didn't die until 3 August 1562, when Oxford was 12. If you think the father was Thomas Seymour (having had his way with the teen-aged Elizabeth) the answer is 'probably not'. Elizabeth was removed from the Parr household in June 1548, so the last time she and Seymour could have been in contact was early June. If there was a pregnancy, and it was normal, the child would have been born in early March 1549. Seymour was imprisoned 17 January 1549 and executed for treason on 20 March. A birth in early March would not be technically posthumous, but would be functionally so, since the child would never see the father.

Identification of Imogen with Elizabeth of York makes a lot of sense. Here is Hallett Smith's description of Imogen:

> She is one of Shakespeare's good women, loving and faithful, patient to an almost incredible degree . . .[6]

And here is Alison Weir's assessment of the historical Elizabeth of York:

> Impeccably connected, ceremonious, fruitful, devout, compassionate, generous, and kind, Elizabeth fulfilled every expectation of her contemporaries. Her goodness shines forth in the sources, and it is not surprising that she was greatly loved. She had overcome severe tragedies and setbacks, and emerged triumphant.[7]

This sounds like Imogen to me .

Belarius, Guiderius and Arviragus. Belarius is a grizzled warrior whose unfair banishment caused him to kidnap Cymbeline's infant sons and flee with them to the wilds of Wales (all this happened 20 years before the action of the play). His identity is revealed early on, and very clearly.

Belarius:	Then was I as a tree Whose boughs did bend with fruit; but in one night, A storm or robbery (call it what you will) Shook down my mellow hangings, nay, my leaves, And left me bare to weather.
Guiderius:	Uncertain favor!
Belarius:	My fault being nothing (as I have told you oft) But that two villains, whose false oaths prevail'd Before my perfect honor, swore to Cymbeline I was confederate with the Romans.

(3.3.60-68)

This passage indelibly marks Belarius as an Oxford figure. Just before Christmas of 1580, Oxford confessed to Elizabeth that he, Henry Howard, and Charles Arundel had been plotting pro-Catholic activities. Howard and Arundel (the "two villains") responded with a farrago of accusations against Oxford. Elizabeth, who was angry with Oxford for impregnating Anne Vavasor, used these allegations as an excuse to have Oxford thrown in the Tower.[8] Note that in the final two lines, 'Cymbeline' stands for Elizabeth and 'Romans' stands for Roman Catholics.

In addition, Belarius refers to himself as a tree in the first part of this speech; this reminds us of the tournament at Whitehall on 22 January 1581, in which Oxford presented himself as "the Knight of the Tree of the Sun."[9]

Belarius, after fleeing to Wales (close to Milford Haven, actually), sets up housekeeping in a cave and raises the king's sons as his own. By the time of the play they have grown to be vigorous young adults. The elder Ogburns speculate on their place in the Ur-cast.

> There is much revealed in *Cymbeline* regarding the sons of the sovereign, the true heirs of Cymbeline's kingdom—that is, to the throne of England. This alone could explain why the play was never printed before it appeared in the First Folio, when the identity of Belarius was obliterated along with that of the dramatist. People would have comprehended too much. To the suspicious and alert it would have been only too obvious that Belarius represented the banished Earl of Oxford and the two boys Elizabeth's two sons. Who else could they have been?
>
> One is puzzled to find Oxford portraying Arthur Dudley, the Queen's son by Leicester, and Southampton, her son by him, as though they were on equal footing; for he certainly considered Southampton Elizabeth's rightful heir. Yet the scene in which Belarius and the boys are introduced (III.3) is Wales; and it was actually to Milford Haven in Wales that Arthur Dudley went in 1580: the "Milford Haven" of *Act III, scene 4*. The sole way we can explain what seems to be an all but superhuman impartiality––to say nothing of such bold candor—is by taking account not only of Oxford's determination to tell the absolute truth, but also of the fact that, while bent upon reminding the Queen that she had two sons, he nevertheless regarded Dudley as a bastard and Southampton as legitimate.[10]

I don't buy it. I don't buy it for several reasons, two of which are: Firstly, Arthur Dudley wasn't important enough to be included in an Ur-cast; he went from Milford Haven to Spain, where he was kept incommunicado for the rest of his life.[11] Secondly, I recoil from any attribution of superhuman powers to the Author, since that is the explanation for his erudition brought forward so frequently by Stratfordians.

In response to the Ogburns' plaintive cry, "Who else could they have been?" I offer the following suggestions.

(1) Guiderius and Arviragus are simply the sons of the historical Kimbelinus. Sometimes a historical figure is just a historical figure.

(2) They represent the sons of Henry Tudor: Arthur (1486-1502) and Henry (1491-1547). This attribution complicates the character of Cymbeline, making him stand for Henry VII as well as Elizabeth and Edward IV.

(3) They represent Lambert Simnel and Perkin Warbeck, pretenders who perturbed the reign of Henry VII. The obvious objection to this assignment is that Guiderius and Arviragus are revealed to be true princes, not pretenders (although the Author is capable of the occasional mischievous inversion[12]).

(4) They represent the sons of Edward IV: Edward, Prince of Wales (proclaimed Edward V but not crowned) and Richard, Duke of York—the 'Princes in the Tower', thought to have been killed by Richard III. They were the brothers of Elizabeth of York (identified with 'Imogen'), so this assignment is attractive in that it preserves the brother-sister relationship between these characters. And just as the removal (by death) of the Princes made Elizabeth of York the natural heir to the throne, the removal (by abduction) of Guiderius and Arviragus makes Imogen the natural heir—strong motivation for Cloten and the Queen. Note that in both cases—historical and dramatic—the sons, though significantly younger than the daughter, would have succeeded to the throne, as males were preferred.

As we have noted, Milford Haven, the place where Henry Tudor started his campaign for the crown, is in Wales.

> Henry took care to emphasize his descent from the ancient kings of Britain, and in particular the legendary Arthur, and the Welsh prince Cadwaladr, who had fought the Anglo-Saxon invaders in the seventh century. He claimed Cadwaladr as his hundredth progenitor, and had his red dragon blazoned on his standard and later used as one of the supporters of the Tudor royal arms.[13]

The Author (himself pseudonymous) had Belarius choose pseudonyms for himself and his two young charges after fleeing to Wales. The name he chose for Arviragus was 'Cadwal', obviously an abbreviated form of 'Cadwaladr'. Guiderius became 'Polydore', presumably a reference to Polydore Vergil, the official Tudor historian. Belarius called himself 'Morgan'; three candidates for this allusion are given below:

> **Morgan Mwynfawr** (d. 665?), regulus of Glamorgan . . . is said to have been a cousin of King Arthur and a knight of his court . . .

> **Morgan Hen** (d. 973), regulus of Glamorgan . . . was the chief prince of the region, and in that capacity attended the English court . . .

> **Morgan** (fl. 1294-1295), leader of the men of Glamorgan, appears, like his fellow-conspirator, Madog, only in connection with the Welsh revolt which came to a head on Michaelmas day, 1294...[14]

It is evident that the play *Cymbeline* is suffused with references to Wales and Welsh imagery, and partially inspired by the career of Henry VII. Scholars have noted that Shakespeare dramatized the lives of all the English kings from Edward III to Henry VIII, with the one exception of the first Tudor, Henry VII. We now see that a play about Henry VII is not missing, just disguised. As are Belarius ('Morgan'), Guiderius ('Polydore'), and Arviragus ('Cadwal').

End Notes

1. Eva Turner Clark, *Hidden Allusions in Shakespeare's Plays*, 3rd Revised Edition, Ed. Ruth Loyd Miller (Kennikat Press, 1974).

2. John Lothrop Motley, *Rise of the Dutch Republic* (New York, 1898, 1931); quoted in Clark, 86.

3. Milford Haven in *Cymbeline*: 3.2.43-4, 3.2.48-9, 3.2.58-60, 3.2.82, 3.4.28, 3.4.41-3, 3.5.7-8, 3.5.130, 3.5.149, 3.5.155, 3.5.159, 3.6.4-6, 3.6.58, 3.6.60-61, 4.2.291, 4.2.335, 5.5.281.

4. Alison Weir, *Elizabeth of York* (Ballantine, New York, 2013), 35.

5. *Dictionary of National Biography* (1968), Vol. XX, p. 240-2.

6. Hallett Smith in *The Riverside Shakespeare* (Houghton Mifflin, 1974), 1519.

7. Weir, 444-5.

8. Mark Anderson, *"Shakespeare" by Another Name* (Gotham, 2005), 165-9.

9. Daniel L. Wright, 'Shaking the Spear at Court', *Shakespeare Oxford Newsletter* 34.2 (Summer 1998).

10. Dorothy and Charlton Ogburn, *This Star of England* (Coward-McCann, 1952), 962.

11. ibid., 1252-56.

12. C. V. Berney, 'The Merchant of Venice: 2004 and 1980', *Shakespeare Matters* 4.2 (Winter 2005), 30-31 'Oxford's Offstage Cameo'.

13. Weir, 164.

14. *Dictionary of National Biography*, Vol. XIII, 907-8.

33

Further Curiosities of *Cymbeline*

In a previous paper[1] I discussed connections between Posthumus Leonatus, the 'hero' of Shakespeare's play *Cymbeline*, and the historical Henry Tudor, victor of Bosworth Field (and thus Henry VII), who was himself born posthumously. Recognition of this connection greatly clarifies the play, revealing a layer of reference to 15th century history, including Welsh references, and the identification of Imogen with Elizabeth of York, who married Henry VII. On rereading Charles Beauclerk's powerful and illuminating book, *Shakespeare's Lost Kingdom*, I find that this Oxfordian author was also aware of the play's Tudorian subtext. Beauclerk writes

> In *Cymbeline*, which can be read as a symbolic history of Britain, Shakespeare's special myth of kingship fuses implicitly with the Tudor conception of its rights in the kingdom. The play's hero, Posthumus Leonatus, after a period of exile on the Continent, returns to Britain via Milford Haven in Wales (the place where Henry Tudor landed his invasion force in 1485).[2]

It is a sad commentary on the quality of Stratfordian scholarship that in all the orthodox material I have read, not one writer comments on this essential layer of meaning in *Cymbeline* (even though the Author keeps nudging the reader with obsessively repeated references to Milford Haven). Stratfordian scholars are presumably of normal intelligence (I hear that they dress themselves, and can eat with knife and fork), but in spite of 400 years of study, they don't know when the plays were written, or what they're about.

I would like to start this paper with comment on a couple of free-standing issues—the legal status of the bond between Imogen and Posthumus, and an expository comment on the latter's education—and then move on to some deeper curiosities hinted at in the text of the play.

Were Imogen and Posthumus married? In the introductory exchange beginning the play, the First Gentleman says of

Imogen "[She] hath referred herslf unto a poor but worthy gentleman. She's wedded, her husband banish'd, she imprisoned . . ." Later, referring to Posthumus, he says " . . . and he that hath her I mean, that married her . . . " Posthumus refers to himself as 'husband' (1.1.96) and to Imogen as 'wife' (5.5.226). Imogen calls Posthumus 'husband' (1.6.3) and twice describes herself as 'wedded' (1.6.2: 5.5.261). Posthumus has been banished—he travels to Rome, but Imogen remains in England; wouldn't we expect a wife to accompany him? And how can Cloten approach her as if she's still available for marriage (2.3.111-24)?

The answer is scattered through several speeches.

Posthumus: I will remain the loyall'st husband that did e'er plight troth. 1.1.95-6

Iachimo: Give me your pardon. I have spoke this to know if your affiance were deeply rooted. 1.6.162-4

Queen [describing Pisanio]
: . . . the agent for his master, and the remembrancer of her to hold the hand-fast to her lord 1.5.76-8

We conclude that Posthumus and Imogen have 'plighted their troth', that is, have entered a precontract, a promise to marry each other, also known as a 'hand-fast'.

Alison Weir explains:

> English sources mention . . . a precontract, a promise before witnesses to marry; once it was cemented by sexual intercourse, it became as binding in the eyes of the Church as marriage. By the fourteenth century, the Church had reluctantly allowed that such clandestine marriages—with no calling of banns or blessing by a priest at the church door—were valid, but only if the promise had been made before two witnesses, which the law required. In practice, many couples considered themselves married on the basis of a promise alone . . .[3]

Posthumus specifically states that their troth-plight was unconsumated[4] and there is no mention of any witnesses, so Cloten—so wrong in his assessment of his prowess as a swordsman—is right on the money when he says to Imogen

> The contract you pretend with that base wretch, . . . it is no contract, none; and though it be allowed in meaner parties . . . to knit their souls . . . in self-figur'd knot, yet you are curbed from that enlargement by the consequence o' th' crown, and

must not foil the precious note of it with a base slave . . .
(2.3.114-122)

Cloten is quite justified in pursuing Imogen to gain the crown—
—her contract with Posthumus can easily be untied by Authority.

Posthumus's Education. We return to the exposition at the beginning of the play. The First Gentleman speaks of Posthumus's childhood:

> . . . The King he takes the babe
> To his protection, calls him Posthumus Leonatus,
> Breeds him and makes him of his bedchamber,
> Puts to him all the learnings that his time
> Could make him the receiver of, which he took,
> As we do air, fast as 'twas minist'red,
> And in 's spring became a harvest; liv'd in court
> (Which rare it is to do) most praised, most lov'd,
> A sample to the youngest, to th' more mature
> A glass that feated them, and to the graver
> A child that guided dotards. To his mistress
> (For whom he now is banish'd), her own price
> Proclaims how she esteem'd him; and his virtue
> By her election may be truly read,
> What kind of man he is.   (1.1.40-54)

This rosy description of a brilliant childhood fits Henry Tudor, but not perfectly.

Henry was four years old in 1561 when Edward IV took the throne. The child was placed in the care of William Herbert, a staunch Yorkist, and was raised in Raglan Castle, in southeast Wales, where he was tutored by the noted scholar Andreas Scotus. Scotus gave his pupil good marks, saying "he had never seen a child so quick in learning." [5]

But Henry's education was interrupted several times. In 1469 his guardian was executed for treason by the rebel Warwick, and in 1470 the boy was reclaimed by his uncle, Jasper Tudor. After the Lancastrian defeat at the Battle of Tewkesbury in 1571, Jasper fled to Brittany, taking Henry with him. In later life Henry complained that "from the time he was five years old he had been either a fugitive or a captive." [5] Though he was well educated, he never had an opportunity to shine at court.

But we know someone who did. Edward de Vere was 12 when his father died, and he was made the ward of court official William Cecil. He was tutored by the preeminent scholars of the time: Thomas Smith, horticulturalist John Gerard, Latinist Arthur Golding, and Lawrence Nowell, who when his charge was 13, wrote "I clearly see that my work for the Earl of Oxford cannot be much longer required."[6] The passage from *Cymbeline* quoted above describes its subject as "a sample [example] to the youngest, to th' more mature a glass that feated them," reminding us of a certain Prince of Denmark who was "the glass of fashion and the mould of form."[7] I conclude that the passage was intended to refer at least as much to 'Posthumus as Oxford' as to 'Posthumus as Henry Tudor'. The Author has subtly supported this conclusion by seeding the passage with *ver* words: **spring** (Latin *ver*), **virtue** (spelled *vertue* in the First Folio), **truly** (L. *vero*), and **glass** (Fr. *verre*).

The Villain. Like the historical Edward IV, the fictional Cymbeline has married a widow who is interested in the advancement of her male relatives, in this case her son, Cloten. He woos Imogen (Scene 2.3) and she rejects him. Humiliated, Cloten vows revenge in a speech so savage it was expurgated from the BBC film of the play.

> *Cloten.* . . . Even there, [at Milford Haven] thou villain Posthumus, will I kill thee. . . . She said upon a time (the bitterness of it I now belch from my heart) that she held the very garment of Posthumus in more respect than my noble and natural person, together with the adornment of my qualities. With that suit upon my back will I ravish her; first kill him and in her eyes; there shall she see my valor, which will then be a torment to her contempt. He on the ground, my speech of insultment ended on his dead body, and when my lust hath din'd (which, as I say, to vex her I will execute in the clothes that she so prais'd), to the court I'll knock her back, foot her home again. She hath despis'd me rejoicingly, and I'll be merry in my revenge. (3.5.130-45)

In my previous paper[1] I gave reasons for associating Cloten with François, duc d'Alençon, who wooed Queen Elizabeth in the period 1578-81, and is widely regarded as one of the most loathsome figures in history.

The Raw Nerve. After the death of Edward IV in 1483, his brother usurped the throne, styling himself Richard III. As the extent of his tyranny became clear, even staunch Yorkists began to look around for candidates to replace Richard. Margaret Beaufort (Henry's mother) could not rule, being a woman, but as the great-granddaughter of John of Gaunt, she had royal (Lancastrian) blood—thus, so did Henry. At some point

Margaret suggested that Henry marry Elizabeth of York, the beautiful daughter of the popular Edward IV, thus uniting the warring houses and ensuring peace for coming generations.[8] This idea was greeted with great enthusiasm, and Henry, exiled in Brittany, promised that if he gained the throne he would marry Elizabeth.

After his victory at Bosworth, Henry did become king, and his claim to the throne rested on three legs. (1) *Descent*. This leg was a bit wobbly, since some of his ancestors were tainted by bastardy. (2) *Conquest*. Though his defeat of Richard was decisive, Henry preferred to be seen as a legitimate king who had disposed of a usurper. (3) *Marriage*. Henry had welcomed the swell of support he received when he promised to marry Edward's daughter, but after Bosworth he became very sensitive to the idea that the people would regard him as 'king consort'—someone who wore the crown not in his own right, but because he had married the princess. The idea that the crown was *his* (and not his wife's) became an obsession with him, so finally (in this context) "he would not endure any mention of the Lady Elizabeth."[9]

In the light of this circumstance, the last five lines of the First Gentleman's speech acquire a curious pungency.

>   . . .   To his mistress
> (For whom he now is banished), her own price
> Proclaims how she esteem'd him, *and his virtue*
> *By her election may be truly read,*
> What kind of man he is.   (emphasis added)

"By her election"—(dramatically) Imogen's choice of Posthumus as husband, or (historically) Elizabeth of York's ascension to the conjugal throne? ("Both" is an acceptable answer.) Are these lines innocuous praise of Posthumus, or is the Author mischievously probing Henry Tudor's raw nerve about his right to the throne? Perhaps there are other passages that will help us decide.

Later in Act I, Cymbeline upbraids his daughter for affiancing herself to a commoner.

Cymbeline.	Thou took'st a beggar, would have made my throne A seat for baseness.
Imogen.	No, I rather added A lustre to it. (1.1.141-3)

Shakespeare Confidential

Again the ambiguity—does *Cymbeline's daughter* mean that Posthumus's worthiness adds luster to the throne, or does *Edward IV's daughter* mean that she (by marrying Henry Tudor) validates Tudor's claim?

Iachimo's statement on this subject is less equivocal.

> This matter of marrying his king's daughter, wherein he must be weigh'd rather by her value than his own, words him, I doubt not, a great deal from the matter.[10] (1.4.14-17)

I think we must consider the possibility that the Author is deliberately taunting Henry VII about his advantageous marriage. Of course, it's preposterous to think that a glover's son from a rural village would dare taunt even a dead king. It's not so preposterous if the Author was a scion of the oldest noble family in England, whose ancestor, the 13th Earl of Oxford, had been the military leader and strategist who won the victory at Bosworth Field that put Henry on the throne.[11]

The 'Heroism' of Posthumus. All through the play, various characters—starting with the First Gentleman (1.1) and ending with Iachimo (5.5) —tell us what a virtuous, upstanding prince of a fellow Posthumus is. But what are his acts? His goodbye to Imogen is relatively harmless, but once he gets to Rome he makes this insane wager with Iachimo, a man he has just met, and a professed womanizer. Iachimo proposes to seduce Imogen, so Posthumus gives him a letter of introduction that stops just short of saying 'This is my best buddy, please go to bed with him'.[12] Imogen wisely rejects Iachimo's advances, but returning to Rome, the cad claims to have been successful. Posthumus retains his faith in his fiancée's chastity during Iachimo's description of her bedchamber, but loses it when the Italian produces a bracelet—the Briton's parting gift to Imogen. And then when Iachimo describes a mole on the girl's left breast, Posthumus goes totally berserk, threatening violence to both Iachimo and Imogen.

> [to Iachimo] If you will swear you have not done't, you lie,
> And I will kill thee if thou dost deny
> Thou'st made me cuckold. . . .
>
> O that I had her here, to tear her limb-meal !
> I will go there and do't, i' th' court, before
> Her father, I'll do something— (2.4.144-9)

The next scene (2.5) is Posthumus's virulent diatribe against all women (to paraphrase: '*This mess isn't* **my** *fault—it's because women are evil*').[13] It is closely followed by the scene (3.2) in which Posthumus's faithful servant Pisanio reads the letter commanding him to murder Imogen as revenge for her supposed adultery. (The previous philosophical unconcern of Scene 1.4—"if . . . you have prevail'd, I am no further your enemy; she is not worth our debate," seems utterly to have vanished.)

Our hero is then offstage until Scene 5.1, when he receives the bloody cloth sent him by Pisanio as 'proof' of Imogen's supposed murder. There's a glimmer of remorse, but characteristically, he lays the blame on Pisanio ("Every good servant does not all commands . . ."). He changes into British peasant garb and fights valiantly against the invading Romans. After the British victory he slips back into Roman-style clothes, and is then taken prisoner. In jail, he yearns for death, but seems to have regained a philosophical calm.

The final scene of the play is like the *dénouement* of a Poirot-style detective story—all the characters are brought together, all secrets are revealed, all mysteries explained. Posthumus is there, as is transgendered Imogen, disguised as the page Fidele. Iachimo confesses that he duped Posthumus, who responds with a wild, self-lacerating speech that ends

> . . . every villain
> Be called Posthumus Leonatus and
> Be villainy less than 'twas! O Imogen!
> My queen, my life, my wife! O Imogen,
> Imogen, Imogen!   (5.5.223-7)

Imogen rushes to his side, to assure him that she is alive—

> Peace, my lord, hear, hear—

—and he responds by savagely striking her, snarling

> Shall's have a play of this? Thou scornful page,
> There lie thy part.

It's a stunning moment. What's going on here? Why this brutal response to an unoffending page? Can it be that Posthumus is as rotten as Cloten? Well, they wear the same clothes, and if you chop the head off one of them, he can't be distinguished from the other, even by his fiancée. Is the Author suggesting a parallel between the historical avatars of Posthumus and

Cloten—namely Henry Tudor and François, duc d'Alençon? Each was a prince who sailed from France, seeking to wed a princess named Elizabeth. Each had a strong-willed mother, politically astute, who schemed to put her son on the English throne.[14] As noted previously,[1] Henry Tudor was literally posthumous, having been born three months after his father's death. Alençon was functionally posthumous, being only four years old when his father died.[15] I find that the parallels are striking—no wonder it's hard to tell them apart!

What does the Author think of Henry Tudor?

First Fact: from Edward III (ca. 1350) to Henry VIII (ca. 1530), the Shakespearean canon contains at least one eponymic play for each of the kings of England—with three exceptions: (1) Edward IV; (2) Edward V; and (3) Henry VII (aka Henry Tudor). Edward IV appears extensively in *3 Henry VI* and in *Richard III*. Edward V was one of the 'Princes in the Tower' who disappeared during the reign of Richard Crookback—he was never crowned. Henry Tudor appears briefly in *3 Henry VI* and in *Richard III* (where he is called 'Richmond'), *but he never gets a play of his own.*

Figure 14 - Henry Tudor

Second Fact: returning to the play *Cymbeline*, from Act 2 on, Posthumus—the character identified with Henry Tudor—acts more like a villain than a hero, threatening violence, ordering a servant to murder his fiancée, making speeches of 'remorse' that seem designed to make him the center of attention, and finally, brutally striking the innocent 'page' who is really the aforesaid fiancée.

Third Fact: not only is Posthumus villainous in his own right, he has a mystic connection with the villainous Cloten (see above). Not for nothing does Guiderius exclaim "Double villain!" as he prepares to chop off Cloten's head (4.2.89).

Consideration of these three facts leads me to believe that

the Author—Edward de Vere, 17th Earl of Oxford—profoundly disliked Henry VII, to the extent that he not only denies him his own play, but casts him (thinly disguised) as a self-involved fool in a fictional play, and makes him the doppelgänger of an avowed villain. This conclusion forms an interesting contrast with the establishment view that Shakespeare was a Tudor propagandist who smeared Richard III to make the Tudors look good.

What is the cause of this intense dislike? The honest answer is 'I don't know'. However, it would be irresponsible of me to lead you this far without at least a suggestion. Keep in mind that the latter days of Henry Tudor's reign were marred by his obsession with raking in more and more cash, and that the military leader responsible for Henry's success at Bosworth Field was John de Vere, 13th Earl of Oxford.[11] Francis Bacon recounts the following anecdote concerning a visit by Henry VII to the Earl at Castle Hedingham.[16]

> There remains to this day a report that the King was on a time entertained by the Earl of Oxford (that was his principal servant both for war and peace) nobly and sumptuously, at his castle at Henningham. And at the King's going away, the Earl's servants stood in a seemly manner in their livery coats with cognisances, ranged on both sides, and made the King a lane. The King called the Earl to him and said, 'My lord, I have heard much of your hospitality, but I see it is greater than the speech. These handsome gentlemen and yeomen that I see on both sides of me are (sure) your menial servants.' The Earl smiled and said, 'It may please your grace, that were not for mine ease. They are most of them my retainers that are come to do me service at such a time as this; and chiefly to see your grace.' The King started a little, and said, 'By my faith (my lord) I thank you for my good cheer, but I may not endure to have my laws broken in my sight. My attorney must speak with you.' And it is part of the report, that the Earl compounded no less than 15,000 marks.

In modern terms, the Earl of Oxford, who had won the kingdom for Henry, and had just feasted him 'nobly and sumptuously', was fined £10,000 for exceeding the number of retainers allowed by the Crown.

If you want to explore the Author's feelings about ingratitude, read *Timon of Athens*. Here's a sample: "I am rapt and cannot cover the monstrous bulk of this ingratitude with any size of words."[17]

End Notes

1. See previous chapter, '*Cymbeline*: the Hidden History Play,' 219-27.

2. Charles Beauclerk, *Shakespeare's Lost Kingdom* (Grove, 2010), 234.

3. Alison Weir, *Elizabeth of York* (Ballantine, 2013), 86.

4. Posthumus says of Imogen "I am her adorer, not her friend" (1.4.69). The *Riverside* glosses 'friend' as 'lover, i.e. paramour'. Later, convinced that Iachimo has bedded her, Posthumus wails "Me of my lawful pleasure she restrain'd, and pray'd me oft forbearance . . ." (2.5.9-10)

5. Weir, 37.

6. Charlton Ogburn, *The Mysterious William Shakespeare* (EPM Publications, 1984), 435-41.

7. *Hamlet,* 3.1.153

8. Weir, 100.

9. Francis Bacon, *The History of the Reign of King Henry VII* (Hesperus, 2007; first published 1622), 11.

10. The 1974 *Riverside* editor glosses the phrase "words him . . . from the matter" as "causes him to be described in terms very wide of the truth" (p. 1525). But the part that strikes the eye is "he must be weigh'd rather by her value than his own."

11. Peter Hammond, *Richard III and the Bosworth Campaign* (Pen & Sword, 2010), 35, 87, 99.

12. The letter reads, "He [Iachimo] is one of the noblest note, to whose kindnesses I am most infinitely tied. Reflect upon him accordingly, as you value your trust"—Leonatus. (1.6.22-5)

13. The most interesting line in this speech comes when Posthumus fantasizes about Iachimo's supposed encounter with Imogen: "Perchance he spoke not, but like a full-acorn'd boar, a German one, cried 'O!' and mounted . . . " (2.5.15-17). The boar was a feature of the Oxford family crest ('O!'), but why a German one?

14. Henry Tudor's mother was Margaret Beaufort, Countess of Richmond and Derby. Alençon's mother was Catherine de' Medici, Dowager Queen of France.

15. Alençon was born 18 March 1555. His father, Henri II of France, died (from a wound sustained in a jousting match) on 10 July 1559.

16. Bacon, 146-7.

17. *Timon of Athens*, 5.1.64-6.

www.ingramcontent.com/pod-product-compliance
Lightning Source LLC
Chambersburg PA
CBHW071657090426
42738CB00009B/1569